THE CAMBRIDGE COMPANION TO
THE BIBLE AND LITERATURE

This *Companion* volume offers a sweeping survey of the Bible as a work of literature and its impact on Western writing. Underscoring the sophistication of the biblical writers' thinking in diverse areas of thought, it demonstrates how the Bible relates to many types of knowledge and its immense contribution to education through the ages. The volume emphasizes selected texts chosen from different books of the Bible and from later Western writers inspired by it. Individual essays, each written specially for this book, examine topics such as the gruesome wonders of Apocalyptic texts, the erotic content of the Song of Songs, and Jesus' and Paul's language and reasoning; as well as Shakespeare's reflections on repentance in *King Lear*, Milton's genius in writing *Paradise Lost*, the social necessity of individual virtue in Shelley's poetry, and the mythic status of Melville's *Moby Dick* in the United States and Western world in general.

CALUM CARMICHAEL is Professor of Comparative Literature Emeritus at Cornell University.

(continued after Index)

THE CAMBRIDGE COMPANION TO

THE BIBLE AND LITERATURE

Edited by

Calum Carmichael
Cornell University

CAMBRIDGE
UNIVERSITY PRESS

CAMBRIDGE
UNIVERSITY PRESS

University Printing House, Cambridge CB2 8BS, United Kingdom

One Liberty Plaza, 20th Floor, New York, NY 10006, USA

477 Williamstown Road, Port Melbourne, VIC 3207, Australia

314–321, 3rd Floor, Plot 3, Splendor Forum, Jasola District Centre,
New Delhi – 110025, India

79 Anson Road, #06–04/06, Singapore 079906

Cambridge University Press is part of the University of Cambridge.

It furthers the University's mission by disseminating knowledge in the pursuit of
education, learning, and research at the highest international levels of excellence.

www.cambridge.org
Information on this title: www.cambridge.org/9781108422956
DOI: 10.1017/9781108386081

© Cambridge University Press 2020

First published 2020

Printed in the United Kingdom by TJ International Ltd. Padstow, Cornwall

A catalogue record for this publication is available from the British Library.

Library of Congress Cataloging-in-Publication Data
NAMES: Carmichael, Calum M., editor.
TITLE: The Cambridge companion to the Bible and literature / edited by Calum
    Carmichael, Cornell University.
DESCRIPTION: Cambridge, United Kingdom : Cambridge University Press, 2019. | Series:
    Cambridge companions to religion | Includes bibliographical references and index.
IDENTIFIERS: LCCN 2019040734 (print) | LCCN 2019040735 (ebook) | ISBN 9781108422956
    (hardback) | ISBN 9781108386081 (epub)
SUBJECTS: LCSH: Bible as literature. | Bible–Criticism, interpretation, etc. | Bible–Influence.
CLASSIFICATION: LCC BS535 .C28 2019 (print) | LCC BS535 (ebook) | DDC 809/.93522–dc23
LC record available at https://lccn.loc.gov/2019040734
LC ebook record available at https://lccn.loc.gov/2019040735

ISBN 978-1-108-42295-6 Hardback
ISBN 978-1-108-43524-6 Paperback

Contents

Contributors

Graeme Auld University of Edinburgh, Scotland

Ruth Blair University of Queensland, Australia

Thomas L. Brodie Formerly Dominican Biblical Institute, Limerick, Ireland

Jeannine K. Brown Bethel Seminary, San Diego

Calum Carmichael Cornell University

James Crenshaw Duke University

Jonathan Fortier George Mason University and Fraser Institute, Canada

Emily O. Gravett James Madison University

Meghan Henning University of Dayton

William J. Kennedy Cornell University

Victor H. Matthews Missouri State University

Geoffrey P. Miller New York University Law School

Todd D. Still Baylor University

Gordon Teskey Harvard University

Steve A. Wiggins Oxford University Press

Abbreviations

AV	Revised Standard Version
BZAW	*Beihefte zur Zeitschrift für die alttestamentliche Wissenschaft*
DBSup	*Dictionnaire de la Bible Supplément*, H. Cazelles et al., eds. (Paris, 1928–)
ELH	*English Literary History*
HLR	*Harvard Law Review*
HTR	*Harvard Theological Review*
JBC	*Jerome Biblical Commentary*, eds. R. E. Brown, J. A. Fitzmyer, and R. E. Murphy (London, 1968)
JBL	*Journal of Biblical Literature*
JEDP	The Y(J)ahwistic, Elohistic, Deuteronomic, and Priestly literary strands in the Pentateuch
JHS	*Journal of Hellenic Studies*
JPSTC	*Jewish Publication Society Torah Commentary*
JR	*Journal of Religion*
JSNT	*Journal for the Study of the New Testament Supplemental Series*
JSOT	*Journal for the Study of the Old Testament*
JSOTSS	*Journal for the Study of the Old Testament Supplement Series*
JTS	*Journal of Theological Studies*
NRSV	New Revised Standard Version
SBLDS	*Society of Biblical Literature Dissertation Series*
VT	*Vetus Testamentum*

Introduction

It is increasingly fashionable for interpreters of the Bible unfamiliar with the original languages and the relevant ancient history to pursue literary approaches. Even the legal material is commonly evaluated in literary terms. No scholarly effort is independent of fashion in the sense of a cultural trend and of idiosyncrasy in the sense of a personal bent. An often unspoken assumption is that because so much research into linguistic and historical backgrounds of the biblical texts has occurred down the centuries little scope is left to say much that is new. There is a measure of truth in this notion. Despite an abiding commitment among a coterie of German scholars, more often than not scholars pay but lip service to the longstanding historical-critical theory about the Graf-Wellhausen JEDP four source make-up of the Pentateuch. The approach's long history illustrates the not infrequent phenomenon of a critical theory perpetuating itself even when its *raison d'être* has been lost sight of. It is, however, precisely a lack of confidence about uncovering new meaning in the original sources that provides a major impetus for this volume. The essays reflect the efforts of scholars who, by and large, not committing to old order ways, enable them to advance imaginative ones of looking at the Bible. The goal is to modify and reshape many preconceived notions about the contents of the Bible and also its role in selected areas of Western literature. Another aim is to stimulate further questioning on the part of the reader. There is good reason to do so. The German philosopher, Friedrich Schlegel, speaks of a classical work as one that cannot ever be fully understood, but those who are educated and who seek to enhance their education nevertheless through engagement with such a work learn more and more.

The sophistication and insights of ancient authors can never be underestimated. An all too detrimental attitude to the past is one the social historian E. P. Thompson voices when he speaks of "the enormous condescension of posterity." Clouding critical judgment, the attitude is born of two contradictory stances on the part of modern inquirers: a tendency to look down on the "primitives" from the height of our progress and, contrariwise, a proclivity to look up to them from the depth of our decadence. Burdened by the complexity of contemporary society and its focus on inwardness, there is admiration for those ancients who seemingly engage in simple, direct, often clever actions free of inhibitions. Both attitudes are largely groundless and distort the ancient texts. Neither stance is embraced by the contributors to this volume.

In uncovering the richness of the biblical texts clearly and engagingly, each contributor demonstrates just how supremely cultured are the ancient authors and those later writers who use the Bible for their own literary creations. Part of the endeavor is to say something new about both and in doing so offer insights pertinent to current fashions. Even where later literary works seem to misuse a biblical source, that need not be a bad thing. The misreading often proves fundamental to understanding a later writer's thinking so that it matters but little what the text may have meant originally. We can, for instance, reflect upon later Western authors' ideas about suicide reflected in their reading of the Bible. Hamlet complains about the Old Testament and wishes God had promulgated no law against the act ("O that the Everlasting had not fixed his canon against self-slaughter"). Shakespeare has in mind "You shall not murder," assumed in his time to extend to self-killing. Few scholars today go along with Shakespeare's understanding of the original commandment but as far as an appreciation of Hamlet's monologue is concerned that is beside the point. Noah curses his son Ham for looking on a father's nakedness when drunk with the consequence that Ham's offspring are to become servants of the descendants of the two other brothers, Shem and Japheth (Gen 9:18–27). Later interpreters used the curse in defense of racial downgrading, viewing the "wicked" Ham as the ancestor of black Africans, the "decent" Japheth of Europeans, and Shem of Semitic peoples. However bizarre the view, it is nonetheless crucial for understanding an influential if abhorrent stance in recent centuries.

No matter how often an ancient text has been studied, respect for the unknown composer calls for ever closer reading. If we acknowledge how difficult it is to read any text and think about it at the same time, a disciplined focus yields new and original results. The philosopher Alfred Whitehead defined a professor as an ignorant person thinking and the image is one worth cherishing. Even if accompanied by an unavoidable measure of naiveté, the exercise of our native intelligence in reading a text enlivens. The goal in this volume is not to emphasize the acquisition of scholarly expertise but to foster search before research. Questions abound. What precisely is the idea present in the texts; to what can we compare the idea in other material, biblical or otherwise, and to what can we contrast it; is it a strange notion in light of our own experience of things; on reflection not so strange but just that the ancient dress makes it appear so? What is puzzling about the material? Why is the curse the penalty for some offenses but not for others? Why is the deity sometimes brought into some texts, legal and literary, but not into others? The greatest thriller (perhaps) before the work of Edgar Allen Poe, the Book of Esther, has no reference to God. Can we formulate our puzzlement? To acquire an eye for genuine problems and a knack for avoiding non-problems constitutes real advance. The pursuit of themes is usually to be avoided. To commit to developing them leaves one vulnerable to looseness of thought, failure to see inconsistencies, and an often fatal tendency to pass over telling details. To generalize is often to omit, even worse, to distort. "Nothing is so useless as a general maxim" warns the English historian Thomas MacAulay; "I care nothing for the systems – only the insights," comments the most influential of all American jurists, Oliver Wendell Holmes; and the contemporary legal scholar Randall Kennedy urges "a skeptical attitude towards all labels and categories . . . and to appreciate instead the unique feature of specific persons and their work."[1]

The aim of the essays is to arouse in an inquiring mind the beguilement of curiosity and the allure of a puzzle laid out in every which way to indicate just how real a puzzle we have engaging our attention. In studying biblical literature, it is relatively easy to concentrate on small amounts of intelligible, largely self-contained material. Eminently desirable is the value of Goethe's remark that "thinking is more interesting than knowing but less interesting than seeing." It is reported that he once threw up his hands in despair when he learnt that the Weimar newssheet he read once a month was to appear bi-monthly. How could he possibly take in so much information? To do so would interfere with his capacity to relate what he read to matters past and present and to anticipate future developments. Today, information comes instantaneously from all over the globe, an enormous encroachment of space – at the expense of time. The words of Ecclesiastes convey the challenge: "Is there anything whereof it may be said, See, this is new? It has been

---

[1] Lord MacAulay, *Miscellaneous Works*, ed. Lady Trevelyan (New York, 1880), 1:100; *The Holmes-Laski Letters*, ed. Mark de Wolf Howe (Cambridge, MA, 1953), 1:331; Gerhard Casper, *The Winds of Freedom* (New Haven, CT, 2014), 52.

already of old time" (Eccles 1:10). Especially pressing is the need to capture change and bring it into the realm of shared understanding. An intimate acquaintance with biblical and outstanding literary texts inspired by the Bible well contributes to such an effort.

Any written text makes a claim upon a reader's attention, sometimes little, other times much. No body of texts has made claims down the centuries to the extent of those in the Bible, especially in the New Testament, and particularly by those who affirm its sacred character. It is not our intent to pursue such a view of the material. The Bible as a sacred text is an ideological construct that conceals its complicated, historically obscure, and multifaceted origins. The process of canonization has tended to erase the very notion of various composers who lived in quite separate periods of time. The secular reader does not make the same assumptions as the religious thinker: that the texts are canonical and therefore authoritative; that they exhibit unity with each part implying every other part; and that the New Testament is a fulfillment of the Old. Yet, to complicate the picture, in order to understand much that is written in the New, we have to heed how the biblical authors, in pursuit of lending authority to their own work, do assume such an interdependence of texts in the Hebrew Bible (or in its Greek translation, the Septuagint). Theirs is an approach that owes much, in fact, to the treatment of Homer's *Iliad* and *Odyssey* as inspired texts containing all wisdom and requiring the application of often convoluted rules to extract it from the Greek texts.

A considerable difference exists between a literary presentation of events and a historical one. Over the past few centuries the historical school of criticism has dominated biblical scholarship with its attempts to detect the historical, social, and political background of the biblical books. But as far back as the eighteenth century, the founder of Utilitarianism, Jeremy Bentham, opined that the historical school represents "erudition deprived of thought." Bentham's claim may be harsh but there is no question that what appears to be historical writing in the Bible is more often than not an indirect mode of communicating ideas of one kind or another. Unlike the Greek, Latin, German, and English languages with their capacity to add prefixes and suffixes to a word – a book can be un-put-down-able – and thereby aid analytical and philosophical inquiry, the Semitic languages do not lend themselves to philosophizing. With no capacity to add prefixes and suffixes, they instead exploit a word's root by modifying it – *'abhadh,* "to perish," *'ibbedh,* or *he'ebhidh,* "to cause to perish," "to destroy." Doing so often deepens and adds complexity to its sense. This characteristic feature of the

Hebrew and Aramaic languages encourages the use of storytelling to convey meaning. Chronological and biographical "facts" are, despite appearances, often only secondarily but brilliantly employed to relay ideas and values.

When we focus on the Bible as embodying different literary products of ancient times and places, the results can be surprisingly different from what orthodoxy of opinion has disseminated down the centuries. The Adam and Eve story illustrates. It can be read not, as it often is, to describe a descent into original sin but to celebrate the rise of humankind from an animal-like state to godlike status with the capacity to know and to discriminate, in a word, to be enlightened. The interpretation of the story as a "Fall" shows up in the time of Second Temple Judaism (530 BCE to 70 CE) and the Church father, Augustine (354–430 CE) makes it a central tenet of Christian belief. Read without Jewish and Christian spectacles, we observe that the author of the story highlights how the *conscious* appreciation of nakedness, a sense of shame, is of the essence of civilization and distinguishes us from the doom of the brutes. Far from being a blot, the awareness is a boon, the greatest there is since all others, cognizance of gender difference and accompanying insight into the manifold complexities of social relations, depend on it. On this reading, the deity represented in the Genesis myth stands, as the gods in early Greek literature do, for supernatural, anti-progressive forces at work in the world, an unsurprising stance given the ancient world's attempts to come to terms with the often overwhelming, harsh conditions besetting humans and animals.

The volume is necessarily selective in content. It takes up texts spanning Genesis through 2 Kings (the Primary History), the Prophetic literature, Wisdom literature, the Gospels, the Pauline letters, and Apocalyptic writings. Equally selective is the limited number of major authors of Western literature and the role of the Bible in their work: Shakespeare, Milton, a few Romantic poets, Shelley in particular, Herman Melville, and contemporary writers like Toni Morrison. The goal is to have readers engage with texts that the contributors assume they may not even have much or any acquaintance with.

In sum, the volume seeks to stimulate questioning about the complex and subtle character of biblical stories, ethical and legal texts, parables and the like, and what has been made of them in later Western literature. I recall a teacher reading Hamlet aloud in class but at no time making a single comment. Come the last act, the last scene, the last line of the play, he closed the book, looked at the class intently, and said, "A good play *Hamlet*, a good play." Bewildered, some pupils read the play again to see why the teacher might think there was anything good in it. There was. The intent of the volume is to communicate the excellence of a past author's thinking and to see the study of the texts as an adventure, to recognize that "there is sleuthing in scholarship as there is in crime, and it is full of mystery, danger, intrigue, suspense and thrills." Vladimir Nabokov underscores the vital requirement: "At a time when American readers are taught from High School on to seek in books 'general ideas' a critic's duty should be to draw their attention to specific detail, to the unique image, without which there can be no art, no genius, no Chekhov, no terror, no tenderness, and no surprise."[2]

---

[2] On scholarly sleuthing, see Harry Wolfson, *Crescas' Critique of Aristotle* (Cambridge, MA, 1929), VI:x; on Nabokov, see *Dear Bunny, Dear Volodya: The Nabokov-Wilson Letters, 1940–1971*, ed. Simon Karlinsky (Berkeley, 2001), 331.

1 Literature in the Ancient Near East and the Bible

STEVE A. WIGGINS

In the broad scope of Western Literature, the Bible fits squarely within what is called Ancient Near Eastern literature. Although the discovery of ancient texts outside the Bible began in earnest only in the 1870s, it has become obvious that literature has been a basic component of civilization itself since nearly the development of writing itself. Valued long before the biblical period, writing took many forms in its early stages. This article will consider three social contexts of ancient literature outside the Bible: empires, influential kingdoms (often under the hegemony of empires), and small kingdoms (mainly in conflict with other small kingdoms). These categories overlap. The smallest kingdoms were seldom truly independent.

First, the large empires of antiquity – Mesopotamian, Egyptian, and Hittite – all produced literary works. The focus here will be on the Akkadian Epic of Gilgamesh. Mesopotamia produced a wealth of literary texts, not all of which have been translated and published even to the present day. Gilgamesh is among the best known and most complete exemplars. For the second category, the kingdom of Ugarit – under Egyptian hegemony for part of its history, but also under the influence of the Hittite empire – produced a substantial body of literature that suggests other similar kingdoms may have done so as well. Surprisingly, some of the most literate compositions derive from such city-states that fell under the control of larger empires. It might be supposed that the centers of power would control the narrative. The surviving examples from smaller cultures, however, show that many literary centers of antiquity thrived without the wealth of empire. Perhaps all literature should be considered local. The third category concerns small kingdoms that rarely asserted their authority outside their borders. Apart from Israel, the ancient home of the Bible, the Transjordanian Moabite kingdom also left a literary legacy. Kingdoms such as Israel/Judah and Moab were rarely independent and rarely important enough to influence other peoples, even at the level of city-states such as Ugarit. All of these varieties of kingdoms, however, produced literature. Even in the smaller, poorer regions literary sensitivity was alive.

LITERATURE

Before considering the specifics of the cultures under discussion, a brief introduction to "literature" is necessary. Ancient writers represent an elite class. As individuals who merited lengthy training in the onerous task of becoming scribes, they were surely intelligent enough to distinguish different types of literature. Victory stelae were different from myths. This is evident in Akkadian, where special cuneiform signs were used only in mythological compositions, or in the (much later) different pointing systems in Hebrew to separate the books of Psalms, Proverbs, and Job from the remainder of the Hebrew Bible. "Pointing" was a system of adding vowels to texts composed of consonants only. Such distinctions demonstrate an awareness of different categories of writing.

Writing in ancient times also required demanding conditions for the survival of documents. Writing materials – initially clay and stone – while durable, could also be fragile. The period of time in which early literature developed was one of frequent turmoil and destruction. Additionally, many ancient sites have never been excavated, almost certainly leaving important information buried to this day. Of the written documents that have been recovered, many of them are the only surviving copies of their literary content. They are often found in a damaged state. None of them survived, passed on by hand, from antiquity to the present, apart from the Bible. Other Ancient Near Eastern Literature, by comparison, had to be rediscovered with all the concomitant difficulties of documents that had become lost for centuries. Many empty spaces, or lacunae, plague the written record, at times obscuring literary traits that may have been incorporated at the time of writing. This is an important respect in which these documents differ from the Bible. Despite its problem areas, the biblical text is virtually complete.

To understand the literature of vanished cultures, some idea of what "literature" is must be established. Among scholarly work in the field, "literature" may refer to any written document of sufficient length, or it may refer to a specific type of document. Since the texts covered in this piece are foundational for writing itself due to their antiquity, their role in defining literature will be considered, along with their own literary character. What did ancient people think that they were writing? Was myth different from literature? What distinguishes history from literature? Questions like these underscore the importance of setting a definition of literature that fits the evidence. This is a particularly vital point since the records themselves do not contain a word that might be considered an equivalent to the modern concept of "literature."

For the purposes of this article, literature denotes written material that was intended to be shared, and therefore was deliberately crafted with some kind of artistic value. The level may not reach what we consider *belle lettres* in modern times, but there is a contextual artistry apparent in the texts we will examine. Consider the difference between simple lists of gods, or even court annals, and a narrative account of a battle left on a victory stele. The latter will be the "public facing" account that demonstrates the success of the king's gods. Some braggadocio should be expected. The reader or listener will be drawn in to some extent. It has the rudiments of a narrative arc. Court annals, according to the biblical book of Esther, are read to help a king overcome insomnia.

While literature purely for entertainment purposes was millennia in the future, story-telling as an art form predated writing. The materials explored here, necessarily briefly, will show evidence of literary crafting, even if for different intended purposes.

Recent analyses of ancient writing establish that a fluidity of texts was normal and that reading literary pieces as "books" is anachronistic. We do not possess the final form of any piece of ancient literature simply because there was no "final form." An exception to this may be the last piece explored here – the Mesha Stele, written on stone and erected (that is, "published") for public display. This may have been intended as a non-fluid text. None of the Epic of Gilgamesh, the Baal Cycle, or the Mesha Stele has an author, as the word is currently understood. For sure they were written down, but they were not authored in the same sense as a modern novel or history is. This is a proviso to be kept in mind when approaching the works under consideration here. With one exception (part of the reason the Moabite Stone was chosen for this study) multiple versions of these texts exist. None was the "fine copy" of pre-computer days.

ANCIENT EMPIRES AND THEIR LITERATURE

The choice of which ancient literary pieces should be given special attention necessarily involves some value judgments. The focus here will be primarily on documents that have some bearing on the literature of the Bible. That does not mean that each piece will have had any direct influence on the Bible. In fact, scholars have agreed that proving dependence is nearly impossible. Direct quotations are extremely rare, and a change of languages and often great distances between cultures are generally involved. This observation must be balanced with the fact that many ancient documents share a similar cultural milieu and therefore possess a similarity borne of this common basic setting. A general survey will help to set the stage.

The earliest writing culture was Sumer, located in what is now southern Iraq. Writing also appeared early in Egypt. The connection between them at this embryonic stage, if any, is obscure. Sumer was eventually superseded by the culture of Babylonia. The first generally acknowledged empire was that of Sargon of Akkad. The Babylonians, it is clear, borrowed literature from the Sumerians. Closely related to the Babylonians but further to the north were the Assyrians. The Assyrians also borrowed literature from Babylonia. This essay does not have the space to tease apart the complexities of how these Mesopotamian cultures differed, but it should be noted that the world of the Bible was frequently dominated by the large empires that grew in Assyria and Babylonia. Scribes in Israel may possibly have known, in some form, various literary pieces such as the Gilgamesh Epic, which originated in Sumer.

Egypt also eventually grew to attain empire status. Israel was often under the hegemony of Egypt. Egypt asserted control over the Levant, along the eastern Mediterranean coastal regions, during much of the developmental period of what the Bible calls "Canaan." This is made clear by the Amarna Letters, a cache of clay tablets containing correspondence between pharaohs of the Eighteenth Dynasty and various rulers in Mesopotamia and the Levant. Other ancient documents also demonstrate Egypt's power in the region. The nature of Egyptian myths was quite distinct from that of Mesopotamian myths.

Although the Hittites are mentioned in the Bible and although their empire rivaled that of Egypt occasionally, their literature seems to have had no impact on the Bible. Hittite is an Indo-European language as opposed to the Semitic language family shared by Mesopotamia and most inhabitants of the Levant. Geographically, the Hittite power-base was concentrated in Asia Minor (present day Turkey) and the literature of that short-lived empire seems not to have penetrated into the Bible. Compared with Mesopotamia and Egypt the quantity of literary materials surviving from the Hittite Empire is not extensive. That may change as further discoveries are added from excavations in the region.

No reason exists for supposing that biblical writers had access, in written form, to the ancient documents uncovered in modern times. At the same time, similarities and parallels demonstrate that some of the ideas and concepts contained in the texts of these empires managed to maintain enough currency to have influenced writers of biblical books. One of these influential documents is the Epic of Gilgamesh from ancient Mesopotamia. Other Mesopotamian literature could be chosen to compare to the Bible as well. The *Enuma Elish*, the Babylonian "creation story," would be an obvious choice, as would the "Babylonian Job." Gilgamesh, however, is a singular literary piece for a number of reasons.

THE LITERATURE OF AN EMPIRE

The Gilgamesh Epic, aside from being one of the most complete of ancient literary documents, is also one known from parts of multiple copies. Clearly, it was a "best seller" of its day and scribes from any number of cultures would have been familiar with it. Parts of it have been found in copies in several locations in Babylonia, as well as Hattusa, Emar, Ugarit, and Megiddo. It also has episodes that resonate with the biblical text, particularly the book of Genesis. Not only that, but the epic can still be read today for guidance concerning the issues it addressed for ancient readers. Few other ancient texts can make that claim. (Ancient "wisdom" texts, however, being largely "secular," may also still contain useful counsel for modern readers, not unlike the much later *Meditations* of Marcus Aurelius.)

Summarizing the action – what modern readers are accustomed to thinking of as plot – is unavoidable in a discussion of ancient literature. The issue of literary genre is particularly salient, if not easily established. The category of "bromance" did not exist in the patriarchal world of antiquity, but the adventures of Gilgamesh and Enkidu may have been the first steps in that direction. It is a nonhistorical epic on the human level with philosophical orientation. Clearly, the many versions of Gilgamesh were shared for entertainment purposes, broadly understood. Indeed, it may have had a function close to modern literature, within its ancient context.

Before beginning the summary of the Gilgamesh Epic, it should be noted that different versions exist (to be discussed later) and some episodes occur in some copies of the story but not in others. The summary here will be of the "Standard Version," although that designation does not have the force of casting a single version as the correct or authoritative rendition. There is no single author and no final version of the epic. It is a fluid text. This is a point to which we shall return. The story line proceeds roughly as follows.

Gilgamesh is king of Uruk, in southern Mesopotamia. For reasons not entirely clear, his people complain to the gods asking them to divert his oppressive behaviors against his own subjects. In typical divine fashion, the gods answer the prayers in a roundabout way. They send a wild man, Enkidu, who will rival, but not best, Gilgamesh in physical prowess. Tamed by a prolonged encounter with a prostitute, Enkidu is humanized and led to the city. After initially fighting Gilgamesh, Enkidu becomes his friend and they wander from their urban center in search of excitement. Pausing at this moment, it is remarkable how modern this storyline (sans deities) appears. The basic plot is a staple of action novels still. One way to define literature might be through a recognition of durability of themes.

Fully aware that there will be consequences for their actions, Gilgamesh and Enkidu head to the famed cedar forests of Lebanon to face off with the monster Humbaba. During their preparations for the coming fight with this fearsome forest guardian, the heroes commission special weapons. This section of the poem resembles the Baal Cycle; when Hadad prepares to take on Yam, the deity in control of the cosmic sea, he also commissions special weapons. On their journey to the forest, Gilgamesh and Enkidu perform daily rituals and Gilgamesh experiences nightly dreams. Humbaba was divinely appointed as a guardian of the cedar forest, and by killing him the pair defy divine decree; the monster protects the forest because the gods have given him that task. The ogre is nevertheless dispatched and the heroes fell one of the famed cedars and return to Uruk. In the city, the goddess Ishtar becomes smitten with Gilgamesh's regal appearance. She proposes to him. Unwisely, he insults her, pointing out that her past lovers have all ended up worse for her attentions. Once again it becomes clear that Gilgamesh had a great deal of influence on other ancient literature. Although not the Baal Cycle, the Ugaritic epic of Aqhat contains a similar scene. Aqhat, a human hero with a divinely made gift-weapon, attracts the attention of Anat, a goddess with some resemblance to Ishtar. Anat covets his bow and makes him promises about his rewards, should he give it to her. He instead insults the goddess with tragic results. This cautionary theme may have been consciously borrowed from Gilgamesh.

Stung by Gilgamesh's rebuke, Ishtar begs her father Anu to give her the bull of heaven to destroy the proud king. Her threats of violence against the gods – she threatens to break into the underworld and release the dead – are likewise reflected in Anat's threats against El in the epic of Aqhat. Enkidu and Gilgamesh together, however, slay the bull and Enkidu adds further to Ishtar's fury by throwing part of the rear quarters of the bull at her. The gods decide one of the two must die, and Enkidu is elected over Gilgamesh. A lengthy deathbed scene, similar to that in the Ugaritic epic of Kirta, is played out. Gilgamesh, devastated, journeys to Utnapishtim to learn why people must die. Along the way he encounters scorpion-men, a wise tavern keeper, and one of the earliest mythological ferrymen, Urshabanu. Ferried across the wide ocean, he meets Utnapishtim and hears the story of the world-wide flood. Only by being flood survivors did Utnapishtim and his wife become immortal. This "Mesopotamian Noah," however, tells Gilgamesh of a plant that will restore his youth. He finds the plant only to have the potential restoration of youth stolen by a snake. He returns home sadder but wiser. This entire final section (tablet XI of the standard version of the series) clearly influenced the development of the primeval narrative of Genesis 1–11, at least thematically.

Several facts about Gilgamesh reveal how ancient epic literature was understood. Multiple copies of Gilgamesh exist, at least in part, and they can thus be compared. What emerges is that no single version represents the canonical Gilgamesh. There is a "Standard Version," followed here, but that is a modern convention based on the fairly late version found in Ashurbanipal's library. Fluidity of texts was the rule. Gilgamesh had previously been a hero represented in Sumerian language poems that do not appear in epic or series form but which clearly predate the Epic. The poems of Bilgamesh, as he is known in them, may be the basis for later elaboration in episodes that did make it into the recognized series.

This history of transmission suggests a certain inchoate nature to ancient narrative. In a sense, Gilgamesh is a fixed character – king of Uruk, monster-slayer, darling of the gods – while, at the same time, details differ among accounts. Such fluidity might be considered an artifact of change over time except that we see similar discrepancies in other ancient literature such as the Ugaritic texts and even the Hebrew Bible. Ancient Near Eastern literature did not consist of final texts. Stories changed with each written retelling. There is not one authoritative version of Gilgamesh. Despite our modern literary sensibilities, we cannot declare that the story played out in any single way. Alternative versions exist, as also with Ugaritic literary texts. The Mesha Stele is different in this regard (which is the main reason for including it here). Comparison with ancient Near Eastern literature indicates a fluidity of narrative that has implications for the Bible. Simple assessments of "what happened" depend on which version a reader is following.

Another fact regarding Gilgamesh is that it was considered a series of episodes, or a set of tablets that went together, already in antiquity. The modern equivalent might be considered long form fiction, such as a novel. Gilgamesh, however, like most other ancient epics, was written as poetry. This series-like quality compares favorably with the Baal Cycle from Ugarit. As a literary piece, Gilgamesh was copied and, to an extent, imitated. The title of the epic changed over time, as did the contents. Nevertheless, the story had broad continuity and currency; parts have been found in Anatolia, the Levant, and throughout Mesopotamia.

The facts concerning the Gilgamesh Epic's preservation indicate that the fixity of literature we associate with either a single autograph copy, such as the Mesha Stele or parts of the Baal Cycle, or with a highly edited collection, such as the Hebrew Bible, is more an impression than an expectation of established "Scripture." The Baal Cycle, as we shall see, is not fixed in the same way as Gilgamesh appears to be, and there are pieces that some Ugaritologists believe should be included in the Cycle. Others disagree. This lack of a stable, canonical version, however, may be considered a basic characteristic of ancient literature.

Reading in antiquity was a specialized skill. The experience of Gilgamesh, in as much as non-elites might have had it, would have been aural. The style of writing was poetic verse, which indicates the likelihood of recitation. We know nothing of the occasions of such public readings, if they even transpired. In other words, although the Epic of Gilgamesh was clearly literature, lack of modern knowledge of its contextual use constrains what might be known about the function of literature in an empire where the population was generally not literate. The multiple copies that have survived indicate that the epic was clearly popular, at least among cultured classes. Andrew George, in the introduction to his translation, makes the point that Gilgamesh is not typically religious literature, but was composed in a world where religion pervaded the everyday outlook in a way that is difficult for modern people to comprehend.

Rather than expend the remainder of the article attempting to cover equally the wide scope of surviving documents from the many cultures of the region, two other explicitly literary texts will be considered in more detail – one is the mythological corpus from the city-state of Ugarit and the other the Mesha Stele of ancient Moab. Neither Ugarit nor Moab was large or affluent enough to have been considered an empire. Ugarit was a prosperous city-state of the northeast Mediterranean. Moab was a rather less developed, land-locked state near the desert that skirmished for borders with ancient Israel, itself a rather small and marginal kingdom.

LITERATURE OF AN AFFLUENT KINGDOM

The Gilgamesh Epic is widely enough known to have appeared in popular editions such as Penguin Classics and general-reader trade versions. Almost unknown among nonacademic readerships stand the Ugaritic Texts. These important tablets derived from a much smaller political entity than the large, wealthy Mesopotamian empires. Ugarit was a small city-state on the Mediterranean coast of what is now northern Syria. It never rivaled the Egyptian or Mesopotamian powers or the Hittite Empire to the north. Nevertheless, Ugarit boasted a literate priesthood and preserved myths that may well have had wider representation throughout the region. These stories are elaborate, detailed, and carefully plotted. They have characters and situations not unlike those of Gilgamesh, but mostly in what seem to be single copies. That means that considerable gaps exist in the stories because of damage to the texts and the action is not always clear. This situation does not inspire modern literary editions for the wider public.

The Ugaritic Texts are less well-known in general, but are among the most important ancient literature to have been reflected in the Bible. Ugarit was destroyed around the turn of the twelfth century BCE, and preserved among the ruins were at least three sizable, multi-tablet mythological, literary texts. The three pieces are known as the Legend of Kirta, the Tale of Aqhat, and the Baal Cycle. As noted in the discussion of Gilgamesh, each of these collections at the very least reflects themes that appear in that Epic. This indicates that ancient literature, like modern literature, was in some sense derivative. The texts from Ugarit may have been adapted to reflect local interest. The same thing appears to have happened with the Hebrew Bible.

While the nature of the Baal Cycle as an actual single literary piece is disputed, it is the longest of the preserved texts from Ugarit and it shows considerable literary awareness. The format of Ugaritic mythological writing also allows for a discussion of the difference between poetry and prose, a distinction not as evident in ancient story-telling as in modern writing. Like Homer, other ancient writers forged epics in poetic form. They were not the means of conveying historical information, and it demonstrates that an awareness of the differences between historical documents (such as the Mesha Stele) and epic tales (Gilgamesh, the Baal Cycle) was recognized already in antiquity. Gilgamesh and the Ugaritic myths were poetic. Prose appears in such documents as the Mesha Stele and long swaths of the Hebrew Bible, as well as court annals and other mundane matters of record.

Although the Baal Cycle may not have been composed as a unified literary epic, the episodes that survive may be fitted together into a recognizable literary sequence. The overall plot appears to be the story of how Baal ("Lord," whose personal name was Hadad) became the king of the gods of Ugarit. As in Greek mythology (which likely borrowed the concept from Semitic precursors), there were different generations of deities. The earlier generation is represented by El (also spelled "Ilu"), whose name is the basic West Semitic word for "God." El is the creator and father of a younger generation of deities. Some interpreters claim Baal is not El's son because there are references to Baal as the "son of Dagan." To argue, however, for strict genealogies of the gods is to miss the protean nature of ancient mythology. It is important to remember that the fluidity of ancient texts belies a final, authoritative version. While it is possible that the story involves rivalry between different families of divinities, that dynamic is not necessary to make narrative sense. All of the characters in this particular myth are gods.

Unfortunately, the opening is missing. The story seems to start with Baal ordered to be subservient to Yam. The senior deity, El, does not actively rule the earth, a role that is left to one of the younger generation of gods. Yam is the god "Sea." Based on cultural context, this casts him in a similar role to Tiamat in the Mesopotamian "creation story," *Enuma Elish*. Like Gilgamesh, *Enuma Elish* also helps set the pattern for other ancient Near Eastern myths, including the Baal Cycle and parts of the Hebrew Bible. (Genesis 1–11, Job 41, Psalms 74 and 104, and Isaiah 27, for example, all show some influence of "sea serpent" mythology.) The story of *Enuma Elish* is well known: the older generation of gods plans the destruction of the younger generation. The younger gods, led by Marduk, prevail in a battle against their mother, the fierce water-dragon Tiamat. Marduk creates the world from her corpse. The Baal Cycle frustratingly suffers from a broken beginning, so we do not have that kind of backstory. Instead we have Yam in charge of the younger generation of deities and a distraught Baal ordered into servitude. This leads to conflict. Baal, with the help of magical maces constructed by the crafty god Kothar wa-Hasis, defeats Yam in single combat. As in Gilgamesh, the explicit narration of the creation of powerful weapons is essential to the story. Sadly, after Yam's defeat, once again the tablet breaks off, leaving any "creation" episode, if it even existed, missing.

Thematically, this first episode of the "cycle" fits well with what follows, and thus the suggestion of a continuous narrative makes sense, although the scenes lack any transition due to the lacuna. Baal, flush with victory, decides to build a palace. He summons his sister Anat, who is artfully introduced in the story. As a goddess enamored of war, she slaughters human armies. When the battle is over, she returns to her home, sets up her furniture like soldiers, and attacks this inanimate "army" as well. Although brief, the scene skillfully presents how she is characterized. The reader or listener has a good idea of what this violent goddess is like. Elsewhere (in the myth of Dan'el) Anat threatens even El, the titular king of the gods, with violence. Such threats of violence were also characteristic of Ishtar in Gilgamesh. Demanding the release of the bull of heaven, Ishtar threatens Anu with violence if her request is not met.

The Ugaritic drama builds suspense as Baal strategically approaches the question of how to request a palace from El. He sends for his sister to join him. Baal's purpose in summoning Anat is to have her assist him in persuading Athirat, El's consort, to plead his cause before El himself. Before they visit the ranking goddess, however, Baal requests a sumptuous hoard of gifts to be made by Kothar wa-Hasis, the craftsman god who had made Baal's weapons to fight Yam. Swayed by the presents, Asherah journeys to El's abode and asks permission for Baal to construct a palace, which El somewhat reluctantly grants. Baal has become the king of the gods. In order to erect a palace, however, he requires El's permission.

It has been proposed, since this episode plays such a major role in the cycle, that the origin of the myth was the building, or dedication, of Baal's temple in Ugarit. A temple dedicated to Baal was indeed unearthed during the excavations of the city. The narrative, as well as additional evidence from the site, make it clear that Baal was the patron deity of Ugarit. It is possible, then, that this is the background to the story.

After the palace built by Kothar wa-Hasis is complete, and a divine feast is thrown, Baal requests a window to be installed. Although the reason is not entirely clear, it seems that he originally feared that Yam might come back and kidnap his daughters through a window and so he had refused to allow one in his palace. Now, however, he decides that his function of controlling thunderstorms requires such an aperture.

Having a window also allows him to project his voice (thunder) over the earth. Once Baal has established his kingship over the gods, he is challenged. The text is uncertain regarding details, but it may be that he provocatively challenges his major remaining nemesis, Mot, whose name means "death."

Mot claims to be the strongest of gods. Here we have echoes of Gilgamesh. In both tales the protagonist has to face the ultimate power of death. In the ancient world gods could die. This was not the usual fate of divinities, but violent death could be a potential threat. The Mesopotamian Descent of Ishtar (based on an earlier Sumerian tale) also explores the death of gods. In another connection to Gilgamesh, both Gilgamesh and Hadad come face-to-face with mortality after an exciting victory. Baal (Hadad) had defeated Yam just as Gilgamesh had defeated the Bull of Heaven. Baal, after receiving a lengthy introduction to the power of death, admits that Mot conquers all. He is ordered to submit and enters the underworld. Baal's death is mourned thoroughly among the gods and the human world experiences drought.

Anat, however, cannot live without her lover Baal. She searches for him and finds his body and buries him. (Her digging of holes in the earth is also reminiscent of Gilgamesh.) After a sacrifice, she informs El that Baal is dead. The immediate concern among the gods is to find a replacement for him. Athtar, a lesser god often supposed to be in charge of fresh water, is proposed but declines the position since he is too small to fill Baal's throne. Anat longs for Baal and confronts Mot. She beats him into pieces. Baal returns from the underworld and is found by Shapash – the goddess "sun" – and Anat. He then engages Mot in single combat. Neither deity, apparently, can subdue the other. El, whose decision is carried to the scene by Shapash, declares for Baal and he is once again established as the king of the gods. Note here that the deity supporting Gilgamesh throughout his adventures is Shemesh, the sun god. Shapash, the Ugaritic sun goddess, like Shemesh, is associated with justice. The Ugaritic "cycle" ends with Baal firmly in charge.

EPIC COMPARISONS

The point of the comparisons made here is not to suggest direct borrowing from Gilgamesh. A copy of at least part of the Gilgamesh Epic was found at Ugarit, and thus the story was known there, but this is not the same as declaring that the Ugaritic scribes – or biblical authors for that matter – consciously lifted episodes from the Epic to fit their own stories.

The Baal Cycle, it is tempting to say, does not have the same level of artistry as Gilgamesh. It is, however, problematic to apply modern standards of literary artistry to ancient texts. As with Gilgamesh, the Baal Cycle (if intended as a cycle) suffers from large lacunae. The story, in keeping with cultural convention, is repetitive, with sections repeated almost verbatim. The same is true of the Gilgamesh Epic. Given the missing pieces it is unclear whether Baal vanquishing Yam served as a "creation myth" for Ugarit or not. Its shared aspect with other creation myths, however, is not in doubt. The Gilgamesh Epic had the benefit of literary polishing. Assyriologists note that Ashurbanipal's library, established to be a repository of Assyrian literary wisdom not unlike the British Library or the Library of Congress, contained versions with literary embellishments that came with the refinement of multiple renditions. The Baal Cycle, to date, is known in a single, incomplete copy. The relationship with fragments will be addressed further along.

The function of the Baal Cycle is debated – it may have had a ritual or liturgical use; at least some Ugaritic tablets seem to have preserved performance instructions, most notably KTU 1.22. The Baal Cycle preserves no explicit rubrics regarding the occasion, but enough hints remain to suggest a formal recitation for at least parts of the poem. Gilgamesh, on the other hand, does not immediately suggest a particular cultic setting. As written literary compositions both pieces were intended to be available to others, fitting with the basic definition of literature used here. The fact that Gilgamesh is known in more than one recension suggests that it [=G] was known beyond its place of origin, but it [=G also?] does not indicate how it was used.

One obvious difference between the two works is that the Baal Cycle is religious literature. The cast of characters consists of gods only. This also points to the likelihood of liturgical use of the Baal cycle. Another point of differentiation is that the "cycle," although somewhat logical, isn't as clearly defined as the Gilgamesh Epic. Both "epics" suffer from lacunae that make a fixed interpretation difficult. Such a grouping of texts may be foreign to the material as well. Although KTU 1.6 (the final tablet of the cycle) begins with an opening line *lb^cl* ("to/of/about/for Baal," indicating perhaps inclusion in a set of texts) it is the only tablet of the standard series with an intact first line. KTU 1.4, in the palace episode, ends with a statement naming the scribe, KTU 1.5 does not, and KTU 1.6 follows directly on from it. Column IV of KTU 1.6 ends with an expanded identification of the writer, suggesting that a larger cycle may have been its context.

With the Baal Cycle (KTU 1.1–1.6) also, fragments such as KTU 1.8, 1.10, 1.11, and 1.133 share characters and perhaps even episodes known from the somewhat probable complete "cycle." Do these represent alternative versions? Scholarly practice tablets? Or, like the Gilgamesh variations, do they point to a fluidity of the narrative? The modern perspective of fixity of texts is a faulty lens. The Bible, for example, differs depending on whether it is a Protestant Bible, a Roman Catholic Bible, or an Eastern Orthodox Bible. Differences in contents may be slight, but they are not identical. As noted previously, fluidity of texts is characteristic of ancient literature. There is no single version.

Stepping outside the context of ancient sacred literature, the expectation of the fixity of texts sometimes depends on modern publishers' practices. Even with the concept of a stable text, corrected printings of a modern book mean that multiple versions may exist under the same title, or even the same ISBN. What any single text says is a function of the impression rather than the fact of a solid final version. Taking this point back to the Bible, consider the "King James Version." It exists in different formats – it was originally translated with the Apocrypha/Deuterocanonical books, but now is generally printed without them. Not only that, but different versions of the King James Bible appeared over time. There is no single, fixed King James Version.

Given these circumstances, expecting a stability of ancient texts that were copied by hand is illogical. The multiple versions of Gilgamesh and the fragments of Baal point to comfort with literary fluidity that contrasts with the modern preference of relative fixity of texts. Ancient texts exhibit more openness than present understandings of literature suggest. An exception to this may be a piece such as the Moabite Stone, which is a war monument. Multiple versions of battle accounts often exist. Famously, the Hittite and Egyptian versions of the battle of Kadesh on the Orontes carry conflicting outlooks of the same event. They were, however, clearly literary endeavors among such forms of writing. On a much smaller scale, the Mesha Stele, or Moabite Stone, is an example of a relatively complete, autograph-version, historically based literary effort.

LITERATURE OF A SINGLE CULTURE

Ancient Israel and Judah shared, along with their immediate neighbors, a political structure that apparently lacked the centrality of a dominant city state. Several limited "nations" maintained some small measure of cultural uniqueness from one another while sharing a general milieu. Israel's nearest neighbors are known as Aram, Ammon, Moab, Edom, Philistia, and Phoenicia. These cultures did not all strictly overlap chronologically nor were they equal in size or influence. Aram, encompassing a fair portion of modern Syria, was probably the largest in land area and exerted considerable political influence on its neighbors. Israel, sharing its northern border with Aram, had frequent clashes with it.

Unfortunately for a survey of a literary variety, not much survives from these neighbors that might be considered *belles lettres*. Inscriptions come to light from time to time, but sources that might compare with the Hebrew Bible or Gilgamesh are rare.

An eastern neighbor of Israel and Judah, Moab, produced an example of a historico-literary text that includes a remarkable modern story easily accessible in the accounts of its finding. The document is known as the Mesha Stele, or the Moabite Stone. It consists of a 34-line inscription commissioned by Mesha, the king of Moab, on the occasion of a divine deliverance from Israel.

The Mesha Stele may seem an odd choice to compare with the serial nature of the Gilgamesh Epic and the Baal Cycle, but it serves as an example of history as literature, or literature as history. If Gilgamesh is an ancient novel, the Mesha Stele is a short story. We consider the account here because it reports on a conflict between the nations that the Bible also represents, and the stele text is relatively complete. Underlying the Mesha Stele as literature is the larger question of history as literature. Although the concept of history as "what really happened" remains current for many people, historians have long acknowledged that any history is a perspective on events – a literary reconstruction. The Mesha Stele illustrates that exceptionally well.

Mesha was the king of Moab in the mid-ninth century BCE. His reign overlapped with that of Jehoram (851–842) of Israel. The inscription on the Moabite Stone commemorates a number of feats, including a victory over Israel that corresponds very loosely with 2 Kings 3, the narrative of Jehoram's conflict with Mesha. The biblical account, replete with miracles and an appearance by Elisha, would not count as history in any strict sense of the word. It has, however, the hallmarks of a literary story: Mesha has withheld tribute from Jehoram. To shore up his strength, Jehoram invites Jehoshaphat, king of Judah, and the unnamed king of Edom, to join him in an attack on Mesha. The three kings, well provisioned, inexplicably forget to bring water. When their armies begin to suffer from thirst, they summon Elisha. The great prophet only responds out of divine regard for Jehoshaphat, a pious king in his eyes. Yahweh would send water down the wadis although it would not rain. The next morning, the Moabites, naively supposing the sunrise reflected in the water to be blood, rush out only to be defeated by the three kings waiting for them. When the Israelite coalition traps Mesha inside Kir-hareseth, he sacrifices his son and "great wrath" comes upon Israel, leading them to withdraw.

Consider this story from a literary standpoint: The *casus belli* involves the withholding of wool as tribute, indicating a lack of precious metal in Moab (metal was required for manufacturing valuable implements of war) – this is not a powerful enemy. Nevertheless, Jehoram invites two other kings to help ensure victory. Experienced warriors would not fail to provision an army with water. A supernatural intermediary is called in and a miracle follows. The Moabites are gullible enough to mistake dawn's early light on the water for blood. The intervention of Chemosh, the god of Moab, decides the final battle for Moab. These elements construct a fine story, but do not measure up as history. Does Mesha do any better?

The Moabite Stone is typical of ancient Near Eastern markers that commemorate the accomplishments of kings. The level of the claims is appropriately modest for a small kingdom. The stone itself was a dedicatory stele for a sanctuary of Chemosh, who delivered Mesha from aggressors in this version of events. The principal instigator was Israel under the Omride dynasty. The inscription describes Omri's incursions into Moabite territory that continued into the reign of Ahab. The stone names only Omri as king of Israel, referring to Ahab as "his son." It is thus difficult to align the Mesha stele precisely with the story of 2 Kings 3. The biblical account, for its part, does not name specific cities apart from Kir-hareseth, and contains several instances of exaggeration and a miracle. According to the Mesha Stele, Moab's fortunes were reversed in Mesha's day and he names specific locations where he attacked to take back land annexed by Israel. He notes that Chemosh delivered him and that his victories were followed by building activities on Mesha's part. In other words, both the Stele and the Kings account contain legendary elements along with their interpretation of history and the two accounts cannot be readily coordinated.

The Mesha Stele has a simple plot: Israel oppresses Moab. Chemosh, the god of Moab, notices their suffering and gives a series of successes to Mesha. After each victory, some kind of dedication is made to Chemosh. Building activity follows victory. This is useful to compare against Gilgamesh despite the obvious differences in character. Both Gilgamesh and Mesha are kings. Both interact with the gods. Clearly, however, although there are elements of divine intervention, the story of Mesha is intended to be largely "historical." It is nevertheless simultaneously a literary product. Consider the narrative arc: Israel oppressed Moab, Chemosh noted this, and Mesha experienced continued success in answering Israel's insults, finally prevailing with the help of his god. The Omrides are cast as villains and Mesha the victim cum victor. There is a satisfying literary development here.

As in the building episode of the Baal Cycle, the Moabite Stone seems to possess a motive of placating a deity through building. Baal's temple in Ugarit is matched by this stele in a comparatively less wealthy nation's building program. The activity of building shows or garners the favor of deities.

The Mesha Stele was not intended as *belles lettres*, but care was taken to cast historical developments in a coherent narrative that show the protagonist – Mesha – in a positive light. The inscription itself, while rare for the smaller kingdoms of this region, follows literary conventions well known from both Egypt and Mesopotamia. These accounts, also intended for public consumption, present themselves with an artistry not required for a simple record of events that had transpired in historical time, such as chronicles or annals. In other words, they portray the kingdom as literate, and proudly so. Not only that, since a victory stele was intended as a "final word" on the episode, the Moabite Stone has the best case here for a fixed text.

Contrasting this literary inscription with the Gilgamesh Epic and the Ugaritic Baal Cycle helps to define Ancient Near Eastern literature. First of all, although not strictly required (as evidenced by other literary compositions), many ancient stories pertained to royalty. Kings were those who could afford to patronize scribes, so literature in cultures with elite power structures reflects literacy as a privilege. While not all literature is mythological, the gods are expected and welcome characters in just about any narrative. Gilgamesh is the son of a goddess, is guided by Shamash, falls afoul of Ishtar, and receives the judgment of Anu. Mesha credits Chemosh with his victory over his troublesome neighbor, Israel. The Baal Cycle is a narrative set in the divine world, but the other two major Ugaritic narratives – Aqhat and Kirta – also present visits from the divine realm.

ANCIENT NEAR EASTERN LITERATURE

Despite the lacunae and accidents of archaeology, the literature of the Ancient Near East was vast. A brief exploration such as this cannot hope to cover the entirety of this large, and continually growing, corpus. Nonetheless, comparing three different types of literature from three different cultures and three differing literary genres is informative. It helps demonstrate the broad range of literary diversity, along with certain commonalities. Ancient literature cannot be measured against current literary preferences. Characters may "change their spots" across, and perhaps within, a single body of literature. Literary series, even when honed over time, do not follow the logic of modern sensibilities. For example, the Standard Version of the Gilgamesh Epic summarized in this chapter excludes a twelfth tablet that is clearly part of the series. Many Assyriologists exclude it as a kind of appendix since Enkidu, who died earlier, reappears in the story. The style and narrative continuity have changed. Nevertheless, some ancients clearly included it as part of the series. The lacuna here is in our knowledge not in the original telling.

Deities do not represent unchangeable entities the way they later will in monotheistic thought systems. They change their minds and sometimes even act in contradictory ways. Ancient texts are not systematic theologies. What occurs in a story has a certain literary contingency about it. That remains true regardless of the instability it may inject into the narrative as a whole.

Ancient literature has much to teach us about both the world and the contents of the Bible. Expecting them to be modern, however, sets a reader false expectations about both form and content. Although literature may derive from settings as massive as empires or as small as provincial capitals, in many respects it is always local. The present day analogy is with publishing, which is located within the "empires" of large cities such as New York or London. The writing, however, originates on a much smaller level – today, the individual author.

Perhaps most importantly, such examinations challenge the stability of texts. Literary fluidity is the rule, not the exception. At least partially because of the status of the Bible – theologically labeled as "the word of God" – the concern with a fixed form of a text has developed in western cultures. The more ancient documents we uncover, the clearer this fluidity of ancient writing becomes. If we learn to recognize the fluidity of such literature we will come much closer to understanding what ancient writers wished to record, and did record, on their own terms.

Further Reading

Bryant, John, *The Fluid Texts: A Theory of Revision and Editing for Book and Screen*, Editorial Theory and Literary Criticism (Ann Arbor, MI, 2002).

Culler, Jonathan, *Literary Theory, a Very Short Introduction* (New York, 1997).

Damrosch, David, *The Buried Book: The Loss and Recovery of the Great Epic of Gilgamesh* (New York, 2007).

Dearman, Andrew, ed., *Studies in the Mesha Inscription and Moab*, Archaeology and Biblical Studies 2 (Atlanta, 1989).

George, Andrew, *The Epic of Gilgamesh: The Babylonian Epic Poem and Other Texts in Akkadian and Sumerian* (New York, 1999).

Gibson, J. C. L., *Canaanite Myths and Legends*, 2nd ed. (Edinburgh, 1977).

Kovacs, Maureen Gallery, *The Epic of Gilgamesh* (Stanford, 1989).

Mroczek, Eva, *The Literary Imagination in Jewish Antiquity* (New York, 2016).

Tigay, Jeffrey H., *The Evolution of the Gilgamesh Epic* (Wauconda, IL, 2002).

Wyatt, N., *Religious Texts from Ugarit: The Words of Ilimilku and His Colleagues*, The Biblical Seminar 53 (Sheffield, 1998).

2 The Primary Narrative (Genesis through 2 Kings)

THOMAS L. BRODIE

The Hebrew Bible's first nine books flow into one another in diverse ways, from the creation of everything (Genesis 1–2) to the destruction of Jerusalem, including the exiling of its inhabitants to Babylon (2 Kings 24–25). At one level the account seems clear. At another it appears repetitive, disjointed, and contradictory. Nor is it obvious what kind of writing it is. Jewish tradition saw the five initial books – Genesis, Exodus, Leviticus, Numbers, Deuteronomy – as Torah, literally what hits the mark, usually translated as teaching, instruction, law, "the law of Moses," and called the other four – Joshua, Judges, Samuel, Kings – prophets, "the Former Prophets." Christians, following Greek terminology, called the initial five books the Pentateuch, literally five-scroll, and called the latter four *historiae*, enquiries or histories.

Recently, beginning apparently with David Freeman, all nine have been called "the Primary History."[1] The title is attractive, and reflects the faith–history connection. Yet "history" is often understood as recounting of specific facts. "Narrative," while reflecting some facts, allows for another focus. So, first a brief look back.

THREE KEY ASPECTS OF BIBLICAL INTERPRETATION

For over two thousand years, and especially recently, branches of biblical study have multiplied, but among them all, three approaches are fundamental: allegorical, literal (literally historical), and literary. The three partly overlap.

The Age of Allegorical/Symbolic Interpretation

Early interpreters read scripture as true, and while some took it literally, most saw it as indicating something more – as symbolic or allegorical

---

[1] David N. Freeman, "The Law and the Prophets," *VTSup* 9 (1963), 251.

(Gk. *allos-legō*, "other-saying"). In Alexandria – the Roman Empire's second city, and cultural capital of Greek literature, pivotal in rendering the Bible into Greek – Philo generally read the text as allegorical. Philo (ca. 20 BCE–50 CE) was prestigious, a leader within Alexandria's 100,000 Jewish community, and his influence was lasting: "[T]hrough men like Clement [of Alexandria] and Origen, Philo's allegorizing achieved a dominant place in the Christian exegesis of the Old Testament ... During the 12th, 13th, and early 14th centuries ... literal ... tendencies rose to the surface like islands in the sea, but they did not survive; and the Middle Ages drew to a close with allegory once more dominant."[2]

The Age of History-Focused Interpretation
(The "Historical Critical Method")

The Middle Ages saw the gradual growth of a multi-faceted spirit of critical inquiry, and Martin Luther (1483–1546) added momentum to it. The Bible provided Luther with a counter-authority to the Pope, but as such, the Bible needed to be clear, and clear meant literal, implying literal history. Church authorities responded in kind. "The Reform shifted interpretation from symbolic to literal. And the Catholics said: 'If you go literal, we'll outdo you.'"[3]

Thus began a centuries-long quest, "the historical critical method" or simply "the historical method," which saw the Bible's authority as resting largely not in what it symbolized but on its reliability as a literal guide to the past, to factual history. Raymond Brown often recounted how his mentor William F. Albright urged him to focus his commentary on John (1966–71) not on theology – even though John was often known as "the Theologian" – but on history.

The search for history led to the effort to identify the text's sources, but since the sources were presumed to be largely lost, the only way to identify them was by looking directly at the biblical text itself and thus trying to detect them. This led to two great waves of proposed lost sources: lost written sources, documents; and lost oral sources, traditions.

---

[2] Raymond E. Brown, "Hermeneutics," in *Jerome Biblical Commentary*, eds. R. E. Brown, J. A. Fitzmyer, and R. E. Murphy (London, 1968), 71:37, 42.

[3] Ernan McMullin, "Galileo and the Church." Lecture given at Dublin City University, June 26, 2010.

First, the Lost Written Sources

In 1753 Jean Astruc, observing variations in the text, proposed cautiously that Genesis consists of two distinct documents that predated Moses, thus explaining how Moses described events before his own birth. Around 1883, Julius Wellhausen, researching Israel's history, adapted Astruc's principle that variation reflects diverse sources and, having resigned from his theological faculty to avoid disturbing candidates for ministry, he proposed that the Pentateuch combined four documents, JEDP – Yahwist, Elohist, Deuteronomist, Priest(ly) – and he visualized these four as illustrating diverse times between Solomon and Ezra (970–450 BCE). The JEDP theory – "the documentary/four-source theory" – has had a long history, but "cannot be tied [to]. . . historical reconstruction"; recent proposals to renew the theory included saying goodbye to J or relocating it to the exile, and moving P from the exile back to the monarchy.[4]

Second, the Lost Oral Traditions

Inspired by studies in popular religion, Hermann Gunkel's commentary on Genesis proclaimed that Genesis reflected the experience of undeveloped people, with short attention spans, and drew not on written documents but on sagas, on oral traditions (a kind of tradition different from that of traditional Judaism).[5] The research challenge was to identify the diverse forms of oral tradition, and having identified the form, to trace the tradition's history back, behind writings, to the original experience, the "situation in life" (*Sitz im Leben*). The tracing of forms became known as *form criticism*. Gunkel did not indicate clearly how to trace forms and traditions, or how to identify oral tradition's mediators ("tradents"). By 1938 the hypothesis of dependence on oral traditions had entered the study of both Joshua (Martin Noth) and John's gospel (Percy Gardner-Smith).

At present, both theories, reconstructing lost written sources, and tracing lost oral traditions, emerge as unduly conjectural, unreliable as bases for history. Links between Deuteronomy and Josh/Judg/Sam/Kgs, once seen as evidence for a further hypothetical source, an independent Deuteronomic History (e.g. Martin Noth, 1943), are emerging as part of a larger network of inner-biblical connections. "The last quarter of the 20th century has seen the development of a crisis in the historiography

---

[4] Thomas B. Dozeman, *The Pentateuch: Introducing the Torah* (Minneapolis, 2017), 159–85, 192.
[5] Hermann Gunkel, *Genesis* (Göttingen, 1901), i.

of ancient Israel, which shows no sign of abating in the early years of the 21st."[6] Indeed, Leo G. Perdue speaks of "the collapse of history."[7] Some factual history is retrievable, largely by moving beyond the biblical texts, especially into archaeology.[8] Such retrieval is important but it is not what Gen-Kgs is about.

The Age of Recovering Symbolic Meaning: Scripture as Rhetoric, as Art

Given the crisis in history, some researchers moved the emphasis from history to the text's message, its theology. However, this bypasses something, as James Muilenburg realized. In 1968, his SBL Presidential address was not as dramatic as Luther nailing theses, but it signaled a comparable shift.[9] He supported identifying forms, ultimately literary forms, but spoke of biblical studies being "isolated ... from ... the literary monuments and peoples of the Near East," and of the need for greater attention to literary factors, including rhetoric, namely "rhetorical criticism."[10]

"Rhetoric" can suggest "hollow rhetoric," but the reality is otherwise. Rhetoric was essentially the art of speaking convincingly. And the way of crafting oral speech was by a studied process of writing, so rhetoric shaped writing. Rhetoric reflected the blossoming of the millennia-long development of writing and communicating. It "encapsulated the most ancient, central and pervasive tradition of verbalization and of thought known to mankind, at least in the West."[11]

Muilenburg's appeal had some impact, and, partly for that reason, the sense that the biblical texts are poetic and artistic writings – a sense already developing – gained some ground.[12] A stream of writers has emerged, and already some of the Bible's perplexing features have become clearer. Muilenburg also highlighted delimitation, identifying where a passage begins and ends.

---

[6] John Collins, *The Bible after Babel: Historical Criticism in a Postmodern Age* (Grand Rapids, MI, 2005), 30.

[7] Leo G. Perdue, *Reconstructing OT Theology: After the Collapse of History* (Minneapolis, 2005).

[8] William G. Dever, *Beyond the Texts: An Archaeological Portrait of Ancient Israel and Judah* (Atlanta, 2017).

[9] James Muilenburg, "Form Criticism and Beyond," *JBL* 88 (1969), 1–18.

[10] Ibid., 2, 8.

[11] Walter J. Ong, *Interfaces of the Word: Studies in the Evolution of Consciousness and Culture* (Ithaca, 1977), 214.

[12] For instance, Robert Alter, *The Art of Biblical Narrative* (New York, 1981).

Muilenburg omitted the vast subject of rhetorical imitation (*mimēsis*; Lat., *imitatio*), although in 1957 Renée Bloch had already flagged the related topic of biblical midrash – searching (Heb. *drš* "to search") for meaning, meaning that may reshape the sense – an area almost completely unexplored: *"complètement inexploré."*[13] Midrash helps open the way to creative rewriting and inner-biblical hermeneutics.

Writing, virtually from its inception, was so rare and valuable that it had been surrounded by an ethos of preservation, an ethos, even when writing something new, of somehow keeping what had already been achieved, already been written. Verbatim repetition was not required. The ideal was combining imitation with emulation (*zēlos*; Lat., *aemulatio*), thus contributing something further. This ethos of preservation was maintained regardless of whether the reader would detect the underlying source(s).

While the Greeks articulated the *theory* of imitation, its practice was followed by almost *all* Greek and non-Greek writers, from those first producing diverse forms of the epic of Gilgamesh to the biblical writers who developed diverse ways of midrash/inner-biblical interpretation. Greek was not alien to the Jewish people, especially its diaspora. Greek became the new language of the scriptures. Methods of citation in Greco-Roman and Jewish writers were indistinguishable.

Biblical scholars often feel skeptical of literary/rhetorical criticism. Even Dozeman's invaluable book *The Pentateuch*, while reporting on literary criticism, does not truly engage it. Nor do many major historians and commentators. Literary issues can seem secondary to history/ theology. But literary issues need to be settled first; they clarify a text's nature, so the text can be used responsibly. They have "operational priority."[14] As it is sometimes said, "First write the history of the writing, and then history itself can be written." The brevity of a death notice may suggest that a family has little to say about someone, but death notices constitute a specific literary/rhetorical form with historical content and, once recognized, their brevity makes sense.

Growing awareness of how biblical writers used extant writings and one another is transforming the quest for sources. Finding extant

---

[13] Renée Bloch, "Midrash," *DBSup* 5 (1957), 1263–81 (1279).

[14] Robert Polzin, *Moses and the Deuteronomist: A Literary Study of the Deuteronomic History: Part 1* (Indianapolis, 1980), 6; Thomas L. Brodie, *Genesis as Dialogue: A Literary, Historical and Theological Commentary* (Oxford, 2001), xxv–xxvii.

sources is not new. In the nineteenth century it was recognized that Genesis 1–9 combines and transforms aspects of Mesopotamian epics.

Efforts to detect the origin of Gen-Kgs by linking it with lost documents and traditions have failed, but, partly because of alarm about being "isolated . . . from . . . the literary monuments and peoples of the Near East," attention is now turning to mainstream writings, including other biblical books, especially the prophets, and the Greeks. The Greeks may seem alien. The closing chapters of Gen-Kgs evoke an archaic world – Assyria, Babylon, Egypt, even, repeatedly, Chaldeans – one where Greeks seem unknown. Yet within seven years of the final episode of Gen-Kgs, the resurgence of imprisoned Jehoiachin (562 BCE), all-conquering Cyrus was moving toward building a record-breaking empire, and soon toward absorbing an unmatched Greek-led blossoming of culture, culture fed by "near Eastern influence."[15] Within this ferment and its new roads, the standout literary monuments were Homer's epics (written ca. 700 BCE), epics bridging east and west. The Greeks saw Homer's works both as sacred writings and as education's foundation. What better challenge for someone composing foundational sacred writings in Hebrew than to reshape and surpass the foundational texts of one's greatest cultural rivals?

The possibility and appropriateness of emulating/surpassing Homer does not prove it happened. However, since the 1980s, criteria for detecting literary dependence are being developed.[16] Already, for instance, "three independent researches" indicate that Gen 24 used Homer's *Odyssey* 6–13.[17] Verifiable literary connections with prophets, Homer, and later writers can help clarify Gen-Kgs' origin.

Connecting with rhetoric sets biblical studies in the context of literary art, and definitions of art often speak of evoking another world, of being symbolic. Literary art engages the world of allegory and symbol in a way that focus on factual history generally does not. It helps open the way for a fuller explanation of many texts and for reconnecting with early biblical interpretation.

---

[15] Walter Burkert, *The Orientalizing Revolution: Near Eastern Influence on Greek Culture in the Early Archaic Age* (Cambridge, 1992), 1–40, 128–29.

[16] See Brodie, *Genesis*, 421–32. On imitation, rewriting, and criteria for detecting extant sources, see also Thomas L. Brodie, *The Birthing of the New Testament: The Intertextual Development of New Testament Writings* (Sheffield, 2004), 3–30, 42–49.

[17] Yaakov S. Kupitz, "Stranger and City Girl: Genesis 24 and Homer's *Odyssey* 6–13," in *The Bible and Hellenism*, eds. Thomas L. Thompson and Philippe Wajdenbaum (Durham, 2014), 117–64 (118).

APPROACHING GENESIS-KINGS

Literary studies encourage attentiveness to a text's final shape, so in reading Genesis-Kings it seems best to approach it as in the Hebrew Bible, as essentially a single unbroken narrative. Surprising breaks certainly occur, but breaks are being increasingly understood. "The biblical writers . . . had certain notions of unity rather different from our own."[18] Biblical narrative often shows truth as "dialogical," combining diverse viewpoints as, for instance, did Dostoevsky.[19] The presence of diverse viewpoints is not surprising. Facts are facts, but God, creation, and living beings, including humans, are complex, difficult to know, as are seemingly simple matters, even about oneself: "I know not why I am so sad," *The Merchant of Venice* (opening line). Gen-Kgs signals complexity by beginning with a creation account that sees humans first in God's image, transcendent (Gen 1), then made of clay (Gen 2) – like opposites, seemingly contradictory. But they are complementary, one of many complementarities between Gen 1 and 2.

A Challenging World: Origins (Gen 1–11)

In the beginning everything looked promising. But the overreaching actions of Adam, Eve, Cain, and others brought change, and a contrast emerged between the human heart and the Creator's. The human heart designed evil all day, so the Lord's heart regretted and grieved (6:5–6), grief so deep as to want to be rid of everybody. "But Noah found grace with the Lord." A worldwide flood ensued; "but God remembered Noah," and re-established humanity. Afterwards, the human heart seems even worse than before, designing evil since youth (Gen 8:21). Now, however, it elicits compassion. God makes a covenant never again to destroy the earth, promising "I will remember," and setting up the rainbow, as a reminder. That covenant was kept. The world was never again flooded away. But centuries later, when Manasseh promoted evil (2 Kgs 21:16), the Lord decided, not in grief but in anger, to cast away Jerusalem and Judah (2 Kgs 24:3, 20). What had gone wrong?

After the flood, Noah's sons seemingly did well. When one son tempted the other two to surrender to the eyes' allure by looking at their father's nakedness – echoing that of the forbidden fruit – the other two resisted (9:18–29). But when humankind, speaking one language, found a plain, they settled there and overreached again, attempting a

---

[18] Alter, *Art*, 133.
[19] Carol Newsom, "Bakhtin, the Bible and Dialogical Truth," *JR* 76 (1996), 290–306.

high-tech tower, to reach heaven and establish their name, effectively to be like gods and define their own name/destiny. Then their language fails and they scatter (11:1–9). They seem lost. Matching that failure is Shem's shrinking genealogy. Its lifespans shorten (11:10–32). And when people set out for Canaan, they failed to arrive; reaching Haran they settled there. "Haran," for practical purposes, is also the name of Abram's youngest brother, who died prematurely. The travelers have settled into dwelling in the memory of past sadness, overshadowed by death.

Overall, Genesis 1–11 moves from a two-part splendid world (Gen 1–2) to a two-part picture of people overshadowed by failure (11:7–9) and death (11:27–32). Gen 6–11 reworks much of Gen 1–5, but shows more awareness of death's closeness. At the center (Gen 6–9) stands a drama of hearts, a human heart struggling with evil, and another heart, sometimes grieving, but always remembering, and always ready to recreate.

The rest of Gen-Kgs builds a narrative that, amid diverse literary forms, remains centered on the heart, not heart as a specific body part, but heart as meaning the whole person, the center, the interior, plus the ensuing external rites, laws, and activities, from tiny to vast. External personal appearances are often omitted; the narrative lets actions speak, lets the reader/hearer fill the gaps. Focus on the heart adds to making the narrative *primary*.

Genesis 12–50: Foundational Portraits

Some basics: Abraham dominates Gen 12–25; Jacob, much of 25–50. Isaac's presence is intermittent (from 17:17–19 onward), rarely leading the action, but highlighted among the Philistines (Gen 26). He is enigmatic.

All three receive calls; these build on each other (12:1–3; 26:2–5, 23–25; 28:10–22). All move from doing well to confrontation/struggle (Abraham, 18:1–33; Isaac, 26:15–25; Jacob, 31–33). All experience blessing/recognition: Abraham, through Rebekah (Gen 24, "a kind of novella"[20]); Isaac through the Philistines (26:26–33); Jacob through Joseph (a novella).

Abram's account, running from age 75 to 175, evokes transcendence. Jacob's, running womb to tomb (dies at 125), approximates down-to-earth biography. This variation develops the transcendent/earthy

---

[20] Nahum N. Sarna, *Genesis* (Philadelphia, 1989), 16.

variation in Gen 1–2. Isaac's enigmatic narrative (Gen 26) – dies at 180 – most resembles Abraham's.

Abraham: A Low-Key Mystery Unfolds

At one level, Abraham's narrative seems matter-of-fact. The Lord speaks a simple command: "Go ... " The destination: "a land that I will show you"; the purpose: to form a nation bringing blessing to all peoples. The previous effort to go to Canaan failed (11:31). But now Abram, Sarai, and Lot move like light at creation: "They set out to go to the land of Canaan // and they came to the land of Canaan" (12:5).

Traversing the land in stages, Abram observes rituals, building altars in Gen 12–13 (preparatory to conspicuous rituals in Gen 14–15?). But amid famine and Egypt's danger, Abram disavows Sarah as wife. God-sent plagues – creation reversed – rescue her from Pharaoh. Later, in a land dispute involving Lot, Haran's son, Abram allows Lot first choice. Lot is careful. He looks around, calculating, and chooses the best-looking land, aware especially of water, "well watered everywhere" (13:5–13). Abram too looks around, but God guides Abram's seeing. He sees not Lot's leftovers, but a land extending north, south, east, west (13:14–17).

This narrative gives land two meanings, land in plain sight, measurable real estate, and land as something else, a reality made visible by God, and made visible after letting go of obvious wealth, for Lot's sake. The difference is elusive but fundamental, and helps account for confusion about boundaries. "The Pentateuch is filled with conflicting boundaries of the promised land."[21] The land is for Abram's children (12:7) but, like land, the idea of children is perplexing. Abraham has no children; his wife is barren. Yet, having indicated land in every direction, God then promises children in countless numbers (13:16). And after Abram risks his life, for Lot's sake, God again guides Abram's seeing. God brings him outside and directs his vision toward the heavens, the stars (15:5). Looking heavenward and engaging the uncountable stars, Abram "believed the Lord," and, "the Lord reckoned it to him as righteousness" (15:6), righteousness being "that sum of integrity and humble submission which makes a [person] ... pleasing to God."[22] Abram's believing in the Lord, his acceptance of God-given sight of the heavens, gives him a new inner quality. The background of the phrase "reckoned as righteous" is a "priest's

---

[21] Dozeman, *Pentateuch*, 240.
[22] *The Jerusalem Bible* (London, 1966), note on Gen 15:6.

formal acknowledgement of a sacrificial gift as properly offered ... [or of] a particular attitude to God [which] is declared correct."[23]

In Abram's case the development of this particular attitude, this new inner quality, is bound up with having a child/descendants. The next event is a searing covenant-making that points both to land and ten peoples from one great river to another (15:7–21). These puzzling accounts (Gen 12–15) – land better than watered land; having a child when old – cannot be reduced to prosaic calculations of land and population. More is involved. Meanwhile, Sarai is coming alive. She had been introduced matter-of-factly as Abram's wife. Then, equally matter-of-factly: "Now Sarah was barren. She had no child." Sarai says nothing. In Egypt, angry Pharaoh tells Abram to take his disavowed wife and go. Sarai still says nothing.

When Abram returns from Egypt – "he and his wife" (13:1) – Sarai's name is not mentioned, neither then nor for years, years eventually including Abram's complaint to God about going childless. Sarai remains barren, beautiful, silent, and unmentioned. But when Abram undergoes the life-changing covenant (15), the narrative returns to Sarai, and adds: she has an Egyptian slave-woman, Hagar (16:1). Finally Sarai speaks. "Go in to my slave-girl" – so that the child would be hers. She is angry first with God; then with Abraham; finally with the pregnant slave-girl who now despises her. She blames Abram, and calls on God to judge him – the first glimmer that she regards God as on her side. Abram gives way. She mistreats the slave so badly she runs away. But an angel reassures the slave and sends her back to submit to Sarai. At eighty-six, Abram's child is born, Ishmael, half-Egyptian.

At ninety-nine, the Lord, under a new name, appears to Abram, with new names for Abram and Sarai – henceforth Sara*h* and Abra*ham* – bringing a new form of covenant, with circumcision, and announcing that Sarah is to have a child! Abraham laughs, and far from fretting as formerly, finds God's gifts too much (Gen 17:17–18). The mood changes (18–19). At Mamre, when the Lord appears to Abraham at ninety-nine, the heat intimates heaven-sent fire. Abraham faces two challenges: standing to provide lavish hospitality, including asking Sarah to bake bread (but did she? 18:6–8); and standing before God arguing about justice (for Lot's family). Afterwards, Abraham verifies: yes, God remembered (19:27–29) – as during the flood. Lot, ever calculating, again misses out on life, unaware even when having sex (19:30–38). His wife,

[23] Claus Westermann, *Genesis 12–36* (Minneapolis, 1995), 223.

focused on what is behind/past, becomes salt/dead, like the Salt/Dead Sea.

Abraham's Gerar visit clarifies what Sodom/Gomorrah suggested. He foresaw the fire, so is a prophet (20:7); he interceded, so is an intercessor, praying, praying also for healing, healing even the barren. Gerar also enhances Sarah, perhaps countering shame from her Egypt experience (12:10–20), and also saving face in Gerar.

Then Sarah brings forth Isaac. His Hebrew name is associated with laughter (17:15–22; 18:9–15; 21:6), prayer (25:21), playfulness (21:9), fondling (26:8) – as if these were part of an extra dimension, evoking (God's) spirit. God has enabled her to laugh, laugh with many others. Her transformation from barrenness to Isaac is also her inner transformation from bitter silence to shared laughter. And at some level, she now seems more clear-eyed than Abraham. Seeing Ishmael play with Isaac, she demands, to safeguard Isaac's inheritance, that "this slave woman with her son" be driven away (21:1). Ishmael will later generate twelve tribes (25:12–18).

For the moment, however, Abraham is distressed. But God promises to safeguard both sons' inheritance. So, rising early, Abraham sends Hagar and Ishmael away, a haunting drama (21:8–21). And when dealing with king Abimelech – just before and after Isaac's birth (ch. 20; 21:22–34) – Abraham, instead of being cowed and expelled, as in Egypt, "possesses a new sense of confidence."[24] Then, when God tests him, commanding him to sacrifice Isaac, Abraham rises early and obeys serenely. When Sarah dies, he mourns, without exaggeration, and gracefully buys a Mamre field (land) that reverberates across Genesis. In sending his servant to find Isaac a wife, he says calmly that "God ... will send his angel ahead of you" (24:7). For Abraham too, Isaac means transformation. His death (25:7–11), amid genealogies and far-flung places (25:1–6, 12–18), implies that God's promises to him involve "the human race."[25]

Jacob: A Working Life: Struggle and Dream

Jacob is calm/quiet, dwells (at home) in tents, loved by his mother, Rebekah, closer to earthly human life than Abraham. Even solving his mother's barrenness is more human than in Sarah's case. It begins when his human father, Isaac, prays (25:21).

[24] Sarna, *Genesis*, 148.
[25] Ibid., 171.

Yet life is challenging. Rebekah, in painful pregnancy, wonders what life is about. In the womb, Jacob struggles with twin Esau – intimating future struggles – struggles even at birth, grasping Esau's heel. The family is divided. Rebekah may love Jacob; but Isaac loves Esau – for wild game. And Jacob gets Esau to surrender his birthright – for red food.

Suddenly, uniquely in Gen 26, Isaac occupies center stage. He echoes Abraham's experiences, implicitly recalling how he had brought unique blessing to Abraham and Sarah. Furthermore, and climactically, the Philistines now recognize him as having a special blessing (Gen 26:28–29).

Normally, Isaac would transmit that blessing to his eldest, Esau. But, when old and blind he transferred it to *Jacob* (ch. 27). He did so unknowingly. But his wife knew.

Rebekah first appeared when aged Abraham sent a servant to find Isaac a wife. Biblical betrothal scenes use a pattern: a man enters a foreign place and meets a woman at a well. However, the writer may "refashion [the pattern] ... radically."[26] Gen 24 (Genesis' longest chapter) has two wells, two meetings, two betrothals. And the text has two levels – like the promises to Abraham of land and children.

At one level, Gen 24 concerns the betrothal of Isaac and Rebekah (second well, Lahoi Roi; 24:62–67). However, it prioritizes Rebekah's emergence at well one (Nahor; 24:1–61): Rebekah demonstrates God's covenant love for Abraham – another form of betrothal (24:12, 14, 27, 49). So Rebekah works at two levels: as an earthly betrothed; and as representing God's betrothal to Abraham.

Likewise regarding the blessing (Gen 27). She is a loving mother, but by contending against something in Esau she is also playing a key role in God's work. Esau's description fits not only a hunter in the wild, but the wild animal itself, covered with hair – thus continuing the serpent/Cain drama: craftiness/cunning, Eve's fixation on (forbidden) food, the Lord cautioning Cain that something is lurking/crouching within him (4:7), and Cain's going out into the field, to kill. Blind Isaac retains his own identity, but shares Esau's world. He loved Esau for the wild meat, and when judging who is present, relies not on listening to Jacob's voice, but on smell (27:22–27), animal-like.

Furthermore, the struggle – Rebekah/Jacob versus Isaac/Esau – engages the struggle, the enmity, declared in Eden, of "the woman"

[26] Alter, *Art*, 52.

and her offspring against the serpent and its offspring (3:15). Rebekah is "the woman." In childbearing she had suffered pain – as was said to Eve. But unlike the punished woman in the garden, no man lorded it over Rebekah, neither in her father's house (Gen 24) nor her husband's (Gen 26:7–11; ch. 27). *Rebek*ah's name is like an implicit play on *brk*, root for "bless." The declaration in Eden allowed that the serpent would strike the heel of the woman's offspring, but Jacob reverses that. At birth he grips Esau's heel. Most of all, while the serpent and Cain brought curse (3:14, 17; 4:11), Rebekah brought blessing to someone who, far from squandering it, as Esau squandered his birthright, cherished it.

The reversal continues. Blessing received, Jacob flees north, and has a dream-vision that intimates reversing Babel (28:10–22). Rather than use high-tech bricks for stone to build a pride-based tower to heaven (11:3), Jacob lays his head on a stone and dreams of a spiritual space, a form of house, with a God-given ladder reaching heaven – not Babel, but Bethel, "House of God," a place to guide him toward seeing that "all the families of the earth shall be blessed" (28:14).

Bethel stays with Jacob, especially in confronting Laban and Esau (31–33). But the years take their toll. He limps, and is silenced by younger men, including some of his own sons. Yet returning to Bethel renews his strength, even when Rebekah's nurse dies amid an evoking of tears; even when beloved Rachel, having already borne Joseph, dies giving birth to a second child. Amid the sadness, Jacob renames the child Ben-jamin ("Son of happy omen" literally, "Son of the right hand," Gen 34–35). And, as hoped at Bethel (28:21), he returns safely to his father, Isaac, who is buried by Esau and Jacob (35:27–29).

Later, however, beloved Joseph is killed – so Jacob's other sons say, deceptively – leaving Jacob old and mourning. Focus moves to Judah, Jacob's fourth son (38). (The first three committed murder or incest). Judah, having helped sell Joseph, goes away, apparently to forget. But he is reminded – as are others – and eventually, to save his father losing Benjamin to slavery, Judah offers himself in Benjamin's place (44:18–34, Genesis' second-longest speech). Judah's speech sparks Joseph's self-revelation, which then reverberates through others, including Jacob, whose heart goes cold until his spirit revives. Jacob blesses Pharaoh, and his own sons, highlighting Judah (even if ironically). Jacob's funeral rites are twofold: the world's best (Egyptian); and home to Mamre – where Sarah laughed – observed uncomprehendingly (50:1–14). And Joseph helps his brothers comprehend their own role within God's intentions.

EXODUS

Exodus stands out in world literature, and rivals the drama of creation. It also moves emphasis from individuals to society, to the Israelites, now numerous but oppressed. The twofold task: pull down Pharaoh's tyranny; and build up the people.

Pulling Down Tyranny (1:1–15:21)
Low-Key Introduction: Initial Resistance (1.1–2:22)
Two deferential midwives undermine Pharaoh's plan. Moses' mother and sister show ingenuity. Moses' resistance involves killing, so, fearing Pharaoh, he flees to Midian, settling with his future father-in-law and tending sheep. Moses' birth account imitates Sargon's, founder of the first true empire. His Hebrew name connects explicitly with being "drawn out" [of water] (1:10), as was Sargon.

Fire and Great Change: The Burning Bush and Creation-Related Plagues (2:23–11:10)
Moses' prophetic call (2:23–4:31, the burning bush) helps him face Pharaoh, and by bringing plagues (Exod 5–11), he effectively invokes (God's power over) creation as favoring justice.

Establishing Remembrance: Passover (12:1–13:16)
Passover establishes a vivid annual festival of remembering, reinforced by a week-long feast of Unleavened Bread. The accompanying teaching is virtually unforgettable, like a sign on your hand or forehead (13:16). Tyranny's fall ends with a song and a dance (15:1–21).

Building (15:22–40:38)
Low-Key Introduction: Basic Needs or Dangers (15:22–18:27)
Building the people in the wilderness begins quietly, emphasizing water and food. Moses' fighting here (against Amalekites) is through outstretched hands. Again a father-in-law appears, but tending people, not sheep.

Fire and Great Change: God's Fiery Descent on Sinai and Creation-Related Commandments (19–23)
No burning bush here, but a fiery mountain, and solemnity evoking God's power over creation, power shown through a double covenant: the Decalogue and the Book of the Covenant.

*Ensuring Remembrance: Writing; Building a Tent That Recalls
God and Contains the Writings (24–40)*

Writing and remembering, already highlighted in the Amalekite inci-
dent (18:14–16), now take center stage, first in writing the laws (ch. 24),
then in building a mobile temple (tent/tabernacle/sanctuary), center of a
drama of remembering and forgetting. Builders recall complex instructions (25–31, 35–40). But while Moses receives God's written tablets,
people forget him, idolize a golden calf, and apostatize (32:1). Moses
invokes God's mercy, and challenges people to choose. Result: grim
division, 3,000 killed. The cloud, signifying divine presence, covers the
tent, and will guide the journey onward (40:34–38), but first inward.

LEVITICUS: JOURNEYING INWARD

The Lord calls Moses from the tent, with a somewhat more inward
message for the people, concerning ritual, including ordination (chs.
1–10); purification/cleanliness, including Atonement (11–16); and holiness ("the holiness code," 17–27). These three parts accord both with
the three increasingly holy places of the tent (outer court; holy place;
holy of holies) and with three stages of holiness in a person, as follows:
Ritual (1–10) may be performed or attended to in a way that is empty –
as the prophets attest – but when sincerely carried out it greatly promotes order and meaning. *Purification*, or removing uncleanliness
(11–16), can be external, but generally deeper. Animals are classed as
clean/unclean (11), as are humans involved with various elements,
including birth, death, blood, sickness, leprosy, and sexual impurities
(12–15). Within that list (12–15), the first and last categories highlight
women: women in childbirth (12) and women's sexual impurities
(15:19–30). *Holiness* (17–27, "the Holiness Code") goes to a person's
deepest level. Here the Bible first formulates clearly " . . . you shall love
your neighbor as yourself" (19:18); likewise "the alien" (19:34). Holiness
includes: ritual sacrifice; marriage relationships; holiness and love; festivals; land and funding; and living that implies two ways: living bringing blessings, or curses (Lev 26).

The basic idea of three stages of holiness finds support, for instance,
in the three sections of Jesus' last will and testament (John 13–17).[27]
One effect of indicating three stages is to challenge those journeying,
and to provide support and a form of roadmap.

---

[27] Thomas L. Brodie, *The Gospel According to John* (Oxford, 1993), 429–36.

NUMBERS ("IN THE WILDERNESS")

If Exodus evokes beginnings, Numbers evokes journeying for almost a lifetime. The narrative is three-part. *The intense gathering* (Num 1:1–10:10). Initially, people seem rejuvenated. The two-part picture of the army (Num 1–2) is as orderly/strong as two-part creation (Gen 1–2): instead of creation's array in seven days (Gen 1), a vast army in twelve tribes (Num 1); and instead of focusing on the tree of life, and by four rivers (Gen 2), focuses on the sacred tent, in four directions (Num 2). Better still, while Eden crumbles in a two-part fall – Adam/Eve, Cain/Abel – the people in Num 3–4 gain strength from a two-part picture of priests and Levites, again arranged around the tent. And while Genesis then gives two complementary genealogies succumbing further to sin and death (4:17–6:8), Num 5–6 gives two complementary chapters on problems of uncleanness/sin/death but, with help from dedicated priests/Levites, people do *not* succumb.

The departure (Num 9:1–10:10) is like an intensified Exodus – with Exodus features: Passover, cloud, trumpet. These elements look forward, even to days in their own land when dramatic trumpets will again bring remembrance: in war, so your God remembers you; and in festivals, so you remember your God (10:9–10).

The Long Journey: From Exuberance to Atonement (Num 10:11–19:22)

The decades-long journey, Sinai to Kadesh, begins exuberantly. Every stage invokes God (10:11–36). But the journey meets difficulties – complaints, crises, quarrels. These echo earlier crises on first leaving Egypt, but now complaints are punished. More is expected. Memories stray: "Remember the fish we used to eat in Egypt for nothing ... the onions and garlic!" (11:5).

Crises intensify: living conditions; administration (11); Moses' Cushite woman (12). Then, disastrously, as a scouts' report generates loss of faith, the people are condemned to dying in the wilderness, leaving the Promised Land to another generation (13–14). Leaders spark deadly power struggles (16–17).

Yet the sense of a deity remains. No matter how destructive the situation, the Lord's glory comes down or appears (11:25; 12:5; 14:10; 16:19; 17:8; 20:6). Legislation also intervenes (chaps. 15, 18–19), placed beside the crises; and atonement (Num 19).

Moab's Plains, Facing the Jordan and Jericho (20–36)

At the desert of Zin, problems intensify. Miriam, who once led the dance, dies and is buried. No water! People unite against Moses and Aaron. The Lord's glory appears, but Moses' response draws a puzzling divine decision: He and Aaron will not lead the people into the land (20:1–13), a puzzle possibly connected with the ambiguity of "land." Exuberance gives way to the shadow of death.

Moses is undeterred. Despite rebuff from Edom, despite Aaron dying, despite losing people in an attack, despite God sending deadly fiery serpents to punish hungry impatient people, Moses holds steady. He sends word, from the Lord, to deal with the serpent of death by looking it in the face (21:4–9).

Moses' leadership continues to slip. Israel marches on (21:10–35). Balaam's effort to bring curse brings blessing; God's prophetic spirit is unstoppable (22:2–24:25).

Another apostasy (25:1–5)! – like another golden calf aberration. A further grim division. Moses' departure beckons. The Lord tells him to climb a mountain and look at the land before being gathered to his people. He and the Lord converse briefly. Joshua is appointed to replace him (27:12–23). The closing (Num 27–36), framed by references to women's inheritance, opens to a world of time (including festivals) and space, and belongs to the land enigma.

Moses' narrative seems finished. But as Leviticus once interrupted the journey and rejuvenated it, so now does Deuteronomy.

DEUTERONOMY

Leviticus and Deuteronomy differ in speaker, audience and content. Leviticus comes from God, Deuteronomy from Moses, Moses remembering – his last will and testament, addressing a later generation. Leviticus spoke of deepening levels: ritual, purification, and holiness. Deuteronomy speaks of wisdom, and apparently of further deepening (age/experience related?), deepening of love, heart, soul, and memory.

> *Part* 1: The travelers lose heart, but a new generation/heart emerges (1:1–4:43).
>
> *Part* 2: Deepening of love, heart, memory. Two options (4:44–chap. 11).
>
> *Part* 3: Love–led law in action ("the Deuteronomic Code"). Two ways (12-30).

Finale: Moses' song, blessing, enigmatic death (31–34; cf. deaths of Enoch; Elijah).

Parts 2 and 3 increasingly integrate remembering, plus love/heart, with law-like realities of ritual and duty. Remembering – a key motif in Genesis: esp. Noah (8:1), Abraham (19:29), Rachel (30:22), Joseph (40:23–41:9) – enables the process. "The central theme in [Deut 8:1–10:11] ... is ... to remember ... not forget."[28]

The picture of two ways reaches intensity in Moses' climactic call to choose life (Deut 30:15–20). Then, as Moses begins to depart – he sings, blesses, and climbs Mount Nebo – he challenges Joshua and the elders not to deviate from the law, "the way" (31:29).

The Two Ways (Jos/Judg/Sam/Kgs)

Having completed the Law of Moses, the narrative emphasizes its application. It shows the two ways in action, vivid pictures, some history-like, of following and not following the law. Links to Deuteronomy are emerging as part of a larger pattern of inner-biblical connections.

JOSHUA AND JUDGES

Joshua describes Joshua's conquest, guided by remembering Moses and leading with the ark carrying the law. Following the law resolves problems (Joshua 1–8). Judges, however, recounts disorder. People generally desert God, then call for help, and are rescued by unpredictable judges, until deserting again and often generating something worse.

"[T]hese two accounts [Joshua; Judges] cannot be reconciled."[29] True, if seen as factual history. But in literary context – that of "the two ways" – they fit perfectly. Their terrible symmetry culminates in their conclusions: twelve-tribe reunion for covenant renewal (Josh 24); and tribal union for civil war occasioned by gang rape (Judg 19–21).

SAMUEL AND SAUL (1 SAMUEL)

Saul is sometimes linked to Greek tragedy, a link reinforced by similarities to Homer's Hector, for instance: conspicuous head/helmet, battle readiness, death in battle, body abused then recovered, a night journey in disguise. But links with Samuel are more immediate. The names'

---

[28] Dozeman, *Pentateuch*, 493.
[29] Dever, *Beyond the Texts*, 629.

similarity – Samuel, Saul – is significant. Through Samuel the Lord calls Saul. Together they frame 1 Samuel, from Samuel's birth to Saul's death. Yet they also form a contrast. Samuel listens, lets no word fall to the ground (1 Sam 3:9, 15, 19), hears sheep and oxen (1 Sam 15:14). His name evokes Hebrew for hearing/listening. Saul's non-listening costs him the kingship (1 Sam 13:13; 15:17–28).

David and Solomon (2 Sam 1–1 Kgs 11)

David has many similarities to Jacob,[30] but is also linked explicitly to Solomon. David (Judah's tribe) and Solomon belong together, father and chosen son. They stand out. They are also very different. Though David makes mistakes and does wrong, he listens to prophetic corrections; he repents, sometimes in tears. He should die, he says, in Absalom's place. Solomon echoes Egypt's splendor. Some of his achievements, including building, are set in the context of leaving Egypt (1 Kgs 6:1; 8:9). His portrait is ambiguous. And at the end there is no ambiguity. On the one hand, Solomon, more than anyone else, resembles the evil-hearted deviant "sons-of-god" who induced the deluge. As "sons of God" they had become some form of strange gods. And Solomon's engagement with foreign wives and their gods went to his core; "And Solomon clung to these in love" (1 Kgs 11:2); the turning of his heart is hammered home (1 Kgs 11:2–4). Both cases effectively involve a change of identity, thus incurring future divine punishments that include limiting life to 120 years and limiting Jerusalem's twelve-tribe kingdom largely to one, Judah (Gen 6:1–8; 1 Kgs 11:1–13). David's adultery, and murder of Uriah, had indeed grossly violated Mosaic law, but David admitted guilt, repented, and personally endured the consequences of his crimes – something Solomon never did. This contrast of hearts is explicit and repeated (1 Kgs 2:1–4; 11:4, 6). Solomon's account echoes the primordial fall.

Israel's tribes had joined the southern monarchy because of David (2 Sam 5:1). They break because of Solomon (and Rehoboam and Jeroboam), thus giving dual monarchy: Judah (Southern Kingdom, capital Jerusalem) and Israel (Northern Kingdom, capital Shechem; then Tirzah; finally Samaria).

---

[30] Philippe Wajdenbaum, "Jacob and David: The Bible's Literary Twins," in *Anthropology and the Bible*, ed. Emanuel Pfoh (Piscataway, NJ, 2010), 149–70.

Truthful Prophets and Idolatrous Kings

The dual monarchy account (28 chapters: 1 Kgs 12–2 Kgs 17) includes an interrupted list of kings that cites annals and uses preset formulae assessing each king, especially regarding worship. Citing annals fits the literary practice of building references to written documents, somewhat as archaism makes narrative sound old. The list reflects aspects of the lists of names in Genesis' genealogies (genealogies that themselves reflect more ancient king lists). In this king list, assessments of kings are essentially negative.

Not so prophets. Prophets may be false, especially kings' prophets, but overall their presence is positive and central. From Shemaiah's message against war (1 Kgs 12:22) to mentioning multiple prophetic reminders (2 Kgs 17:13), the monarchy account emphasizes prophets, especially how prophets or prophet-like speakers faced kings.

In fact, the torso of the dual monarchy account consists of the Elijah-Elisha narrative (1 Kgs 16:29–2 Kgs 13, virtually twenty chapters), a distinct eight-block narrative distilling and transforming almost the entire Primary Narrative into an account of a matched pair of prophets: Elijah, evoking the transcendent; and Elisha, more earthly, biography-like.[31] Elijah arrives out of the blue, invoking the creator, and later disappears into heaven. Elisha enters as a strong young ploughman driving twelve yoke of oxen, and exits as bones in a tomb.

Elijah and Elisha move emphasis from negative kings to prophets who bring God's word, justice, care, and healing. For instance, Elijah's narrative begins by telling how King Ahab's Baal-related marriage and chaotic worship generated king-related building that killed two sons, but Elijah brought a clear sense of God's supremacy, then introduced harmony and kindness, and finally restored a widow's son to life (1 Kgs 16:29–17:24), one of three increasingly clear revivals from death (see 2 Kgs 4:8–37; 13:14–25).

The final dual-monarchy chapters (2 Kgs 14–17) emphasize Samaria's general failure to follow law or prophets (17:13). And so Assyria deported the people, turning Samaria into something alien. The northern tribes were lost. It is not far from Samaria to Jerusalem.

---

[31] Thomas L. Brodie, *The Crucial Bridge: The Elijah-Elisha Narrative as an Interpretive Synthesis of Genesis-Kings and a Literary Model for the Gospels* (Collegeville, PA, 2000).

Final Contrasts (2 Kgs 18–25) Hezekiah/Manasseh

Jerusalem fell not to Assyria but to distant Babylon. The context contrasts good and evil: faithful Hezekiah, listening to Isaiah; and evil Manasseh (2 Kgs 18–21). Hezekiah brought Jerusalem a conduit of water (20:20); Manasseh, a stream of blood (21:17). Manasseh provokes God into envisaging another Samaria: "I will stretch over Jerusalem the measuring line for Samaria . . . I will wipe Jerusalem as one wipes a dish, wiping it and turning it upside down" (21:13). The Hezekiah-Manasseh account implies that Jerusalem's fall involves both mystery-like providence (Hezekiah/Isaiah) and punishment for evil (Manasseh).

Josiah/Other Kings

The end seemingly continues the contrasts, but in varied form (2 Kgs 22–25). The reader is ready for the fall, but not for what precedes it: the two-part wonder of finding and implementing the book of the law/Torah during Josiah's temple repairs (22–23). "De Wette realized [1806] that the discovery of the long lost law book of Moses was a literary fiction."[32] This fictional nature of Josiah finding the law fits with the traditional fictional account of Moses writing it.

The power of the finding is heightened by its presentation and content. The presentation is dramatic. First, the surprise. Then the tension around recognition and Huldah's authentication (22:8–20), echoing classic recognition scenes and the Joseph narrative. The scene's position, penultimate within all of Gen-Kgs, achieves maximum dramatic effect.

The finding's content evokes key elements of Gen-Kgs, especially the focus on the heart. The picture, at the end, of Josiah as "turned to the Lord with all his heart . . . soul" (23:25), responds to both the crisis of alienated hearts in the beginning, before the deluge (Gen 6:5–6), and the heart emphasis at the center, in Deuteronomy (esp. 6:4–6).

The account does not say what eventually happened to the book. The final kings are negative (23:31–25:26), broadly contrasting with Josiah. However, the first deportation is so imposing (24:13–16) – treasures, plus eighteen-year-old king Jehoiachin (Josiah's grandson) with his mother and eunuchs, and many others – that readers may reasonably hope the precious book will not be forgotten, even if it is again hidden.

Certainly, Jehoiachin did not stay hidden. "In the 37th year" of Jehoiachin's exiled imprisonment (562 BCE), the new Babylonian king

---

[32] Dozeman, *Pentateuch*, 507.

took him from prison to sit on a throne above the other kings. This is no petty promotion. The details of Jehoiachin's emergence (25:27–30) interweave three moments of resurgence – of Joseph from prison (Gen 41), of Jehoash hidden in the temple (2 Kgs 11–12, esp. 11:3), and of Josiah discovering Moses' law. Jehoiachin's emergence implies a setting where, despite losing the temple, the book could survive and inspire the exiles.

The end is elusive. Does it matter that the two-part account of destruction (2 Kgs 24–25) balances and reverses aspects of the two-part account of creation (Gen 1–2)? Certainly, the people of Judah maintained their identity, most obviously as refugees in defeated Egypt (24:7; 25:22–26), and as deportees in ascendant Babylon (562). And Abraham's children seemed to be everywhere (Gen 25:1–18). As for the actual copy of the discovered Torah: Whether intended or not, the absence of a clear statement about its location may tend to draw the reader into wondering about it, and then of asking the more basic question: whether it is written in the heart (Deut 6:6).

The Primary Narrative is not an intellectual proposition. It is encyclopedic, a song in the heart, at times sad, but a song nonetheless.

Further Reading

Finkelberg, Margalit and Guy G. Stroumsa, *Homer, the Bible and Beyond: Literary and Religious Canons in the Ancient World* (Leiden, 2003).

Goldhill, Simon, *The Invention of Prose* (Oxford, 2002).

Grabbe, Lester, ed., *Did Moses Speak Attic? Jewish Historiography and Scripture in the Hellenistic Period* (Sheffield, 2001).

3 Reading Biblical Literature from a Legal and Political Perspective

GEOFFREY P. MILLER

Human societies cannot function unless some people exercise coercive force over others. Basic to all societies, therefore, are the twin questions of when individuals may legitimately exercise power and how that power should be embodied in social institutions. These issues are central to the work of modern political and legal philosophers such as John Rawls, Robert Nozick, Joseph Raz, Ronald Dworkin, and H. L. A. Hart. They are basic also to the work of many of their predecessors – Marx and Mill in the nineteenth century; Kant and the Federalist Papers in the eighteenth; Locke and Hobbes in the seventeenth; Hooker and Machiavelli in the sixteenth. Christian, Jewish, and Arab thinkers of the Middle Ages occupied themselves with the topics, as did Cicero and others in the Roman Empire. Ultimately, political theory is traced to the Greeks – Plato and Aristotle, active in the fourth century BCE. Strauss and Cropsey's history of political philosophy is controversial in other respects, but it is in the mainstream of opinion when it concludes that the "political works of Plato and Aristotle are the oldest works devoted to political philosophy which have come down to us."[1]

In books, articles, and working papers published over the past two decades I have argued that the ancient world has bequeathed another work, possibly more ancient even than Plato and Aristotle, which also sets forth a sophisticated political theory. The author of this work is a great political thinker – possessed of remarkable capacities of systemization, balanced in judgment, profound in insight, and capable of setting out a coherent justification for the authority of law and a conceptual framework for strong but limited government power. What is this ancient work of political theory? It is not one that has lingered in the dusty obscurity of a library of ancient books. Nor was it recently unearthed in an archaeological expedition and translated for the world.

---

[1] Leo Strauss and Joseph Cropsey, *History of Political Philosophy*, 3rd ed. (Chicago, 1987), 1–2.

It is a book with which nearly all of us are familiar, at least to some extent: the Bible.

Deep insights about law and government are found throughout the Bible, both the Old and New Testaments. I will focus, however, on the Primary History – the great narrative extending from Genesis through Second Kings that traces the history of Israel from earliest times through the fall of the Southern Kingdom in 586 BCE. This narrative of the relationship between Israel and its God is a great monument of the human spirit, a magnificent work of literature, a rich repository of wisdom, a practical guide for living. It is also an amazingly sophisticated political theory – an extended and systematic analysis that justifies political authority, demonstrates the necessity of law and government, explores the nature of power relations in families, argues that nationhood is the best form of political organization, identifies self-governance, centralized institutions and sovereignty as the essential elements of nationhood, and claims that constitutional monarchy represents the best form of national government.

As an argument for the legitimacy of government in general and for constitutional monarchy over other forms of governance in the ancient world, the Bible's Primary History also contains important information about law. The explicit law codes contain the elements that constitute the *corpus juris* – the body of law – in any modern society: constitutional rules, legislation, administrative rules, rules of procedure and litigation, and a legitimating principle or rule of recognition that identifies a norm as having the quality of law. But the legal content of the Bible is not limited to propositions set forth as rules. The narratives in the Book of Genesis contain an extended set of precedents in the form of stories about the Patriarchs of the Israelite people – stories that set forth rules appropriate for the social and political environment in which formal legal functions of the state were weak and principal responsibility for maintaining social order fell on nonstate actors and institutions.

It is not at all surprising that the Bible deals extensively with law and government. Although the saving acts of God are at its core, the Bible is also relentlessly curious. Its pages offer pithy and intriguing observations about topics as diverse as language, culture, cosmology, meteorology, cooking, fashion, geography, commerce, diplomacy, history, family relationships, viniculture, animal husbandry, warfare, architecture, and much else besides. Given that government and law were ubiquitous in the lives of the peoples of ancient times, as they are today, it would be surprising if the Bible did not take an interest in these topics as well. And there can be no doubt that the Bible does display such an interest. The biblical text is chock full of laws – not only the Ten Commandments but also detailed codes of law that cover many topics both religious and secular. Legal materials are so pervasive in the Bible that the Jewish tradition refers to its first five books as "Torah" – law.

When the Bible is not discussing law, it is often dealing with politics. The books of Samuel and Kings tell of intrigues within the royal courts; Judges describes the political activities of tribal leaders; Joshua chronicles a period of military rule; Exodus, Leviticus, Numbers, and Deuteronomy recount the leadership of Moses. Even the book of Genesis deals with political issues insofar as it concerns authority in families. Politics is everywhere in the Bible's Primary History.

The Bible's interest in politics and law is not merely historical. It is also theoretical. Interspersed in the Bible are many examples of speculative thought: The first chapter of Genesis still commands respect from cosmologists, while, outside the Primary History, the Bible's Wisdom Literature enquires into many deep and challenging philosophical questions. There is no reason that the Primary History would not also engage in thinking about political themes. In fact, explicit examples of such thinking can be found in its pages: Samuel's warning about the ways of kings is one example (1 Sam 8:11–18); Jotham's parable of the trees is another (Judg 9:7–15).

The Bible, moreover, displays a distinct propensity to express ideas about politics and law in symbolic form. The hand is a symbol of power (e.g., Exod 15:6, 15:12; Pss 17:7 18:35, 21:8), the staff a mark of authority (Gen 38:18, 49:10; Exod 17:5; Num 17:2). The rainbow represents God's covenant with Noah (Gen 9:13–16); the mark of Cain demonstrates God's vow to protect the life of that figure during his wanderings (Gen 4:15). Mount Zion refers to Jerusalem, the land of Judah, the tribe of Judah, or the Israelite people. Figurative usages sometimes go beyond mere correspondences between narrative elements and features of the world: parables and fables create whole systems of symbolic meaning organized to bring out points or observations about the political world (see Judg 9:7–15; 2 Sam 12:1–4; 2 Kgs 14:9–10).

THE ROLE OF NARRATIVE

There is a great deal of explicit legal material in the Bible in the form of the great law codes of the Torah. But the Bible's political and theory is largely embodied in narratives rather than in discursive analysis.

To appreciate these ideas, it is necessary first to unpack the narratives to extract their legal and political meaning.[2] Once brought to light, these ideas reflect a sensible set of rules and principles appropriate for the governance of an ancient society – and, in many respects, appropriate for the governance even of modern political and legal systems.

Narrative offers advantages as a means for recording and transmitting information in a culture where many people are not literate. People in the agricultural areas of ancient Israel would have had little need for reading and writing; most of their affairs could have been conducted orally. If they needed to record or understand anything in writing, scribes could be hired. Literacy, moreover, was expensive. It required training, a luxury that poorer families could ill afford. And, unlike Egypt, which possessed papyrus, the peoples of ancient Israel did not have a readily available medium for memorializing written texts (pottery fragments were cheap but awkward; scrolls were expensive).

In a society where literacy was uncommon and the media of writing costly, much of the information important to the organization of the culture would have been recorded and transmitted orally, in the form of stories. Stories – narratives – have excellent mnemonic qualities in that they are easy to recall and can be used as "tags" for recalling other items. The story line calls to mind other ideas that would be difficult to recall, or to recall fully, if presented in purely discursive form. The artistic quality of narratives further enhances their communicative force. Many bible stories rank among the great works of human literature. Discursive political analysis lacks the punch. Narratives are better suited to the task of wide dissemination. Even if every member of the audience did not understand the political issues, some would get the message. We can say of the Bible's political theory, as Hobbes said of Thucydides, that "the narration itself doth secretly instruct the reader, and more effectually than can possibly be done by precept."[3]

Narratives had advantages other than ease of assimilation and memorization. Because they presented a history of the Israelite people, these texts could claim the imprimatur of legitimacy that is associated with

---

[2] This approach is, in a sense, the converse of Calum Carmichael's method, which sees many biblical laws as commentaries on the biblical narratives. See, for example, Carmichael, Calum, *Law and Narrative in the Bible: The Evidence of the Deuteronomic Laws and the Decalogue* (Ithaca, NY, 1985). This chapter presents the biblical narratives, not as frameworks on which the structure of biblical law is constructed, but rather as themselves being embodiments and expressions of law.

[3] Quoted in Martha C. Taylor, "Implicating the Demos: A Reading of Thucydides on the Rise of the Four Hundred," *JHS* 122 (2002), 91–108, 92.

historical events deemed relevant to the people's self-concept. Additional authenticity could be achieved by associating a message with figures already endowed with traditional authority – Abraham, Jacob, Moses, and so on. If people already accepted Jacob as an important ancestor, they were more likely to credit the message associated with things Jacob is said to have done. Etiologies – stories that explained the origins of things or traditions – also provided legitimacy. By associating a narrative with some element or condition known to the audience from their world, the message of the narrative gained credibility because of that connection (e.g., Gen 9:12–16; Josh 4:6). Etymologies validated narratives in a similar manner: the audience would be familiar with the word being explained, and, by associating it with the bible story, would accord greater credit to the other elements of the story (e.g. Gen 4:25, 5:28–29, 19:22, 32:30; Exod 2:10). The use of items from popular culture also enhanced authenticity: If someone discovered a familiar song or proverb in the text, he or she was more likely to view the narrative as authoritative.

Narrative, moreover, is a flexible means for framing simplified models of human society. We use narratives today for that very purpose. Economists' research papers specify models of economic activity, inhabit those models with agents who act according to specified criteria, and examine how the agents behave under the conditions of the models. The biblical narratives do essentially the same thing. By selecting the characters and the physical setting in which those figures interact, the Bible isolates the question under consideration and focuses attention on its resolution. The reader knows only the details that the texts supply.

Like other modes of expression, narratives have deficits as well as advantages. Narratives are inherently more ambiguous than discursive approaches, and accordingly can be subjected to multiple interpretations (although even discursive approaches can support multiple interpretations). Counter-narratives can modify or cancel a narrative by placing the first text in a different context. Despite these drawbacks, the advantages of narrative are sufficiently pronounced as to make it plausible that the Bible might use this medium to express and investigate ideas about law and government.

Several reasons help explain why interpreters to date have not fully appreciated the Bible's political theory. First, most interpreters approach the Bible from the standpoint of religious faith. Even contemporary secular interpreters of the bible are often educated in seminaries or other religious institutions, and therefore tend to reflect religious attitudes in their interpretations. Given this perspective, a political interpretation is not to be expected. Further, biblical scholars are trained in the disciplines of languages, theology, and biblical history but are rarely experts in the fields of politics, law, or political theory. They are unlikely to recognize political meanings in the texts they interpret because they are not attuned to issues that are central to those other disciplines. Much biblical interpretation, moreover, is influenced by the great theorists of the past. Those scholars continue to exercise an influence on biblical interpretation, one that may sometimes discourage unconventional approaches.

Why is the legal and political theory of the Bible conveyed in the form of narratives when the theory developed in the Greek world takes the form of discursive theorizing? The Greeks were hardly strangers to narrative: Homer is one of the great intellectual monuments of world culture. Even Greek philosophy was not devoid of narrative. Plato dismissed poetry as a means for conveying truths about the world but expressed his own ideas in the form of dialogues. Although Plato's rhetoric might be dismissed as a convention used to tease out different views on philosophical questions, his choice of medium was important, in some sense, to the message he sought to convey. Aristotle abandoned the dialogical style, but he recognized the potential for narrative-like figures of speech to communicate information effectively: In the *Poetics* he commends metaphor for its capacity to sharpen analysis and to convey information to an audience in a compact form. Nonetheless, it remains true that there are significant differences in style and presentation as between Greek and Israelite political theory.

We cannot know the reason for these differences between Greek and Israelite thinking about legal and political issues, but several conjectures are possible. The simplest explanation is simply that of path-dependence: Similar societies can evolve in different ways depending on unforeseeable or random events. There is no reason why theoretical discourse in Israel should have assumed the same form as that in Greece, even if conditions in the two regions were similar. Social and political conditions may also have been influential. Many Greek philosophers were itinerant thinkers who roamed the Greek cultural region in search of patrons. This factor would have influenced them to develop and express ideas in a form that could readily be transferred across national boundaries. Israel, in contrast, does not appear to have supported a population of itinerant teachers. Given this circumstance, political ideas in Israel could have assumed a different form than the form that developed in Greece. Geopolitical factors may have influenced rhetorical choices as well. Over the course of its history, Greece became a world empire interested in exporting its culture and its ideas to the lands it had conquered. This process of cultural transmission worked best if the ideas in question were framed in discursive form that could easily transmit across cultural boundaries. Thus, Greek thinking, as it evolved, may have developed in more general and abstract forms accessible to people everywhere. In contrast, Israel became an inward-looking society, operating under foreign domination and concerned with the preservation of its own traditions. In ancient Israel, rhetorical conventions that focused on the people's legends and cultural history could have been a preferable means for transmitting and embodying in the culture basic ideas about politics, governance, and law.

THE BASIC JUSTIFICATION FOR GOVERNMENT

Political theorists in the Western tradition have famously derived principles of government and law from a "state of nature" – a posited primordial condition in which government and law are absent, and where people act as separate individuals in pursuit of their own ends and objectives. State-of-nature ideas are present in the early modern theories of Locke, Hobbes, and Rousseau; they recur, in modernized form, in the work of the twentieth-century political philosopher John Rawls.

The Bible also presents a state of nature theory, but it is one that stands in dramatic contrast to these later works. According to the Bible, the natural state – the condition of human beings at the very beginning – is not one of anarchy. According to the Book of Genesis, the first human beings were Adam and Eve, and before their fall, they lived in conditions that were the opposite of anarchy. The setup of the Garden of Eden story – the very beginning of time in the human sense – generalizes the analysis to all humanity: Whatever happened to Adam and Eve is relevant to everyone, everywhere, throughout history. A similar message is conveyed by the geographic setting, which locates the Garden as the source of four great rivers, and implicitly as the center of the human world.

The Garden is a civilized place, protected against incursion and governed by a rule of law clearly stated and vigorously enforced. It is home to human beings and animals living in harmony with one another. And it is a venue for productive activity. Adam and Eve are not on vacation; it's their job to keep and tend the Garden. God rules the Garden as a just, benevolent, and powerful monarch who allows his subjects freedom of action but also expects them to obey the few rules that God does impose. The Bible, in short, presents the Garden of Eden as an idealized political entity – a simplified model of an actual political system that highlights the features pertinent to the point that the text seeks to convey.

The Bible's presentation of the natural condition of human beings as one of government and law is both morally appealing and factually more accurate than the account provided by early modern and modern political philosophers. People have never lived in the state of radical individuality posited by Hobbes and others. We are fundamentally social animals, and as such, it is our natural condition to live in relationship with others in relationships structured by rules of authority. Rather than deriving political obligation from an unrealistic and unconvincing condition of anarchy, as in later Western philosophy, the Bible locates the origin of political obligation in a system of social relationships that both establish and are constituted by that obligation.

Within this setting, the Eden story explores fundamental justifications for the exercise of political authority. To begin with, Adam and Eve are obligated to obey the rules of the Garden simply because God announced them. God, being the deity, is entitled to absolute obedience from his human subjects. God, moreover, is both extremely powerful and likely to become angry if Adam and Eve transgress his rules. Adam and Eve would be wise to obey his commands even if they disagree with them. But these authoritarian justifications for political obligation are supplemented by rationales more appealing to modern sensibilities. Adam and Eve have a wonderful life in the Garden. All of their needs are met; they are secure and safe from harm; they get to walk around naked all the time. In portraying the wonderful existence God provides for his creations, the Bible supplies a utopian theory of obligation. Given the manifest benefits of life in Eden, it is more than reasonable that Adam and Eve should accept the simple, non-onerous requirements that go along with living in such an ideal place.

Although the Bible presents human beings as inherently related to one another through government and law, it also contains an impressively sophisticated account of anarchy – the condition in which government and law are absent. This condition is explored in the Dark Age texts of the Book of Genesis – the account of humanity between the time of Adam and Eve's expulsion from the Garden of Eden to the re-establishment of government and law after Noah's deliverance from the Flood. These narratives expand the analysis of the Eden narratives by asking whether human beings can achieve a good and decent life in the absence of government and law. They do so by describing an experiment in which people interact strategically in an environment where the benefits of cooperation can be shared by all, but where defection is always possible. The Dark Age texts reject anarchy and conclude that government and law are essential to human flourishing.

CONSTITUTIONAL LAW

All legal systems operate according to fundamental rules that govern everything else. The Bible also contains a sophisticated body of constitutional law, one that sets forth fundamental rules but also offers a justification for why these rules should be accepted as primary to the organization of a legal system.

I have already mentioned the philosopher John Rawls, whose *Theory of Justice* is one of the great landmarks of Western political theory. Rawls' book had a major impact on political thought, in part, because it presents a compelling thought experiment designed to identify basic principles of political justice. Rawls' insight is that a fair set of political rules will have the following feature: It would be agreed to by rational people who lack knowledge about their endowments in society. In other words, you are asked to agree to a set of political norms without knowing whether you are rich or poor, male or female, young or old. By depriving people of knowledge of their endowments, Rawls creates the essential conditions for an arrangement that should be accepted as fair by everyone. Rawls calls this decision process the "original position" and the restrictions on knowledge the "veil of ignorance."

The Bible sets forth an astonishingly similar decision process. After their departure from Egypt, the Israelites wander in the desert until they come to Mount Sinai. Having escaped their oppressors in an enormous rush, they have virtually no possessions. They did receive some gold from the Egyptians on their way out of town, but gold is of little use in the desert. They have no idea of when (or even if) they will ever arrive at a place of safety. And they have no knowledge of the position they will eventually occupy in the Promised Land – whether they will live near the sea, or inland, whether their lands will be fertile or barren, large or small – or whether, as in the case of the Levites, they will have no extensive tribal lands at all. In these conditions, the Israelites receive their fundamental law and voice their approval of the constitution that God is establishing for them. The setting of Mount Sinai thus replicates, in narrative form, the specifications for fair decision that Rawls would formalize thousands of years later. The Israelites' unanimous agreement to these laws underscores the Bible's claim that the laws so established are fundamentally fair to all concerned.

The foundational laws given to the Israelites on Mount Sinai are not the only constitutional rules set forth in the biblical narratives. Another example is found in Exod 17:8–13. A band of Amalekites attacks the Israelites in the wilderness near Rephidim. Joshua, on Moses' order, leads the Israelite forces fighting the enemy while Moses, Aaron, and Hur look down from the top of a hill. The Israelites win the battle when Moses holds up his hands, but when he lowers his hands, the Amalekites prevail. The problem is that Moses can't hold his hands up for ever. When Moses grows tired, Aaron and Hur take a stone and put it under him so that he can sit. Then they hold up Moses' hands – one on each side – until sunset, allowing Joshua's forces to utterly defeat the enemy.

The tableau depicted by the text symbolizes a constitutional rule. The United States Constitution declares the President to be the Commander-in-Chief of the military and gives him or her the power to make treaties (subject to confirmation by the Senate) but it also gives Congress the power to declare war, to raise taxes, and to make rules for the government of the nation's military. The Exodus account provides an analogous distribution of war powers in the government of ancient Israel. Ultimate authority over military operations lies in the king, symbolized by the figure of Moses who orders Joshua to engage the enemy and who then oversees the battle from atop a hill. The hill symbolizes Jerusalem, and the stone that Aaron and Hur put under Moses represents the royal throne. Joshua, here as elsewhere, represents the military leader – the field commander of Israel's fighting force. He exercises moment-by-moment control over military operations: Moses supervises from afar, but he doesn't make strategic decisions in the field. Aaron, here as elsewhere in the Bible, stands for the country's religious authorities. Hur (an otherwise mysterious figure) represents the king's bureaucracy. The text uses these figures to establish a political compromise recognizing that the religious and civil authorities are equally responsible for the successful conduct of the war. The delegation of authority to these figures is represented by Aaron and Hur holding up Moses' hands; their exercise of authority is explained in the detail that Moses becomes too tired to keep his hands aloft on his own. Others in his government must help the king carry out his constitutional responsibilities. Overall, the text sets forth a rational and sensible set of constitutional rules for the conduct of military operations within the context of Israel's monarchy.

CONTRACT LAW

Among the many fascinating texts in the Bible are stories that describe the making, performance, and breach of contract. These include Abraham's purchase from Ephron the Hittite of a burial ground for his wife, Esau's sale of his birthright to Jacob, the performance by Abraham's servant of a contract of agency to procure a wife for Isaac, Jacob's employment agreement with his father-in-law, Jacob's sons' negotiation and breach of a peace treaty with the Shechemites, Jacob's fraudulent procurement of Isaac's blessing, and Jephthah's vow to perform a sacrifice in exchange for a military victory. It appears that these stories served the important social function of embodying and culturally transmitting rules of customary law that responded to the problems of contract formation and enforcement in a society without an established state, or one in which the state failed to exercise effective central authority. Indeed, the social importance of this legal function helps to explain why these stories survived and passed through the oral tradition to be collected in the national epic of the Israelite people.

The story of Jacob and Esau illustrates some of the advantages that the narrative confers as a source of customary law. These two are twins, but Esau has the birthright as first-born. Esau becomes a hunter and Jacob a farmer. Esau comes in from the field feeling famished and finds Jacob with some lentil stew. Esau asks Jacob to share the meal, but Jacob refuses to give him any food until Esau agrees to sell him his birthright. Even when Esau indicates a willingness to sell because he is at death's door, Jacob insists that he first swear an oath. Esau swears the oath, and Jacob gives him the food.

In modern terms, this story describes a contract for sale in which Esau and Jacob exchange Esau's birthright for a mess of pottage owned by Jacob. It is noteworthy that Esau, after swearing an oath and selling his birthright, never denies that the deal is binding as a matter of contract. The story thus conveys the rule that a contract is legally binding even if it is made under conditions of grossly unequal bargaining power. This contract might not be enforceable under today's law, either because it would be considered to have been negotiated under duress or because it would be deemed unconscionable. Whatever its present-day merits, however, the birthright rule was sensible under what we know of the circumstances of the time when it evolved. In a situation with no state, no court, and no authoritative written system of records, contracts had to be privately enforced if they were to be enforced at all. Private enforcement often means that the individual or his family must resort to violence, and violence raises the possibility of feuds. The upshot is that a disagreement over the meaning of a contract was exceedingly costly in such a setting. The customary law set forth in the Jacob–Esau story helped to minimize this risk. As long as a party has sworn an oath, and thereby has engaged in the formality needed for a promise to be legally binding, the deal could not thereafter be challenged on the ground that the consideration given in exchange was inadequate or that the contract was negotiated under conditions of unequal bargaining power.

PROPERTY LAW

Property is the institution through which a society assigns rights in resources. One function of social organizations is to administer these rights: to define the right in question, to assign it to a holder or holders of title, and to enforce the right against others. These functions were just as important in ancient times as they are today. It is not surprising, therefore, that biblical texts deal extensively with issues of property.

No system of property rights will be effective unless the resource in question is clearly and objectively identified in some durable medium that can be consulted in the event of disputes. Evidence from the Bible suggests that the devices for identifying property boundaries were not too different from methods used today. In some cases, property was defined by means of a "metes and bounds" description that links borders to known landmarks. The Bible contains metes and bounds definitions of Israel's sovereign claims vis-à-vis neighboring states (Num 34:1–12; see also Gen 15:18–21) and for the claims of the various tribes within the Promised Land (Josh 15–19). Metes and bounds strategies are also used to define private lands: an example is the plot of land purchased by Abraham as a tomb for his wife, described as "the field of Ephron in Machpelah, which was to the east of Mamre, the field with the cave that was in it and all the trees that were in the field, throughout its whole area" (Gen 23:17).

Metes and bounds, however, are by no means a perfect solution to the problem of defining property boundaries. They depended on physical landmarks that themselves could change or disappear; and if not written out they might be forgotten or distorted in the event of a dispute. One means for dealing with the latter problem was to embed the description in a story or other artefact of popular culture: Descriptions could be recorded in oral traditions carried forward by families or clans. The monuments of choice were stones, which had the virtues of being readily available, reasonably heavy, and impervious to rot or other forms of deterioration over time. Single stones appear to have been used in urban areas; for rural properties, more extensive structures such as cairns or standing stones were employed (Gen 31:45–46). These larger monuments would have been easy to find in undeveloped lands where single stones could be lost or lack distinctive identity as property markers.

Despite these advantages, monuments also had obvious deficiencies as devices for identifying the borders of real property. One problem, not present for metes and bounds descriptions, is that monuments could be moved by unscrupulous neighbors. That the surreptitious repositioning of boundary stones was a problem in ancient Israel is evidenced by the many biblical statements disapproving the practice (Deut 19:14; 27:17; Job 24:2; Prov 22:28; 23:10; Hos 5:10). Cairns and standing stones would have been more resistant to covert repositioning; but in rural areas, someone intent on committing a fraud would have greater opportunity to work without being observed. Boundary monuments also had the disadvantage that they did not identify the owners: Even if they remained in their original positions, a fraudster could falsely claim that he or she was the true owner. Perhaps for this reason, property agreements were sometimes sealed by communal meals or oaths sworn to family deities (see Gen 31:53). Such rituals would have helped to give content to the mute testimony of the stones.

A more effective strategy, where technologically feasible, was to record the description of the property in a written deed, and then to deposit the document in some repository of records where it could be accessed to resolve disputes over ownership. Jeremiah 32 contains a description of such a recordation system in use in Jerusalem during the final days of Judah as an independent country. Jeremiah purchases land in the territory of Benjamin for seventeen shekels of silver. The purchase price is weighed out – presumably on an official scale used to combat later claims of fraud (Jer 32:9; compare Gen 23:16). The transacting parties signed the deed in the presence of witnesses, who also affixed their signatures. Two copies of the deed were prepared: One was left unsealed, and the other was encased in some sort of seal, presumably in such a way that if the seal were broken, it would be obvious to any later observer that the document had been tampered with (Jer 32:11). Both copies were then given to Baruch son of Mahseiah – apparently a government official – who was to place them in a clay jar so "they may last a long time" (Jer 32:14).

All workable systems of real property provide assurances to the counterparties that their efforts to buy and sell parcels of real estate, if conducted according to proper legal form, will be effective at transferring title. To achieve this objective, the law must distinguish between actions that have the legal effect of conveying title and those that are merely preliminary (such as negotiations that end without an agreement). In the common law, the issue is addressed through the requirement of "delivery": the parties must undertake some formal, objective action recognized as sufficient to convey title. At one time, the transfer of real property at common law was accompanied by a ritual known as "livery of seisin," which involved the actual handing-over of a twig or clump of earth symbolizing delivery of the real estate in question. The biblical law of real property also imposed formalities of delivery. Probably, at one time, both parties were required to walk the boundaries of the property in the presence of witnesses (cf. Gen 13:17); later the law recognized that delivery could occur symbolically through the handing over of a sandal (Ruth 4:7). In the story of Jeremiah's purchase, the law recognized as sufficient for delivery the signing and sealing of a deed in the presence of witnesses (Jer 32:1–15).

FAMILY LAW

The family was a fundamental institution of society in biblical times, even more so than it is today. It is not surprising, therefore, that the Bible sets forth rules governing power relations in families and regulation of transfers of wealth within families. The most important context for intra-familial wealth transfers was then – as now – the conveyance of property on death. I previously mentioned that conveyances of intangible personal property present problems of delivery, since the resource in question has no physical form. The problem is acute in the case of wills because the testator cannot testify as to his intentions after he or she is dead. The Bible addresses this problem by requiring that the testator engage in unequivocal objective actions as prerequisites to an effective transfer. This requirement served the purpose of reducing the risk of after-the-fact disputes over inheritances – a purpose so important that even fraudulently induced blessings were effective at conveying patriarchal rights so long as the parties observed the requisite formalities.

The narrative of Isaac's last will and testament illustrates these principles. The story assumes that a precondition to the effectiveness of a will is that the testator would kiss the intended object of his bounty.

Rebekah, who wishes the birthright to go to Jacob, knows this fact and knows that Isaac intends to bequeath the birthright to Esau. She counsels Jacob to place goatskins on his hands and neck – a stratagem that works when Isaac kisses Jacob and, convinced that he is dealing with Esau, conveys his blessing to the disfavored son (Gen 27:39–40). The message of the story is that the testator's objective and observable action of kissing the intended object of his bounty is sufficient to render a testimonial gift valid and binding, even if the gift is procured by fraud. The Bible is willing to accept occasional instances of unfairness in order to guarantee the security and durability of wills, an essential objective if the dangers of violence and feud are to be avoided in a society in which the central government is weak or absent.

CONCLUSION

This essay has presented a theory of biblical interpretation that focuses on narratives as repositories for ideas about law and government. Key to this methodology is to unpack the narratives by understanding their symbolic meaning. I have illustrated the application of this strategy in a variety of contexts: the justification for government and political obligation, constitutional law, contract law, property law, and the law of the family. Many other examples and many other areas of law could be interpreted using the same approach. I hope to have convinced the reader that this approach represents a perspective that can serve as a valuable supplement to other strategies of biblical interpretation.

Further Reading

Carmichael, Calum, *The Spirit of Biblical Law* (Athens, GA, 1996).
Levinson, Bernard, *Legal Revision and Religious Renewal in Ancient Israel* (Cambridge, 2008).
Miller, Geoffrey P., *Ways of a King: Legal and Political Ideas in the Bible* (Göttingen, 2011).
Morrow, William S., *An Introduction to Biblical Law* (Grand Rapids, MI, 2017).
Rawls, John, *Theory of Justice* (Cambridge, MA, 1971).
Watts, James W., *Reading Law: The Rhetorical Shaping of the Pentateuch* (London, 1999).

4 Biblical Law and Literature

CALUM CARMICHAEL

LAW IN THE OLD TESTAMENT

The laws in Genesis through Deuteronomy are attributed to the legendary lawgiver Moses – with two exceptions. After the devastation caused
by the Flood, the deity communicates laws for the new world about
killing animals and humans (in that order, Gen 9), and also the Decalogue (literally the Ten Words, not necessarily identical with Commandments) given at Mount Sinai for the new Israelite nation (Exod
19–20). All the laws, whether articulated by Moses or the deity, are part
of a continuous narrative, the Primary History, stretching from Genesis
through 2 Kings. Both the legal and the literary material focus on first
time occurrences, on events at the beginning of the world and then of
the Israelite nation. The composition, more or less, relays chronologically these events and their impact on later history up to the exile of the
nation to Babylonia in 586 BCE. The presentation of laws and narratives
together is a well-wrought literary product of unknown writers who
impose ideal ethical and legal standards on problems arising in the
narrative traditions.[1]

We know nothing about the writers responsible for setting out the
narratives and the laws in the Primary History. They are most likely
associated with scribal schools but there is little point in speculating
about their education, attachments, or standing in society. What we
can say is that their work is a product of the world of rhetoric and
instruction in wise dealing. Their purpose is not, as is commonly
thought, primarily to set down law codes to govern their society.
Instead, in the interests of bolstering national identity, probably in the
post-monarchical, exilic period, they compose laws to "correct" past
wrongdoing as described in ancient (even to the scribes) stories.

---

[1] Comparable is how later Islamic standards infuse laws current in Arabia in the
seventh century CE.

A commitment to the laws they articulate by a newly formed nation promises a future time of peace and rest from enemies for the Israelites. Biblical laws reveal a spirit both nationalistic and universalistic. Foreign nations will "hear all these statutes, and say, surely this great nation is a wise and understanding people" (Deut 4:6).

When the deity gives rules after the Flood and at Mount Sinai, and when Moses gives rules for national life, the judgments anticipate events that occur long after the time at which the rules are articulated. In a notable example, Moses' rule about kingship concerns an institution that comes into existence long after his time. The rule prohibits a monarch from multiplying horses, wives, silver, and gold (Deut 17:14–20). Moses anticipates how King Solomon will do precisely that (1 Kings 10, 11). Such foresight is, in fact, the writers' own hindsight at work. They survey the past and judge that what happened could have been anticipated. Historians adopting this stance become prophets looking backward. In his predictive theory about American law, the jurist Oliver Wendell Holmes writes: "The prophecies of what the courts will do in fact, and nothing more pretentious, are what I mean by the law."[2]

The Primary History tells sequentially of origins: the beginning of the world, of humanity, of the Israelite nation's founding fathers, of its religious institutions, of its prophetic leaders, and of its monarchical rule. The positioning of the law collections within the narrative stream shows a similar interest in origins. The fresh beginning of the world after the Flood brings the rules about bovicide and homicide to counteract the violence that caused the deity to flood the earth (Gen 9:3–6). The start of the Israelite nation after the exodus from Egypt brings us the Decalogue (Exod 20). The various rules in Exod 21–23 look back initially on the conduct of the fathers of the nation; the ritual instructions in Exod 24–40 look back on the post-exodus wrongdoing associated with the worship of the Golden Calf; the laws of Leviticus take up the religious offenses associated with, initially, Jacob's family; and the laws of Deut 12–26 anticipate new life in the land of Canaan and the later monarchical period.

The rules fit a universal trend whereby many or most groups produce bodies of instructional counsel and, grounding it in the highest authority, locate its origin as far back in time as possible. The Israelite nation's biblical rules are no exception. The term "authority" (from

[2] Oliver Wendell Holmes, "The Path of the Law," *HLR* 10 (1897), 461.

Latin *augere*, "to increase, exalt") hints at the strength added behind the scene. In ancient Israel, the anonymous writers ascribe authority to a fictional Moses and to the deity as the ultimate source of law. Such ascription conveys the mystery and the unknowability of the origin of laws, in Sophocles' words, "They are not of yesterday, or today, but everlasting. Though where they came from, none of us can tell" (*Antigone*, lines 445–46).

THE DECALOGUE

The placement, sequence, and function of biblical laws are not best understood in terms of societal application. Especially illustrative is the way in which the Decalogue comes into existence. Issuing directly from God in a dramatic setting on a mountain and depicted as a mythical event, it is a scribal invention, an imaginative, intellectual quest chiefly intent on fashioning a divine origin for Israel's laws. To communicate that its contents are ageless, the Decalogue's delivery evokes the beginning of the world. The "voice" that Moses hears at Mount Sinai – "And God answered him by a voice" (Exod 19:19) – conjures up the "voice" that spoke to create the world in Gen 1. The accompanying smoke, fire, lightning, and thunder invoke the chaos of the newly created universe. Like the ten pronouncements in Gen 1 that God uttered to bring order to the initial chaos, the ten pronouncements in the Decalogue order relations first between Israelites and God (in four of them) and then among humans in general (in the following six).

The Decalogue in Exod 19 is given at a point in time when the Israelite nation is itself being created. This "historical" setting explains why the Decalogue's first part (or tablet) gives directives about worship to be observed by the incipient nation. The broader context for specific provisions is such that God anticipates that after the delivery of the Decalogue (Exod 20) the Israelite people, in their first collective action as a newly formed nation, will commit apostasy and rebel against him. At their request, Aaron, acting for Moses who is absent on the mountain for a long time, fashions a golden image of God in the shape of a calf (Exod 32). Aaron builds an altar before the image and has the people recognize the calf as the numinous "being" who led them out of Egypt. Aaron applies the distinctive name Yahweh to it and sets aside a special day to worship it with sacrificial offerings. Anticipating and opposing these developments, the initial four pronouncements of God's first tablet address the wrongs. The people must acknowledge not some personified, paranormal object but an invisible numinous being,

Yahweh, as the deity who took them out of Egypt. They must not worship gods other than this unseen Yahweh, or produce any artefacts and attribute divinity to them. They must never apply Yahweh's name inappropriately and finally, ordained by Yahweh to counter Aaron's special day, they must honor the "true" God Yahweh on the Sabbath day (Exod 20:2–11).

In the narrative, God's response to the making of the Golden Calf is one that is intent on destroying all the people and starting over again with Moses as the progenitor of new generations. Moses argues, however, that by doing so God would lose his reputation among the Egyptians and he appeals to him not to proceed. The foreign nation would view the destructive act as dishonoring Abraham, Isaac, and Jacob/Israel, the first ancestors of the present generation. God had just delivered their descendants from enslavement in Egypt and had promised to increase their numbers in every generation, including the present offending one (Exod 32:11–14). Moses' appeal to a higher, internationally acknowledged value to honor a nation's forebears induces a change of heart and God permits (most of) Aaron's generation to survive.

In making sense of how the laws appear at different points in an ongoing saga, certain striking features emerge. The laws focus on first-time occurrences of some problem and reveal, in line with how history writing at all times imitates previous history writing, an interest in issues that show up repeatedly from generation to generation. The topic of honor owing to forebears illustrates the focus on first-time events. Moses' successful appeal to honor Israel's ancestors at the climax to the making of the Golden Calf prompts the Decalogue's author to turn back to the Garden of Eden story about the very first two generations of humankind (Gen 2–4). That is when the issue of honoring forebears first arose. Cain is the first son ever to have parents and he is also the first son ever to dishonor them when he murders their offspring, his brother Abel. The switch of focus from the new nation's first generation in Exod 32 back to humankind's first family members explains why the initial topic of the second tablet's six "Words" enjoins offspring to honor their father *and* their mother (Exod 20:12–17). The switch also explains why, most puzzlingly, the topic of murder follows. Cain is the first person ever to commit murder.

The second tablet continues to focus on the first family by unpacking the moral and legal injunctions implicit in God's interaction with it. After the commands to honor parents and to refrain from murder, there are injunctions against adultery, stealing, vain testimony, and coveting. The choice of these particular offenses can be readily explained. Following his misdeed, Cain becomes the first person ever to conclude a marriage. Its institution is traced to God removing a rib from Adam and creating Eve from it: "Therefore shall a man leave his father and his mother, and shall cleave to his wife: and they shall be one flesh" (Gen 2:24). That no spouse exists for Cain at this point in time highlights the ancient author's primary interest not in facts but in mythical origins, in this instance, the institution of marriage. The "history" of the fictional first humans is an interpretive exercise to communicate not actual events but the mysteries of human beginnings. Cleaving and becoming one flesh in marriage mirrors the creation of Eve from Adam's body and carries an implicit prohibition: union with another is divinely ordained and adultery is an offense against the created order.

The ensuing topics, stealing, vain testimony, and coveting, also take up troubling events in Eden. These occur immediately after the union of Eve and Adam in one flesh. She covets the prohibited fruit from the tree of knowledge of good and evil and proceeds to steal it and to share it with Adam. Cross-examined by God about the theft, each utters vain testimony (Adam blames God for giving him Eve and Eve claims to have been beguiled by the serpent). God then expels Adam and Eve from Eden to prevent them similarly coveting and taking this time from the tree of life. Eating its fruit would make them gods and guarantee them ever-lasting life. After the expulsion from the garden, the corresponding desire for "higher" life is to be anticipated and the Decalogue combats coveting a neighbor's enviable possessions, house, wife, field, male and female servants, ox, ass, or anything of a neighbor's that is superior to what the human addressees have.

SACRED (RITUAL) LAW: THE JOSEPH STORY AND THE DAY OF ATONEMENT

Sacred or ritual law invites special attention. As nature is always the same, so rough divisions in legal systems are perennial: public affairs; land; persons, that is, birth, marriage, family, status, succession; trans-actions; crime; and procedure. An unsurprising result is that in most societies similar social, political, and economic problems arise and similar rules appear. To seek unique features in any system, we look to ritual law because it expresses a community's distinctive identity with its festivals and solemn as well as joyous occasions.

Engaging the attention of anthropologists since the beginning of the nineteenth century, the origin and strange features of many ritual practices prove difficult to comprehend. For one thing, they are embedded in a community's peculiar history and experience and are not easily researched, especially the further back in time we go. We are, however, fortunately able to solve puzzling aspects of biblical rituals in a way often denied to us in the study of rituals of other cultures. The narratives again richly illuminate because rituals are often stories that have either been contracted or expanded from an initial set of narrative events and then dramatized. The Day of Atonement for the forgiveness of wrongdoing is an example (Lev 16). One impetus for the ritual is resistance to "what is done cannot be undone [MacBeth's murder of Banquo]" (*Macbeth*, Act V, scene 1, line 75). At all times there is longing that somehow the impossible can be achieved and the wrong "wiped out." The ritual in Lev 16 attempts to do just that.

Like a few other areas of law, contracts for instance, ritual institutions attract baffling formalistic features the more complex and significant the issue. The ritual in Lev 16 requires animal sacrifices: burnt ones to honor the deity and sin offerings to "remove" past sins. Once a year, the high priest dresses in a linen coat and enters the most sacred part of the sanctuary to offer sacrifices for sin. With much splashing of blood, he makes atonement on account of "the uncleanness of the sons of Israel." As well as atoning for their transgressions, he also atones for those of his own priestly house. An especially perplexing aspect of the ritual designates one goat to be a burnt offering and a second live goat to be dispatched to the wilderness on its own with no human accompaniment. The live animal is thought to go to a mysterious demonic being Azazel. (The word "scapegoat" is derived from an attempt to understand this Hebrew word as the goat, *'az*, that goes away, *'azal*.) The word Azazel is known only from this ritual and the goat sent to Azazel is never seen again. The two actions with the two goats remove the people's sins for the past year, but on what basis has been decidedly difficult to decipher.

The story of Joseph in Gen 37–50 handsomely explains the ritual because its elements dramatize the reaction of Joseph's brothers to their sin against him. To cover up their evil role in his disappearance from the pit into which they cast him, they present counterfeit evidence to their father to suggest that a wild beast killed him. In reality, they had slaughtered a goat and dipped Joseph's coat in its blood, an act that, from a later priestly perspective, renders them unclean. Joseph, in fact, is still alive, but neither his brothers nor his father know anything about how Midianite traders took him from the pit and sold him in Egypt as a slave.

The Joseph saga concerns the first family ever of (Jacob) Israel. The history of their descendants dominates the literature of the Hebrew Bible. A universal phenomenon is that the doings of the first members of any nation or group are of enduring interest and inspire the ritualizing process. So many wrongs in the story are done by the brothers, by Joseph, and even by their father Jacob/Israel. These prompt judgments that already emerge in the exercise of justice as the story unfolds. The story ends with the brothers' request to Joseph that he forgive their bad treatment of him but Joseph tells them only God can do that. The Day of Atonement ritual, in turn, devises a procedure that has their descendants imitate their ancestors' actions to cover up their wrongdoing. At the same time, later Israelites are to remind themselves of their own many wrongs during the past year. The story's climax has God transform the ruin facing the first family into welfare for all. The ritual's aim is to achieve similar redemption for later generations confronting their own transgressions.

The overriding viewpoint in the Joseph story is that God turns evil into good (Gen 50:20), a manner of thinking that also dominates not just the Day of Atonement but the entire sacrificial system. Rituals commonly address negative events with a view to recalling them and then, reversing the wrongdoing, promote beneficial outcomes. Comparable is the common understanding of the old and widespread "eye for an eye" response to a hurt when the recipient, or whoever acts for the wronged person, inflicts a similar wrong on the culprit to recall the misdeed in order to achieve closure for it. Near Eastern texts also relay rituals that eliminate impurity or evil with symbolic actions to evoke it and remove the affliction. Illness, for example, is transferred to an object such as an animal or a figurine, which is then disposed of somewhere. Rituals achieve their goal by acts mirroring the negative ones in focus. The stance, imitating in order to oppose, points to a universal phenomenon: *Per quod quis peccat, per idem punitur,* "By what things a man sins, by the same also he is tormented" (Wis 11:16); "According to the sin it is proper to render satisfaction, so that the sin caused by gluttony is corrected by fasting, and what garrulity allows should be cast out by silence, and thus contrary is cured by contrary" (PL 113, 371); and "Medicines are usually made of opposites" (Aristotle, *Nic. E.,* 2.31).[3]

[3] On Near Eastern rituals, see D. P. Wright, *The Disposal of Impurity: Elimination Rites in the Bible and in Hittite and Mesopotamian Literature,* SBLDS 101 (Atlanta, 1987), 39–43.

Scholars who study the ritual of the Day of Atonement assume that it has a long and complicated history and incorporates a rite (or rites) belonging to distant, probably pre-Israelite times. The matter is less complicated. The ritual is a creative product of reflection on a seminal event in the nation's own history, namely, the brothers' killing of a goat to cover up their wrongdoing after they threw Joseph into a deep pit and then lost him. Their insidious action that followed with his blood-soaked garment convinces their father that his favorite son has died as the victim of a wild beast. The ritual, in turn, incorporates precisely the role of the slaughtered goat and the use made of its blood in order, legitimately, to deflect wrongdoing of whatever kind. The high priest's surprising non-priestly clothing (*ketonet*) in the temple is sullied by sacrificial blood in order to evoke Joseph's special bloodstained coat (*ketonet*), the coat that signified his supreme standing in the family.

These cultic actions serve to recall the evil event by imitating it with a view to deriving good from it. The role of the second live goat mimics the brothers' attempt to remove any suspicion of their wrong-doing by attributing it to a non-existent animal, which, in the ritual, is conveyed in the role of the demonic figure of Azazel. By re-enacting the transfer of the brothers' evil deed to a goat, the ritual serves to remove sin and bring about forgiveness, which, as Joseph himself claims, only God can grant.

Details of the ritual bring out aspects of the brothers' ruse. Someone "at hand," not some named individual, sends the goat off to the wilder-ness. The animal somehow makes its way to an "inaccessible or cut off" land. The odd details serve to bring out the brothers' evil genius in having a goat metamorphose, via the lie they tell to Jacob, into a wild beast (Lev 16:21, 22). The place where the goat in the ritual goes to the demonic being is a reminder that Joseph visited his shepherding broth-ers in the wilderness where evil befalls him at their hands, and also where predatory wild beasts attack from their remote, cut-off parts of the territory. In line with the fiction, the word Azazel most likely draws attention to its special character as something like "fierce, demonic goat" (from a reduplication of the letter zayin to obtain *'ez'ez'el*, also pronounced *'az'az'el*, where the word for goat, *'ez*, is highlighted and the word *'el* added to express the idea of "godlike might").[4] Fantastically, an innocent, herbivorous animal, a goat, becomes an evil devourer of a human being. A domestic animal metamorphosing into a sinister one

---

[4] See Baruch Levine, *Leviticus*, JPSTC (Philadelphia, 1989), 102.

has a parallel in the Joseph story. In the pharaoh's dream of impending agricultural disaster, thin cows devour fat ones in order to convey, so Joseph interprets, future famine (Gen 41:17–24). Like the brothers' goat, the cows become possessed of an out-of-character demonic make-up.

The ritual provides the Israelites with an annual means to confess wrongdoing and achieve forgiveness. Standing over the live goat, the high priest places the confessed individual and collective sins of the people upon its head and dispatches it to the wilderness. In the story, the brothers did confess their mistreatment of Joseph in his presence but they were not aware of who he was (Gen 42:21–24). Later, they attempted to seek forgiveness from him but Joseph tells them that only God can grant it. The strange rites of the Day of Atonement become intelligible in light of the story. No human like Joseph can grant absolution but the Israelite deity can by his numinous presence in the sanctuary and by cultic actions that mirror salient aspects of the brothers' sins against Joseph and their father. To stabilize errant human ways, the sanctuary ritual serves as a form of theatre to alchemize evil into good.

LAW IN THE NEW TESTAMENT

Characteristic of moral teachers at all times is that in enunciating moral rules they are not subject, as lawmakers are for legal rules, to the demands of definition, proof, and the like. Moralists commonly take wrongs known to the law and treat them expansively. Jesus' teaching illustrates: Anger is murder and looking upon a woman with desire is adultery (Matt 5:21–30). His primary focus is moral and ritual law, being largely indifferent to more technical areas of law, civil and criminal procedure, for instance. Like the rabbinic authorities of his time, he recognizes that a few first principles can sum up an entire religion: "You shall love your neighbor as yourself" (Lev 19:18; Luke 10:27). At the same time, however, as in Rabbi Ben Azzai's statement that "you should run to do the lightest duty, for one duty draws another after it, and the reward of a duty is a duty" (*m. Ab.* 4:2), Jesus also insists that no matter how seemingly minor a rule it has the same validity as a major one: "One jot or tittle shall in no wise pass from the law, till all be fulfilled" (Matt 5:18).

The literature of the New Testament reflects early stages in the formation of a sect. Absent is the range of human relations to be found in the Old Testament. It is thus often unwise to compare the legal ideas of the New Testament with those of the Old. Despite this reservation and the additional one that enormous changes in law take place over the centuries – for example, "eye for an eye" becomes monetary reparation – the importance of the Old Testament's role in the New is considerable. This is so because New Testament writers use the Old Testament ideas to express and lend authority to their own ideas.

Many problems yield solutions only when we take into account legal thinking of the time. The bewildering accusation that Jesus is "a glutton and drunkard, a friend of publicans and sinners" (Matt 11:19) is intelligible once we see that his accusers attempt to bring him under the law of Deut 21:18–21 about a rebellious son who will not obey his parents and is characterized as "a glutton and drunkard." Talmudic jurisprudence has the severity of the law apply to the son, not on account of mere revelry, but only if he surrounds himself with godless associates. The gluttony and drunkenness cited in the accusation against Jesus is because the Old Testament prohibition includes these two vices in its characterization of a rebellious son (*b. Sanh.* 70b).

Jesus makes use of the "eye for eye" formula (Lev 24:19, 20) in his pronouncement about turning the other cheek (Matt 5:38, 39). He uses the directive solely to take up that aspect of the law of assault which, by his time, also concerned itself with the intangible wrong of insult. A person by then could receive compensation not just for physical damage to his person but also for emotional distress. As in the earliest codification of Jewish law, the Mishnah, an injured person could claim compensation for an attack on his dignity over and above any injury sustained: "If a man wounds another, he is liable on five counts, for injury, for pain, for healing, for loss of time, and for the indignity inflicted" (*m. B. K.* 8:1). In quoting the "eye for an eye" formula, Jesus addresses himself solely to the wrong of insult as when someone shames a person by slapping him on the cheek, a gesture that is the standard illustration in ancient sources of an attack on one's dignity. Jesus' attitude is a conservative one in that he opposes bringing the incorporeal wrong within the orbit of the courts. Instead of seeking monetary compensation, he counsels meekness in the face of an indignity rather than reacting aggressively: "whosoever shall strike you on your right cheek, turn to him the other also." He would not have opposed assault or murder being dealt with by punitive legal remedies.

Although Jesus is primarily a moralist, he shows a sophisticated knowledge of law and its workings and also, where necessary, consummate skill in communicating ambiguous meaning, the mark of an effective lawyer in a political situation. In one instance, two groups normally greatly opposed to each other, the Herodians, who are loyal to the Roman government, and the Pharisees, who reject it out of hand, hypocritically come together to entrap him. Their hostile question, "Should we pay tax to Caesar or not?" is designed to test where he stands on the issue of recognizing the reigning Roman power. The question poses a dilemma (Mk 12:13–17). To counsel payment would enrage the Pharisees and to oppose it the Herodians. Jesus squares the circle with a clever reply: "Render to Caesar the things that are Caesar's and to God the things that are God's." Contributing to the common misconception that secular and religious authority are separate domains, his declaration cleverly distinguishes *in appearance only* the demands of government and those of religion. His response is a skillfully disguised rejection of Caesar's reign and an affirmation of the Pharisaic position. (Despite the frequency in the Gospels of occasions that depict hostility between Jesus and the Pharisees, they fundamentally share the same beliefs. At play is the universal phenomenon of "the narcissism of small differences." People do battle with those who are most like them.) Jesus' fundamental stance is that everything is ultimately under the control of the deity and thus the emphasis is on the final clause. Hearing their own position affirmed, Herodians and Pharisees are satisfied.

Equally shrewd is the instruction Jesus gives to Peter when a temple official inquires as to whether his master pays the temple tax (Exod 30:13, 38:26; Matt 17:24–27). Peter is unsure but says yes to satisfy the inquirer. Privately, Jesus puts before Peter the syllogism: "Of whom do kings of the earth take toll [poll-tax], of their own sons or of strangers?" Peter gives the correct answer: members of the ruling family are exempt from paying tax and only the nonmembers pay. It follows that, like the priests serving in the temple, Jesus and Peter (standing for the other disciples) are exempt from paying the tax because he and Peter are sons of God, the temple's sovereign.

The matter, however, proves to be complicated. The claim of special priestly status that Jesus asserts for himself and his disciples is not one they should openly declare for it would give offense. They must none-theless not give up their status and belief in their superior standing. To do so, however, requires extraordinary skill. They will both pay and not pay the tax. To avoid illegality, Jesus furnishes an example of a legal dodge, that is, a move that might pass muster for getting round an irksome requirement should the matter ever be subject to formal judi-cial scrutiny. Peter is to find in the mouth of the first fish he catches a shekel with which to pay the half-shekel tax owed by Jesus and Peter in fulfillment of their obligation as Jews of seeming ordinary standing. The money in the fish's mouth is lost property. It is therefore legally theirs but economically and psychologically not really theirs. By proffering the coin to the temple authorities Peter and Jesus will pay the tax in a formalistic sense only, the collectors being none the wiser (or even interested in the source). Free from having to disburse from their own pockets, Jesus and his disciples remain true to their higher, if sensibly concealed, status.

The dodge is one that in actual life is virtually impossible to accomplish without resort to deviousness and deception. It is why the story involves a miracle. As a master with disciples, Jesus has to furnish the perfect example of how to avoid giving offense while at the same time preserving his and their freedom as divine sons in a higher service. The master's instruction about the fish is specifically addressed to his intimates, whereas the directive about Caesar's tax addresses hostile parties. In contrast to esoteric wisdom, worldly wisdom requires a general, ambiguous response so that both claims appear to be valid.

PAUL AND THE LAW

More systematically than Jesus, Paul in his letters to different communities of believers makes pronouncements that impinge directly upon legal matters. His contribution to the New Testament's understanding of law is radical. Trained as a rabbinical scholar, he combines legal subtlety and imaginative daring. His starting point is the notion that Christian believers undergo a passage from death to life in the sense that in their contemporary existence they die with Jesus and rise with him to new life. Important to emphasize is their new position in life in regard to the law: "Therefore if any man be in Christ, he is a new creature: old things are passed away; behold, all things are become new" (2 Cor 5:17, cp. Col 3:10; 1 Pet 1:3, 2:2; *b. Yeb.* 22a, 48b). Paul's notion of new creation comes from the institution of conversion to Judaism current in his time, an experience perceived to profoundly affect the convert's status. All previous biological and legal ties are miraculously gone.

From the limited knowledge available to us, the rabbinic doctrine appears solely to affect laws pertaining to marriage and inheritance. If a brother and a sister convert, for example, they are no longer brother and sister and, in principle, they are free to marry. The problem for the rabbinic authorities is hardly surprising. The outside world could not be expected to understand the profound belief in the miracle of new birth. The rabbis consequently take the position, as does Paul, that any union recognized as incestuous by other societal groups should not in fact take place. Their fear is that outsiders might perceive Jews and

Christians as given to licentiousness. Paul's discussion about a union between a man and his father's wife in the Corinthian community is a case in point: "It is reported commonly that there is fornication among you, and such fornication as is not so much as named among the Gentiles, that one should have his father's wife." Astonishingly, the community is proud of this union between a man and his (divorced or widowed) stepmother. The reason for their pride is their belief in re-creation. Paul condemns their religious boasting as much as their behavior (1 Cor 5:1–6). They should no more make a display of their new freedom than Paul himself once made a display of strict adherence to Pharisaic law.

Deeply influenced by Jewish upbringing about how proselyte baptism makes a newborn being, Paul extends the idea of a convert's narrow freedom from certain laws (those pertaining to marriage and inheritance) into an all-embracing scheme. "All things are licit," is his remarkable claim (1 Cor 6:12). That being said, Paul's ultimate focus is the responsibility that comes with the freedom granted to believers who become newborn. Paul insists on adherence to two ethical stances. First, the believers must think through their intended actions, for example, whether to commit to marriage or to celibacy, or whether to pursue litigation against a fellow believer or to settle without going to court (1 Cor 6–7). They must ask themselves if their conduct chimes with their new-found spiritual well-being. Second, as members of a new sect they must carefully evaluate their conduct by considering its impact on fellow members who may be easily confused. Might they eat food that has been offered to idols and might they cultivate ecstatic speech (1 Cor 8, 12)? The members must themselves judge whether or not the conduct contributes to the community's well-being and advancement. The Pauline combination of freedom from the law and responsibility in exercising this freedom, while intellectually and spiritually demanding, stands nonetheless as a major, inspiring achievement.

Despite Jesus' strict view that every rule should be heeded no matter what kind of duty it entails, there is no indication that it governed his conduct or that of his followers. Reasons for this less than absolute position are readily explicable. The strict stance is an exceedingly demanding one. Moreover, Jesus' attack on the hypocrisy of those who ostentatiously display their adherence to rules, prayer in public places, for instance (Matt 6), probably had the unintended effect of devaluing the rules themselves. Jesus' crucifixion must also have affected attitudes. As the early Jewish-Christian movement grew, and especially under the influence of Paul, it was necessary to smooth the way for Gentile converts, for example, to drop the daunting ritual requirement of male circumcision (Acts 15). With Paul as the leading proponent of the new faith, the affirmation of Jesus as the Messiah became the unconditional requirement and a replacement for the previous affirmation of the law as the supreme guide to life. Believers' chief duty was to live, not under the prevailing ritual and moral law, but through their belief in Jesus as the Messiah.

LEGAL IDEAS IN THE TEXTS

The biblical legal and literary sources are rich in challenging, stimulating topics that express sophisticated legal ideas of perennial interest. In Gen 19, Abraham pleads with God not to destroy all the inhabitants of Sodom but to separate the innocent from the wicked. In doing so, Abraham affirms the justice of individual responsibility over and against the regrettable, if often necessary but fundamentally unjust, application of collective accountability. In Gen 38, a conflict of law with principle emerges when Tamar acts in a higher cause by breaching the ban on adultery and incest in order to fulfill the sacred duty of obtaining a child to remedy her dead husband's lack of a line of descent. She does not engage sexually with Judah's son Shelah, whom Judah has kept from her and to whom she is bound in inchoate marriage. Instead, in disguise, she seduces her father-in-law Judah because he, as head of the household, is the obstacle to the prescribed levirate marriage. In 1 Sam 8, there is also recognition that sometimes authoritative sanctioning of evil is necessary to accommodate human sinfulness. The deity decides to institute kingship, contrary to his position that he alone should govern. In Deut 25:5–10, the sanction of shaming punishment is applied to a man (the levir) who refuses to raise up a child to his dead brother by conceiving a child with the widow. In Num 5:11–31, appeal to conscience in controlling conduct is the major feature of the Bitter Water test for a woman accused of adultery where clear-cut evidence is lacking. Deut 25:1–3 has a rule that points to our concept of human rights. If a person has been found guilty of a punishable offense and subjected to a beating, its application must be restricted to a certain number of stripes. The offender's dignity is at stake and he must not be degraded in public by excessive striking.

Popularly expressed as "an eye for an eye," the *lex* or *jus talionis* reflects an old and widespread response to a hurt. It is far from being an attitude unique to the world of the Old Testament. What is unique is the fuller biblical formula in which the phrase is embedded: "life for life, eye for eye, tooth for tooth, hand for hand, foot for foot." This particular articulation does not, as is usually interpreted, mean that varieties of offenses should receive varied but equivalent penalties. The meaning here is narrow and expresses exactly what it says: intensified death or aggravated capital punishment, that is, systematic mutilation of an offender's corpse *after* the carrying out of a death sentence. This formulation is found, for example, in the rule in Deut 19:16–21. The offense focuses on Naboth's ghastly death wished for by King Ahab and duly arranged by his wife Jezebel. Hiring false witnesses to accuse him of apostasy, she acquired Naboth's vineyard by having him put to death for the alleged crime (1 Kgs 21, 22). Naboth was stoned to death outside his city and dogs tore his corpse apart. In mirroring fashion, the punishments befalling King Ahab and Jezebel – dogs lick up his blood and no more was left of her than "the skull and the feet and the palms of her hands" – avenge the fate of the innocent Naboth (1 Kgs 22:38; 2 Kgs 9:30–37). (1 Kgs 21, 22; 2 Kgs 9).

At every turn we come upon advanced notions that show up in all later ethical and legal thinking. Lack of information, or misinformation, about some matter can excuse an offense. King Abimelech takes Sarah as a wife because he has been misled into believing that she was a free woman (Gen 12). On the other hand, lack of knowledge on account of deficient understanding may not excuse, as when a prophet proclaims, "My people are destroyed for being without knowledge" (Hos 4:6). Human creatureliness and lack of insight can sometimes mitigate accountability, as when God in that magnificent universalist work, the Book of Jonah, declares: "Should not I spare Nineveh, that great city, wherein are more than six-score thousand persons that cannot discern between their right hand and their left hand; and also much cattle?" (4:11). The use of the curse as a sanction points to a distinction not much acknowledged today between a punishable deed and a sin. Where earthly authorities cannot directly punish certain kinds of wrongdoing – offenses carried out in secret, removing a boundary mark, sexual acts committed within a family, or the rich oppressing the poor (Deut 27:15–26) – a sanctioned curse is (alas) the second-best means of dealing with them.

RULES ABSENT IN THE BIBLICAL TEXTS

Certain rules we might expect to see in the sources are absent. One reason for their absence in the text is not their nonexistence but that they are so taken for granted that the lawgiver is not motivated to spell them out. No rule states the grounds for slavery, how to conclude a marriage, or how to proceed with a divorce. There are no rules on the transfer of property (but note the reference to an antiquarian rule about granting a right to acquire a dead relative's land in Ruth 4:7), the conclusion of sale, lease, hire, or liability for defects. It is taken for granted that there is no limit on a man being married to several women concurrently but a woman to one man only; also her exclusion from priestly office. Another reason for absent rules is that biblical legal material is not meant to be comprehensive or even governing in a practical sense – even though later institutions of religion have made the original text into comprehensive, governing conventions.

Reflecting on the origin and content of moral rules can be a demanding exercise. As with the omission of many fundamental laws, we must reckon again with what is self-understood. There is no exhortation to love a child or a spouse. The inclination is taken as "natural." Certain injunctions, on the other hand, may have been committed to writing because of difficulty observing them. There is to be no coveting another's desirable possessions (Exod 20:17). An injunction may also reflect a contentious origin. One is to love God with heart, soul, and might (Deut 6:5). The injunction's background probably in part reflects the opposition of the northern tribes to the political power concentrated in the southern Judean temple in Jerusalem. Seeking independence from the oppressive Judeans, the northern tribes set up two sanctuaries and placed images of the Golden Calf in each. The intent was to evoke the Yahweh they had known and worshipped in the Jerusalem temple, which itself contained divine images (1 Kgs 12:12–33). The political defectors are not apostates but worshippers of the same deity Yahweh. The Judean authorities are behind the writing of the Primary History and their bias underlies a narrative that attributes apostasy to secessionists where no rejection of Yahweh exists. The injunction to rely on inward human attributes, heart, soul, and might (intensity of emotion), may be a response to the worship of outward images in the Northern sanctuaries.

We should be careful not to read certain rules back into the biblical texts. Claiming a biblical duty to procreate or a prohibition against suicide illustrates. Procreation is not articulated as a duty but rather as a blessing (Gen 1:28), which is quite different from a duty. The obligation to procreate began in Greece (because of the Persian wars), spread to Rome, thence later to Jewish and Christian circles but as a duty it is not biblical. An ordinance against suicide is not found in either Old or New Testament. Samson's suicide is extolled (Jud 16:27–31) and

Judas' is accepted in Matthew's account (but not in Luke's quite different one in Acts 1:15–21) as the appropriate capital penalty for someone
betraying a fellow Jew to an oppressive, largely foreign power (Matt
27:3–5). Judas did what law and religion required: He fully repented his
misdeed and returned his ill-gotten gain to the sanctuary. Later Jewish
tradition read a prohibition of suicide back into Gen 9:5, which
demands someone's blood for murdering another person, and Christian
tradition read it back into Exod 20:13, which prohibits murder of
another person.

Aulus Gellius, a linguistic and literary scholar of the second century
CE, tells how one day he came across a difficult legal term in an ancient
epic. So he asked a professor of literature what it meant. But he also did
not know and advised Gellius: "I would have you believe me when I say
that Quintus Ennius learned this, not from a study of poetry, but from
someone skilled in the law. Do you too, then, go and learn from the
same source as Ennius." So much that has been puzzling about both the
laws and the narratives in the Old Testament becomes clear when we
assume that the laws are the key to understanding legal and ethical
problems in the narratives.

Further Reading

Bartor, Assnat, *Reading Law as Narrative: A Study in the Casuistic Laws of the
Pentateuch* (Atlanta, GA, 2010).
Carmichael, Calum, *The Spirit of Biblical Law* (Athens, GA, 1996).
Carmichael, Calum, ed., *Studies in Comparative Legal History*, Collected
Works of David Daube, vol. 2, *New Testament Judaism*, vol. 3, *Biblical
Law and Literature* (Berkeley, CA, 2000, 2003).
Carmichael, Calum, ed., *David Daube's Gifford Lectures*, vol. 1, *Law
and Wisdom in the Bible*, vol. 2, *The Deed and the Doer in the Bible*
(Conshohocken, PA, 2008, 2010).
Matthews, Victor H., *Manners and Customs in the Bible* (Peabody, MA, 1988).
Samji, Karim, *The Qur'ān: A Form-Critical History* (Berlin, 2018).
Sanders, E. P., *The Law, and the Jewish People* (Philadelphia, 1983).

5 Kings, Prophets, and Judges

GRAEME AULD

OVERVIEW

Together, the three books Judges, Samuel, and Kings tell the larger part of the story of Israel and Judah as more-or-less independent nations on their own land. Their principal focus is on "rule," good rule and bad rule: mostly royal rule (by kings), but also "rule" by judges and deliverers, and even by prophets. God too "rules" in these books, but as judge rather than as king. Together with the book of Joshua, they constitute the subset of the Hebrew Bible called Former Prophets and the start of the historical books in an English Bible.

Judges starts where Joshua finishes, with the death and burial of Joshua, under whose leadership Israel had gained her land – and the warning that, with the passing of the conquest generation, people were no longer aware of what Yahweh their God had done for Israel. The larger part of the book (chs 3–16) tells at greater length how a handful of "deliverers" saved Israel from a series of external foes and reports quite briefly on a series of five men who in turn "judged Israel." The latter part of the book (17–21) concentrates instead on problems that threaten Israel from within. Kingship makes a brief explicit appearance in the heart of the book (8–9): victorious Gideon (also known as Jerub-baal) refuses Israel's offer of monarchy while behaving as if he had accepted it; and his son by a concubine Abimelech (his name means "my father is king"!) is briefly king in Shechem in the central mountains. Then its absence becomes the focus of the final chapters. Through these, we read a fourfold refrain: "in those days there was no king in Israel." The first and last of these go on to state, "each person did what was right in their eyes" (Judg 17:6; 21:25). In the book of Kings, every king would be assessed as doing right or evil "in Yahweh's eyes." The actions recounted toward the end of the book of Judges leave readers in no doubt that "right in their own eyes" – and the absence of kings – was very wrong.

Samuel reports the beginning of settled kingly rule in Israel. It opens with the birth and early development of Samuel (1 Sam 1–3) and reports the rise and fall of Israel's first king, Saul (1 Sam 9–31). But the figure that dominates forty of its fifty-five chapters is David: from his secret anointing by Samuel, through his uneasy relationship with Saul, to his acceptance as king first by Judah and then by the rest of Israel, early external successes, his fateful adultery with the wife of one of his leading warriors whose death he then contrives, and growing tensions within his household and mirrored in his kingdom. Though known as "Samuel," its contents suggest "[The Book of] David." Moses may feature across four of the five books of the Torah or Pentateuch; but no biblical character is delineated in such detail as David.

Pace picks up again in Kings: its forty-seven chapters tell a tale that spans some twenty generations. Solomon, David's second son by Bathsheba, succeeds him, is proverbially wise, builds the temple in Jerusalem, enjoys international connections, but is corrupted by the religious implications of the many concomitant marriages (1 Kgs 2–11). The kingdom he inherited from David is divided between (the majority of) Israel to the north and Judah (ruled by his successors) to the south. Each of these kingdoms will have nineteen kings before they collapse: Israel first, conquered by Assyria; and Judah, overthrown by Babylon some seven generations later. The central third of the book (1 Kgs 17–2 Kgs 10) is dominated not by kings but by two prophets, Elijah and Elisha. The apostate character and subsequent demise of Israel is portrayed as a warning that Judah should have learned from (2 Kgs 17).

THE BOOK OF DAVID

King David, his royal line over four centuries in Jerusalem, and the whole issue of kingship in Israel are together the main subject-matter of Judges, Samuel, and Kings. David himself dominates both books of Samuel. But many issues relating to his reign are seen more clearly from the part-earlier, part-overlapping story of Saul. When David becomes king of all Israel, he captures Jerusalem, defeats the Philistines, and brings into Jerusalem the sacred "ark" – symbol of divine presence (2 Sam 5–6). He then proposes to the prophet Nathan building a house for the ark, only to receive the divine response that Yahweh needs no house but will create "a house" for David (meaning "a royal line") "for ever." "For ever" is used more densely in 2 Sam 7 than any other biblical context: Nathan's words read like a promise that will not be recalled. No such promise was made to Saul at the time he was anointed king; but when Samuel told him of his rejection by Yahweh remarkably early in the story (1 Sam 13:13b–14a), he said: "The Lord would have established your kingdom over Israel for ever, but now your kingdom will not continue." And this issue of kingship "for ever" is anticipated even earlier in the book. At the time of Samuel's birth and childhood, rule in Israel was exercised by Eli, hereditary priest at Shiloh. But in light of the gross failings of his sons, he was told by a man of God that the earlier grant of priesthood "for ever" to his family was now anathema to Yahweh: instead "those who honour me I will honour; and those who despise me shall be treated with contempt" (1 Sam 2:27–36). In as far as 1 Samuel was written as a prequel to what follows, its stories of promises to Eli and Saul being revoked invite us to read even the much-repeated "for ever" in the account of David and Nathan as conditional – like a modern contract with tenure for life, unless voided by bad behavior.

Many of the great David-stories concern his relations with women. The first of these is preceded by a huge female chorus. After young David had killed Goliath, the giant Philistine champion, Israel's homecoming forces were greeted by women chanting: "Saul has killed his thousands, and David his tens of thousands" (1 Sam 18:6–7). All Israel and Judah loved David, but Saul was furious. When he found that his daughter Michal was among the hero's admirers, he tried to bring David down by offering marriage and setting her bride-price at a hundred Philistine foreskins – but this challenge was met; and, now his wife, Michal helped him escape her father's agents. Saul had already used his daughter against David; the next time we hear of her, he has given her to another man – in circumstances that are not explained. After Saul's death, David demands her return as part of his negotiations to succeed him in the north. We last see her watching the celebrations through a window as the divine ark is brought into Jerusalem; but this time she despises his behavior – and, significantly, she is now identified as Saul's daughter and not as David's wife. She scolds him for exposing himself as he dances, but he assures her he will be honored by the other women who see him. No longer is she seeing him like the majority of women; and her return to his "house" anticipates the fate of the ten concubines he left in Jerusalem when he retreated during Absalom's revolt. Absalom had intercourse with them "in the eyes of all Israel"; and when David returned he had them confined "living as in widowhood." So too Michal had no child till the day of her death.

Nabal (or Fool) is seen by many critics as a double of Saul (1 Sam 25). Between two episodes during Saul's hunt for David in the arid southern regions when the hunter came into the power of the hunted

(1 Sam 24; 26), we find David providing "protection" for the rich Fool and his flocks. Denied access to the party at the end of shearing, he moves to take revenge but is intercepted by Nabal's wife. Abigail is beautiful and has "taste": she meets David with donkey-loads of provisions and wins him over in one of the longest and deftest speeches in the book. Nabal is a fool; but, when David becomes king, he should not have this death on his conscience. After the party, she tells Nabal what she has done, and he has a (divinely induced) heart-attack. Abigail becomes David's wife: They are well matched.

Bathsheba is the most famous of his wives, and yet she remains elusive. Almost every aspect of the story in 2 Sam 11–12 is ambiguous: What sort of washing did David see her engaged in; did she come to him willingly when sent for; did her husband Uriah (one of David's officers, the Thirty) suspect why he was brought back from the battlefield and sent home to sleep with his wife; why did David mourn their baby before he died and not afterwards? In striking contrast to Abigail, accentuated by the length of the whole telling, Bathsheba says not a word. Her only reported utterance is her two-word message to the king, "I'm pregnant": enough to set deception and murder to follow adultery. Through all the subsequent troubles in David's family, she is absent from the scene (2 Sam 13–20). When David is on his deathbed, his eldest surviving son, Adonijah (son of another wife), claims the throne. Only then does she find her voice (1 Kgs 1) – or at least voices Nathan's strategy: Had not David promised that her Solomon would succeed him? Once Solomon is on the throne, she is happy to voice Adonijah's request of the new king (1 Kgs 2). Presumably, she is confident this request will be his last: His unwise petition is for Abishag, the latest of his father's bedmates. Solomon reads a request for even one woman from his father's harem as a continuing claim on the throne and has him killed.

Is David careless or complicit over the rape of Tamar by her half-brother Amnon (2 Sam 13)? His love for her has made him sick, and he asks his father if Tamar may come and make "heart-cakes" and feed him. In light of the Song of Songs (4:9–10), we may suppose these should have been suspect as less medicinal than aphrodisiac. But David gave his permission, and Amnon forced himself on her. Absalom was her brother; he had Amnon killed and fled to exile; brought back to Jerusalem through the skill of an unnamed wise woman from Tekoa (2 Sam 14), he launched a rebellion but perished in the civil war (2 Sam 15–18).

Other women play important, if briefly told, parts in the unfolding royal story. The Queen of Sheba (1 Kgs 10) has a much larger role in post-biblical story-telling (she is named Bilqis in Islamic legend).

Huldah is the prophetess consulted by good king Josiah (2 Kgs 22). Athaliah in Jerusalem is a royal agent of the Baal-cult (2 Kgs 11). Only Jezebel, her counterpart in Samaria, is more fully narrated within Kings (1 Kgs 16–2 Kgs 9) – and has become proverbial. It is earlier in our story that we find a cluster of characters more like the women around David. Deborah and Jael are named, but not the mother of Sisera, their enemy (Jdg 4–5). Jephthah's daughter (Jdg 11), the mothers of Samson and Micah (Jdg 13; 17), the Levite's abused concubine (Jdg 19), and the medium at En-Dor consulted by Saul (1 Sam 28) all play important roles but are not identified by name. Hannah (1 Sam 1–2), mother of Samuel, is exceptional. In the following narrative of the Davidic line in Jerusalem, kings' mothers are normally named but not described.

But David's character is also explored in his dealings with Saul and his son Jonathan and with his own lieutenants, Joab and Abishai; in his murderous Negeb raids when a client of the Philistine king of Gath; and in civil war with his own son Absalom. We readers read twice (1 Sam 13:13–14; 15:17–26) about Samuel voicing the Lord's rejection of Saul as king; but each encounter had been private, for he does agree to save the king's face and accompany him as he leads his people in worship. Similarly, Samuel went privately to Bethlehem to anoint David as the next king (1 Sam 16:1–13). We already know what the main characters only gradually intuit through the comings and goings reported in the second half of 1 Samuel.

The rule of his house over all Israel outlasted David only one generation. Solomon (1 Kgs 2–11), although builder of the temple in Jerusalem and proverbially wise, himself sowed the seeds of division; and his son, Rehoboam, was too feckless to prevent the split. 1 Kgs 12–2 Kgs 17 offers a synchronic account of the house of David in Jerusalem and Judah in the south and the remainder of Israel in the north over two centuries till Israel's incorporation into the Assyrian empire. Then the final chapters of Kings report on David's last eight successors in Jerusalem till the house of David too fell, this time to the Babylonians. This conclusion pays closest attention to good kings Hezekiah and Josiah (2 Kgs 18–20; 22–23), both explicitly compared with David.

ISRAEL AND JUDAH SEPARATE

The dynastic principle operates much more successfully in south than north. All the kings of Judah belong to the family of David. The line passes from father to son (or occasionally from brother to brother) over some four centuries. Three kings are removed by conspiracy but are replaced by another member of the family. Even when queen mother Athaliah rules on for six years after the death of her son, after eliminating all but one of his heirs, this is a single isolated pause in the otherwise orderly succession; and she is overthrown in a putsch organized by Jehoiada the priest who had protected Joash, one of her grandsons, from her purge. Exceptionally, her reign is described as "over the land" and not, as regularly, "over Judah." The great majority of these "sons of David" are assessed as having "done what was right in the eyes of Yahweh" – four had "done what was evil," while one more had "not done what was right." In a few cases, David is explicitly cited as setting the standard by which the ongoing generations are judged. The criteria are never spelled out; but he had secured Jerusalem as his capital and brought there the ark, where the divine presence was encountered – and he is never associated with worship at "high places" or service of "other gods."

In the north, however, there are several dynasties over only a couple of centuries. Jeroboam is succeeded by his son, but Nadab is quickly overthrown by Baasha. His son Elah soon shares Nadab's fate; but Zimri the assassin is quickly overthrown by Omri the army chief. Omri is succeeded by three of his family: by Ahab his son, then by Ahab's sons Ahaziah and Jehoram. J[eh]oram is overthrown by Jehu, whose rapid chariot ride to power has given our language "driving like a Jehu." He is followed by four generations of his family: Jehoahaz, J[eh]oash, Jeroboam, and Zechariah. Shallum strikes Zechariah down and becomes king in his place, till he shares the same fate at the hands of Menahem. Menahem is succeeded by Pekahiah, his son; but he is overthrown by Pekah, his army chief. An invasion by Tiglath-Pileser, king of Assyria, captures the northern and eastern districts of Israel; and Hoshea becomes king of the heartland centered on Samaria, till Shalmaneser suspects him of treachery, imprisons him, and finally incorporates Samaria into his empire. The nineteen kings represent seven families; and only Omri and Jehu were followed in the throne by more than their own son. The story is complicated and violent, but a single uniform judgment runs through it all: each "did what was evil in the eyes of Yahweh; he did not depart all his days from any of the sins of Jeroboam son of Nebat, which he caused Israel to sin."

Assyrian inscriptions continued to refer to northern Israel as "the house of Omri" even after his short-lived dynasty had been overthrown. But the book of Kings never uses this phrase and speaks instead of "the house of Ahab," his son. At the same time, the narratives in 1 Kgs 16–22 make plain just how circumscribed was his authority. The towering figures in these chapters were Jezebel his wife and Elijah the prophet. The Ahab-problem is first adumbrated in a couple of sentences (1 Kgs 16:30–31):

Ahab son of Omri did evil in the sight of the Lord more than all who were before him. And as if it had been a light thing for him to walk in the sins of Jeroboam son of Nebat, he took as his wife Jezebel daughter of King Ethbaal of the Sidonians, and went and served Baal, and worshipped him.

A few verses later, we learn of Elijah proclaiming to Ahab at their first reported meeting,

As the Lord the God of Israel lives, before whom I stand, there shall be neither dew nor rain these years, except by my word.

Elijah declares to the king that it is he and not the king that is Yahweh's agent. It is he who stands before Yahweh, like the spirit among the host of heaven who volunteered to deceive the same Ahab. Normally, prophets state that they are proclaiming "the word of the Lord." Elijah instead asserts his proximity to Yahweh in the divine council and claims control over the rain by his own word.

The development of the northern story is nicely illustrated when we compare two biblical accounts of Jeroboam. The older one is preserved only in the Greek Old Testament. In it, Jeroboam is an ambitious man, married to a relative of Pharaoh's wife and with a power-base in Ephraim near Shechem, who is ready to rule over most of Israel when Rehoboam follows reckless advice and loses much of what he inherited from his father Solomon. This account is limited to Jeroboam's role within the story of Rehoboam and offers no information on how he went on to rule in (northern) Israel. Its main components are re-ordered in the expansive retelling of the Jeroboam story we read in 1 Kgs 11–14 in Hebrew and English Bibles. The acted parable of a cloak torn into twelve tatters had reinforced a divine warning in the older version but is remodeled as a (conditional) promise offered to Jeroboam while still in Solomon's service. In this expansion, the divine promise once made to David is restated in Jeroboam's favor because of Solomon's misdeeds; and the Lord says to Jeroboam what Abner had once said to David: "and you shall reign over all that your soul desires." However, once he becomes king in Shechem, he sets up a rival cult to Jerusalem. A bit-part in the story of one of Jerusalem's kings becomes the pattern for all of northern Israel's kings: every one of his successors followed him in "the sins he caused Israel to commit." He founded no dynasty but established a pattern.

The larger story of the fates of Israel and Judah is reflected in several of the lesser details. Jehoshaphat of Judah responds positively to an invitation from Ahab of Israel to campaign together against Aram for the return of

Ramoth in Gilead (1 Kgs 22). This is the first occasion since the split in the kingdom that the house of David has made common cause with Israel. Ahab is wounded in the battle and dies; Jehoshaphat lives on. After the next joint battle against Aram at Ramoth, Joram son of Ahab is wounded – but survives only to be overthrown by Jehu. On this occasion, his ally Ahaziah also outlives him, though not for long. There are also two instances of conflict between the kingdoms. Asa of Judah has to buy help from Aram to force Baasha of Israel to "desist," and then outlives him. And later, even when Jehoash of Israel succeeds in destroying a section of the wall of Jerusalem, defeated Amaziah of Judah outlives him for fifteen years. Israel is by far the larger partner; but when dealing with Judah, whether in cooperation or competition, its kings always lose out.

Each of these Judah/Israel episodes is recounted within the narrative of the southern kings. This is most obvious in the cases of Asa (with Baasha), Ahaziah (with Joram), and Amaziah (with Jehoash). However, the story of Jehoshaphat, Ahab, and Micaiah son of Imlah is also thoroughly integrated within the whole history of the south. No corresponding account of cooperation or conflict between south and north is told within the report of a northern king. Despite first impressions, the synchronic account in the larger part of Kings resulted, not from splicing together two once-independent reports, but from supplementing the story of the south. The chronology of the successors of David in Jerusalem stands on its own: When he succeeds (mostly) his father, we are told the age of each new king and how many years he reigns. We still see this clearly in the book of Chronicles, which tells only the connected history of the southern kings and provides the same information. In Kings, however, we are not told the age of each northern king at his accession, but only in which year of the reign of their southern counterpart they come to the throne and how long they then reign. We need the southern data to understand the northern. After Solomon, we find the same number of kings in Israel as in Judah (nineteen). The connected story of separate Israel is less a northern record, and more a southern construct. The purpose of this supplement is spelled out in a lengthy epilogue after the fall of Israel's last king has been reported (2 Kgs 17): Israel was a mirror in which Judah should have seen itself and learned. The core of the argument is in vv. 18–20:

> Therefore the Lord was very angry with Israel and removed them out of his sight; none was left but the tribe of Judah alone. Judah also did not keep the commandments of the Lord their God but walked in the customs that Israel had introduced. The Lord rejected all the

descendants of Israel; he punished them and gave them into the hand of plunderers, until he had banished them from his presence.

The story of Jehoshaphat invited by the king of Israel to make common cause in Gilead is one of the longest episodes in the book. Jehoshaphat first pledges solidarity with Israel, then requests enquiring of Yahweh's word before going further. Four hundred prophets give support to the campaign, but Jehoshaphat asks if any prophet was missing. Micaiah, who normally speaks against the king, first adds his voice to the supporters on the advice of the officer who summons him. When challenged to speak only the truth, he reports he has seen Israel scattered on the mountains and reinforces this first vision with a second – that Yahweh has sought a heavenly volunteer to be a lying spirit in the mouths of the prophets. As a result of his counsel, Micaiah is to be imprisoned till Israel's king returns in peace – if that happens, he retorts, Yahweh has not spoken by him.

This narrative plays a strategic integrative role. First, it sounds many echoes of stories of the house of David from start (David) to finish (Josiah). A key feature of this whole account is the many dozens of words that are used only twice, or only in connection with two kings. Many of these pairings occur in clusters; and by this measure, the story of Ahab, Jehoshaphat, and Micaiah is the most interconnected story of all. Micaiah's vision of "all Israel" as "sheep" without a "shepherd" (1 Kgs 22:17) recalls images uniquely associated with David: he was appointed to "shepherd Israel" (2 Sam 7:7) and he called his endangered people "these sheep" (2 Sam 24:17). In the same verse, "these have no master [literally lord or lords]" again evokes David – for it is most often he that is addressed "my lord king." Ramoth-Gilead reappears only once, again as the goal of a joint campaign against Aram. The prophets are asked if the king of Israel should "desist" from his planned action (1 Kgs 22:6, 15), and Ahab's predecessor Baasha is the only other subject of this verb – and within the account of Asa of Judah (1 Kgs 15:21). "Hide" and "chamber" (1 Kgs 22:25) are repeated only when Joash is saved from his grandmother Athaliah (2 Kgs 11:2). And the two kings "seek" Yahweh through Micaiah "the prophet" (1 Kgs 22:7–8) as Josiah will do through Huldah "the prophetess" (2 Kgs 22:13–14), while "in peace" is uttered three times in the exchanges between Micaiah and the king of Israel and reappears only in the response of Huldah to Josiah.

The Micaiah narrative also has key links with the immediately surrounding chapters in which prophets play a larger role than kings. The rivalry between Micaiah and the 400 prophets is echoed in the story of Elijah at Mt Carmel in competition with 450 prophets of Baal and 400 prophets of Asherah; but here the account includes the mass slaughter of the rival prophets (1 Kgs 18). Several features of the Micaiah story also reappear in another campaign east of the Jordan undertaken by Jehoshaphat and Ahab's son (2 Kgs 3). This time the prophet is Elisha, Elijah's successor. Finally, Jehu usurps the throne of Israel, so bringing to an end the house of Ahab (2 Kgs 9–10) and emulates Elijah with a further massacre of prophetic servants of Baal.

WHEN PROPHETS RULED

The prophets Micaiah (1 Kgs 22), Isaiah (2 Kgs 19–20), and Huldah (2 Kgs 22) do play a significant role in the reigns of Jehoshaphat, Hezekiah, and Josiah, kings of Judah, as do Nathan and Gad in the time of David (2 Sam 7; 12; 24). But prophets named and unnamed, singular and in groups, play a much greater role in the story of northern Israel. The two larger-than-life figures are Elijah (1 Kgs 17–19; 21; 2 Kgs 1–2) and Elisha, his one-time assistant (2 Kgs 2–9; 13). Theirs is the only biblical instance of prophetic succession; and their personalities are more clearly delineated than several of the kings of Israel with whom they dealt. We may speculate that prophetic charisma could not readily be passed on, but, whatever the reason, the only other instance of non-royal (or non-patriarchal) succession in the Bible is from Moses to Joshua. Not only so, but Elijah at Horeb recalls Moses on the mountain of God, and Elijah and Elisha crossing the Jordan riverbed dryshod recalls Moses at the Sea of Reeds and Joshua crossing near Jericho. Given these other parallels, Elijah caught up into heaven may echo Moses buried where "no one knows." Both were last seen near the northeast end of the Dead Sea; and neither had a grave that could become a pilgrim-shrine.

While the biblical prophets from Isaiah to Malachi are known for their words, Elijah and Elisha are better remembered instead for their actions. They are channels of divine power rather than bearers of the divine word. They bring healing to a widow's child or to the commander of the armies of the king of Aram, provide the basics for survival in some poor families, and save a town from invasion. Elijah and the prophets of Baal at Mt Carmel, Elijah confronted by his god at Mt Horeb, the transfer of the divine spirit from Elijah to Elisha, and Elisha and the healing of Naaman, the general from Aram (or Syria), are just some of the great prophetic narratives set (mostly) in the north. Their role as national leaders is anticipated by Samuel.

Many important themes of Samuel and Kings are introduced in
1 Sam 1–8, though these chapters are far from typical of the whole.
They open with a woman's story. Hannah, many years without child,
takes the opportunity of the annual pilgrimage to make a vow: If she be
granted a male child she will dedicate him for his whole life. At the first
pilgrimage after Samuel is weaned, she brings him to the care of Eli the
priest who had been witness to her vow at the temple. In a prayer, she
sings about Yahweh her God, who turns things upside down – who
makes poor and makes rich, brings low and also exalts (2:7). In the
climax of her song (2:10b),

> Yahweh will judge the ends of the earth:
> he will give strength to his king,
> and exalt the power of his anointed.

Hannah, as she dedicates at the temple her small son who will become a
prophet and the Lord's agent in instituting kings, sings about the divine
role of a future anointed king. Hannah asks for and receives a son; and
Israel asks for and receives a king (1 Sam 8–10). Because the name of the
first king, Saul, means "asked (for)," it is often supposed that the
Hannah story originally led up to the birth of Saul. Be that as it may,
her song about kingship was probably appended to 1 Sam 1 long after
that narrative identified her son as Samuel.

The young temple servant is contrasted with the rascally sons of Eli,
who treat with contempt both the offerings made to God and the
worshippers who bring them. Their father's rebukes go unheeded, and
an unnamed man of God pronounces before him an extended oracle of
rejection. There is an even fuller account of young Samuel's night-time
"audition" in the temple: Eli becomes persuaded that the voice calling
Samuel is God's, and Samuel admits to the old priest that he has been
informed that "the iniquity of Eli's house shall not be expiated by
sacrifice or offering for ever."

Samuel was called as prophet in immediate proximity to the divine
"ark"; and this portable container of the divine presence becomes the
principal actor in a major account (1 Sam 4–6) of war between Philistines and Israel. Brought into the battle by Eli's worthless sons, the ark
is captured and both sons killed – the news causes old Eli's death. It is
brought into the temple of Dagon in Philistine Ashdod; and, next morning, Dagon is found on his face before it and the people of Ashdod are
suffering painful tumors. A way is found to return this dangerous ark
with suitable gifts to Beth-shemesh in Israel. There is pleasure at its
arrival and sacrifice is offered; but many people are killed by the Lord,

and the ark is passed on to neighboring Kiriath-jearim – it will be collected from there by David (2 Sam 6).

After some twenty years, the people of Israel are concerned about their relationship with the Lord. Samuel convenes them at Mizpah and judges them there. The gathering provokes a hostile Philistine response, and Israel demands of Samuel that he not cease praying for them. The Philistines are duly vanquished, and many cities are returned to Israel. Samuel appoints his sons as judges in his place; but they prove as worthless as Eli's, and the people ask him to appoint instead "a king like all the nations." The divine answer to a displeased Samuel is that they have rejected God not Samuel: He should do as they ask, but first warn them how a king will behave. They reject the warning, and Samuel is instructed to listen to them (1 Sam 7–8).

Hannah had sung of the potential of a king, and Eli learns that the divine promise to his fathers of priesthood "for ever" is now revoked by God. Senior priests will later play a key role when Joash and Josiah start their reigns as children (2 Kgs 11–12; 22–23). Hannah had sung of the potential of a king, and her son delivers a warning about how kings will (and do) behave. The ark, which will be hidden in the most holy inner sanctum of Solomon's temple (1 Kgs 8), is introduced as a potent and unmanageable force. After its return to Israel, it is barely mentioned till David brings it to Jerusalem. In two of the next episodes, Samuel is judging his people and having success against the Philistines, but then presiding at the selection of King Saul by lot. Both are located at Mizpah, in Benjamin territory north of Jerusalem; and Mizpah will reappear at the end of Kings as the center of administration, once the Babylonians have destroyed Jerusalem and plundered its temple (2 Kgs 25:22–26).

PREQUEL TO THE ROYAL STORY

The book of Judges provides a rather wary prelude to the narratives about kings and prophets in Samuel and Kings. Though often described as a bridge linking these books with Deuteronomy and Joshua, the traffic is mostly in one direction: Most of its contents look forward rather than backward. The title given to it is derived from the second and third of three introductions (1:1–3:11). In a time when what the Lord had done for Israel under Joshua was no longer remembered, Israel abandoned their god and served Baals and Astartes; God responded by giving them over to plunderers. In their distress, judges were raised up who delivered them; and this cycle was frequently repeated. Each episode is like a miniature of the following royal story and shares the values spelled out in detail on the fall of northern Israel. The report of the first named deliverer pulls out all the stops. Israel's evil deeds (serving gods other than Yahweh) led to him giving them over to service of a foreign king. But when they cried out to him he raised up Othniel, known already from Joshua. Yahweh's spirit came on him, he judged Israel, went out to fight with Cushan "the Doubly Bad," and had success resulting in a land at rest for forty years. The following stories may have had independent origins; but the (unlikely) name of this opponent plus the use in a short account of many words and phrases we will meet throughout the book, though never again so many of them together, makes it likely that this prelude to the stories of the deliverers has been contrived by the author of the collection. It introduces themes that follow and includes at the start a leader associated with the land of Judah, in the south.

The next deliverer was Ehud, a left-handed "Benjaminite" (the name suggests either southerner or right-hander). More double meanings follow in a tale reporting the nice trickery with which Ehud dispatches fat Eglon, escapes, and calls out his people who secure the Jordan crossings against escaping Moabites. A curious short note follows: Shamgar son of Anat (name of a Canaanite goddess) struck down 600 Philistines, and he too delivered Israel. No tribal affiliation is given, and he may not have been Israelite – perhaps just a case of my enemy's enemy being my friend.

Next time Israel are made over to Jabin, also familiar from the book of Joshua; and the divine answer was mediated through Deborah, described first as prophetess, third as judging Israel, while "wife/woman of *lappidoth*" is a puzzle. Barak, her commander, will only move against rival Sisera if she goes too; and she agrees, warning him that his will not be the glory, for Yahweh will make over Sisera to a woman. Sisera's forces are routed and he flees toward home. Jael, wife of a Kenite (or smith), gives him "sanctuary"; but kills him once asleep by a tent-peg in his head, then shows him off to the pursuing Barak. Already the longest single episode in the book so far (4:1–24), this narrative is now capped by a substantial victory song in praise of Yahweh (5:1–31), sung by Deborah (and Barak). The god's power demonstrated at (the mountains of) Seir and Sinai is first acknowledged. But this is not a song of the cult: It should be sung where people gather, as at watering places. The narrative had spoken only of forces from Zebulun and Naphtali, and the song gives these tribes special praise. But it has first listed Ephraim, Benjamin, Machir, Zebulun, and "Issachar faithful to Barak" among "the people of Yahweh," before blaming Reuben, Gilead, Dan, and Asher for staying away. Special credit is again given to Jael, before the song turns dramatically to Sisera's mother waiting for the return of her warrior son and encouraged by her ladies to suppose that the delay is due only to the division of the spoils from which her own neck will benefit. And it ends in all brevity:

> So perish all your enemies, o Yahweh.
> But may your friends be like the sun as it rises in its might.

A still more detailed episode of deliverance (6–8) is introduced by a longer statement of the blight caused by nomadic raiders. Yahweh's messenger greeted Gideon in fulsome terms as he was skulking in a wine-press. Commissioned to deliver Israel from Midian, he pleaded first that he was least among the weakest clan in Manasseh. After multiple episodes of reassurance, he moved against the invaders and terrified the Midianite camp into flight by a noisy stratagem. Naphtali, Asher, and all Manasseh were called out in pursuit. Finally, Ephraim too were called out. Protesting they should have been involved at an earlier stage, they were calmed by Gideon's charm.

Victory and pursuit east of the Jordan showed Gideon a changed man. Offered hereditary rule over Israel, he appeared to refuse it but did institute a collection for a golden ephod, which Israel worshipped in his town. He had seventy sons by many wives; but, when a secondary wife from Shechem bore him a son, he called him Abimelech ("my father is a king")! The note about Gideon's burial in the tomb of his father aligns him with only Joshua and Samson in the book of Judges. Anticipating David, and Jeroboam, and Jehu, each of whom started a new royal house, Abimelech had himself made king of Israel at Shechem. Just one of Jerubbaal's seventy sons escaped the slaughter, and this Jotham addressed the lords of Shechem from the top of mount Gerizim (later sacred to the Samaritan community) in a memorable anti-royal parable of the different trees approached to be king, and then escaped his half-brother. The remainder of this lengthy chapter catalogues the several bloody stages through which Jotham's prediction to Abimelech and Shechem of their mutual destruction came to its culmination.

The next larger section of the book (10–12) opens more ambiguously in Hebrew than in NRSV: "And there rose after Abimelech to deliver Israel Tola son of Puah." No external oppressor is mentioned, and the suggestion may be that it was from the experience of Abimelech that Israel required deliverance. Tola is the first of five figures listed in almost formulaic terms as having each judged Israel for so many years, two at the start of the section and three at the end. The notes about Tola and Jair are followed by a detailed account of Israel's continuing apostasy from Yahweh in favor of the gods of all their neighbors. Israel then repented comprehensively, and Yahweh became impatient over the trouble they were having. When Ammon were called out against them, the leaders of Gilead wondered who would head their response.

The story backtracks to Gilead's (legitimate) sons expelling Jephthah, his son by a prostitute (an echo of Abimelech or the shorter Jeroboam story?). He had gone off and became leader of a group of "empty fellows." Under pressure from Ammon, Gilead's elders asked Jephthah to be their "head"; energized by Yahweh's spirit, he moved against Ammon, but first vowed to offer in sacrifice whoever came through the doors of his house to greet him on his return. His victory is quickly noted; but the tragic tale of the sacrifice of his daughter, his only child, is sketched at greater length. Ephraim again complained at not being involved from the beginning. Jephthah was less diplomatic than Gideon; and it came to civil war by the Jordan, with the men of Gilead unmasking the fugitives from Ephraim who could not pronounce "shibboleth" properly, but only say "sibboleth." The first mention of Jephthah "judging Israel" comes in the last sentence we read about him.

Samson (13–16) anticipates Samuel (1 Sam 1–2; 7) in several ways, first of all in being born to a previously barren woman. Yet, while Samuel would be "asked of" Yahweh by his mother, Samson's mother receives her divine instructions out of the blue from Yahweh's messenger, rather like Gideon. A man of great strength, provided he kept the Nazirite vow undertaken by his mother and did not cut his hair, each story about him starts with desire for a Philistine woman. Delilah is the only one of his women who is named. After she coaxes out of him the secret of his hair, he is blinded and shackled to a mill. His strength returns as his hair grows; and, summoned for his captors' entertainment to a great feast, he is able to pull down their temple on himself and them – killing more at his death than in his life. Burial in his family tomb follows; and there is not another burial in biblical story until Samuel.

If Samson anticipates Samuel, he also anticipates Saul and David. Samson is wholly defined, and Saul and David are importantly defined by their role in conflict with Philistines. And an unusual Hebrew idiom involving the divine spirit is found only in narratives about these three characters. NRSV offers different translations of the associated verb; and this unfortunately masks the deliberate comparison: "rushed on him" (Judg 14:6, 19; 15:14); "possessed him" (1 Sam 10:6, 10); "came on Saul in power" (11:6); "came mightily upon David" (16:13). Divine spirit is also credited with the success of Othniel, Gideon, and Jephthah.

If death and burial of Joshua and Gideon were followed by deplorable behavior, it was no less so after Samson's end. In the final chapters of Judges, the key place-names evoke the narratives that follow in Samuel: Bethlehem, Gibeah, Jabesh, Shiloh. The story of Micah and his mother goes from bad to very much worse in just a few sentences; but, if Gideon's death was followed by a bad example of kingship, Micah and his mother exemplify a time when there was no king – and people set their own standards. Micah moved to improve the situation in his house-shrine by installing as priest a Levite from Bethlehem in place of his son: Yahweh would do good by him. The repeated notice that in these days there were no kings this time introduces talk of the Danite tribe seeking land for itself; and that again implies setting its own standards rather than following Yahweh's. Micah then loses his Levite and his cult-objects to equally disreputable Danites, according to a thoroughly discreditable tale about the origins of northern Dan, where King Jeroboam would set up one of his two shrines in opposition to Jerusalem. We may wonder what Jephthah might have said to Micah's mother, had they ever met. Would he have reproved her for being careless with solemn words: She uttered a blessing on the thief she had cursed before Micah confessed to the theft? Or would she have chided Jephthah for carrying out his vow at the cost of his daughter?

The next reminder that we are in a time of no kings introduces a new tale but with familiar elements. This time, the Levite is resident in a distant part of the Ephraim hills, and his connection with Bethlehem of Judah comes through his concubine. She returns there to her family, having rejected him or become angry with him or prostituted herself (the ancient texts offer different explanations). After four months he goes to Bethlehem to persuade her to return with him and is generously welcomed by her father. When he finally tears himself away after days of hospitality, it is close to evening. As they reach Jebus (or Jerusalem), his servant presses him to stop for the night; but the Levite insists on continuing another few miles, and they end up in Gibeah, home town of King Saul.

An old man returning from the fields gives them hospitality in his house, but their evening is interrupted by the town's riff-raff, who demand sex with the Levite. The householder offers his daughter and the visitor's concubine instead; and, when this is refused, the Levite simply pushes out his concubine. They abuse her through the night and leave her fallen at the door. Getting no answer from her in the morning, her master puts her on his donkey. On reaching his home, he anticipates Saul and the yoke of oxen, cuts the woman in twelve pieces, and sends her throughout "all the territory of Israel." All Israel gathers at Mizpah, hears the Levite's story, and determines to move against Gibeah immediately. Benjamin refuses to hand over the scoundrels from Gibeah and send their own forces to the town. Benjamin has the first success, and Israel take themselves weeping before Yahweh, presumably again at Bethel. Encouraged to try again (this whole situation is reminiscent of Josh. 7–8), they fail once more; but they succeed the third time. Many further details of the end of the ambush and flight of Benjamin are added.

The next cause of national weeping before Yahweh at Bethel is that one tribe is now lacking from the people, a situation made more acute by the oath Israel has taken at Mizpah to refuse intermarriage with Benjamin. Jabesh in Gilead had not participated in the campaign against Gibeah – its people are put to the sword except for four hundred young virgins that are provided to the defeated Benjaminites, who are also invited to snatch girls as they dance at an annual festival at Shiloh. No surprise that the book of Judges ends by repeating in full its comment on the beginnings of the scandalous tale of Micah and his mother: "In these days there was no king in Israel; all the people did what was right in their own eyes."

A brief note about a change in circumstances for Jehoiachin, Judah's last king now blinded and in exile in Babylon, ends the book of Kings. The whole final chapter also serves as conclusion to Jeremiah, and several idioms used in the final note have significant echoes in one or both books. Readers have long debated whether it brings a positive or negative conclusion to the story of David's house. The fate of Jehoiachin, blinded and hence unfit for kingship, resonates with lame Mephibosheth (2 Sam 9) – the one son of Saul to outlive the catastrophe on Mt. Gilboa (1 Sam 31:8–13). Was the promise of continued eating at court a benefit to be enjoyed, or a perpetual mockery because it was financed from their own land?

The kings in Jerusalem, whatever their qualities, ruled not because they embodied these qualities but simply in succession to their fathers. A few were ousted but always replaced by another member of the royal Davidic house. We catch an occasional glimpse of ability among the northern kings: Omri secured greater popular support than his rival pretender and not only became king but also founded Samaria as capital city, a city whose name would long outlive the kingdom. However, for depictions of charismatic leadership, sometimes but not always attributed to divine spirit, we look to the narratives about Saul and David, and the deliverers in the book of Judges.

Further Reading

Auld, A. Graeme, *I & II Samuel* (Louisville, 2011).

Auld, A. Graeme, *Life in Kings* (*Ancient Israel and Its Literature* 30) (Atlanta, 2017).

Bodner, Keith, *Jeroboam's Royal Drama* (Oxford, 2012).

Nelson, Richard D., *Judges: A Critical and Rhetorical Commentary* (London, 2017).

Niditch, Susan, *Judges* (Louisville, 2008).

Sweeney, Marvin A., *I & II Kings* (Louisville, 2007).

6 Prophetic Literature

VICTOR H. MATTHEWS

Gods in the polytheistic religions of the ancient Near East represent and are personified as the forces of nature. In order to plan for the future in an agriculturally based region, it is thought essential to determine the willingness of the gods to bring rain in its season or to provide fertility to a community's herds of animals. Furthermore, it would be inconceivable for a ruler to send his army to war, or to build a temple or other public building without first consulting the gods, and no diplomatic arrangement could be negotiated without first viewing and deciphering the omens. At that point, it would be necessary to invoke the gods as treaty partners in the proposed endeavor. Persons who could interpret visible symbols of the gods' intentions formed part of the priestly community and were prepared for their role only after years of training and study of the omen texts. However, when a message came directly from the god(s), it became the task of a prophet to serve as the spokesperson for the deity. What we know of prophets can be found in the cuneiform texts and other records discovered at various sites in the Middle East and in the received biblical text.

Because the extant record of prophetic activity in the Bible achieved its present written form during the Persian and early Hellenistic periods,[1] we tend to see it as the sum total of what we now classify as prophetic literature. In fact, there are also sections of chronicled narrative in the books of Samuel and Kings that contain descriptions of a number of prophets and their messages that represent a different genre than the traditional prophetic books from Isaiah through Malachi. For example, the prophetic characters in the accounts of the kings are sometimes portrayed as "wonder-workers" (see Isaiah in 2 Kgs 20:1–11) or miracle workers (Elisha in 2 Kgs 4).

---

[1] Karel van der Toorn, *Scribal Culture and the Making of the Hebrew Bible* (Cambridge, MA, 2007), 173.

With regard to the more familiar prophetic works, it should be noted that it is quite likely that there existed in antiquity a body of prophetic sayings from which the scribal editors drew in much the same way that they used lost reference works like the Book of Jashar (2 Sam 1:18) or the Book of the Annals of the Kings of Israel (1 Kgs 14:19). What we have in the received texts of the Bible are quite possibly the edited accounts of prophetic activity based on cultic and administrative documents and at least portions of the collected sayings of the prophets as they were embedded into biblical narrative and canonized.

Biblical and non-Biblical prophecy from the ancient Near East, in all of its manifestations, is simply a somewhat equivalent form of divination translated through human words and gestures. Since, however, prophets did not undergo the long training of cultic practitioners, who relied on a body of referenced omen texts, prophesy is better described as "intuitive divination" in contrast to "technical divination."[2] In point of fact, what separates prophecy from priestly ritual practices, including extispicy (examining the entrails of sacrificial animals) or other means of reading divinely inspired omens (dreams, flights of birds, unusual natural phenomena), is that prophets do not need to be members of a guild of religious practitioners or operate within a cultic context based on learned skills. Thus they are not held to rigid standards of ritualized behavior or speech. What they are measured by is the perceived veracity of their message and their strict adherence to the god they serve. That task contrasts with relying on reading omens that has more to do with assessing whether the god(s) will support the contemplated activity rather than concerning itself with predicting the future. In this context, the prophets serve as spokespersons for a god and they gain their authority and notoriety in society from that association.

It is likely that both prophetic activity and divinatory practices have their origin in the basic desire of humans to know the will of the god(s). Thus divine messages "received" and transmitted through priests and prophets answer such questions as: "Should we go to war?"; "Is this the proper place to build a temple?"; or "What sort of sacrifice is necessary to assuage the anger of the god(s)?" The recording of these messages in letters or collected sayings then becomes the basis for what we term "prophetic literature," a diverse body of literary forms that at its heart serves to demonstrate to devotees the active interest of the god(s) in human activities and endeavors.

---

[2] Jonathan Stökl, *Prophecy in the Ancient Near East: A Philological and Sociological Comparison* (Leiden, 2012), 38.

Prophets, including those in Israel, and their audience did not operate in a social vacuum. They were part of a living community that encompassed the entire Near East and were culturally influenced by contact with the complex societies throughout the Levant. As all human communities do, they shared information and cultural artifacts, including literature of all kinds. As a result, when they experienced traumatic as well as joyous events they drew on what they had learned from other cultures. In reacting to these events, an effort was made to sort out the more inexplicable aspects of their life by turning to divination or prophetic figures to provide divine reassurance or warnings. The messages of these prophets address a wide range of topics, but one primary task was to signal to their community and its rulers their obligation to respond to the commands of the god(s). And, in the case of the Hebrew prophets, that meant strict adherence to the terms of the covenant with YHWH.

These prophetic figures, some of whom were indeed part of the established cultic community and some who operated quite independently, delivered their messages in a variety of ways. There were no gender barriers, with both male and female prophets delivering the message of the god(s), sometimes in ecstatic form (having seemingly lost conscious control of their body or normal speech). Many of these prophets operated in a more formal fashion, writing letters to the king or transmitting their words through an official. And, some are portrayed addressing an audience in public places or staging unusual performances that were uncharacteristic of the religious figures associated with the temple community. In this way, they were able to draw audiences and provoke questions about their message (see Ezek 4; Amos 1–2).

With these remarks as introduction, and in order to understand the basic characteristics of prophetic literature found in the Hebrew Bible, it is necessary to examine the social and cultural setting contributing to its development as well as the prophetic traditions that are found in documents from ancient Mesopotamia. Letters, such as those found in the eighteenth century BCE Mari archive, have provided us with evidence of prophetic activity long before the Israelites emerged as a distinct people. The personal names of these non-biblical prophets seldom appear in the Mari letters, which may indicate that they were considered members of a sacred social class whose names could not be spoken. However, their speech is deemed acceptable and valid by the authorities, and their warnings from the god(s) appear to be taken quite seriously.

The Mari correspondence describes several types of prophetic figures. Those that could be labeled as professional prophets are called the *āpilum*. They are associated with the royal court and are spokespersons for a particular god. They regularly convey messages from their specific deity to kings and other officials, and there is no evidence of their first going into a trance-like state before speaking. It is also the case that more than one message or warning was sometimes necessary to get the proper reaction from the monarch. In one case (A.2731:1–44), the *āpilum* rather testily tells the king of Mari that he had "repeatedly" reminded him to send livestock to the sanctuary of the god Addu.

Interestingly, the *āpilum* are cognizant of the importance of the setting when they make a public statement. Demonstrating this critical factor is a letter written by a local official that describes how the *āpilum* first stand at the palace gate and then later at the door of a political opponent of Mari's ruler, denouncing him in the name of the angry god Marduk.[3] The lack of any public outcry against the prophet by the audience is recorded by the sender of the letter and serves as an excellent model for Isaiah's behavior when he confronts King Ahaz at a similarly strategic location just outside the walls of Jerusalem while the king is preparing for a siege (Isa 7:3–9). Clearly, the setting matters when voicing the word of a god.

In addition to the *āpilum*, there were nonprofessional or lay prophets, some of whom were members of the cult community, and others who were simply members of the general public. Thus their daily responsibilities or vocations are occasionally interrupted by prophetic speech, but prophesying is not their primary function. The most often attested of these lay prophets, who are officially associated with a particular temple, and who deliver their divine messages during ecstatic performances, are referred to as the *muḫḫûm* and the *assinnu*. The *muḫḫûm* (a title based on the Akkadian word "to rave") are both male and female, and are described as "raving" or being transformed in most instances into a prophetic frenzy during ritual events. Similarly, in the biblical texts there are also examples of recognized prophets and other persons who are transformed into an ecstatic state by music (2 Kgs 3:15), dancing (1 Kgs 18:26), or a combination of the two (1 Sam 10:5, 10).

The *assinnu* prophets are tied to the cult of the goddess Ishtar-Annunītum. They appear in the Mari texts to be associated with her more martial aspects and only occasionally produce prophetic speech in

---

[3] Martti Nissinen, *Prophets and Prophecy in the Ancient Near East* (Atlanta, 2003), 73–74; ARM 26 371.

a state of ecstasy. Based on what is reported in the texts containing their messages, they deliver understandable (not requiring an interpreter) words of warnings to the king (ARM 26 213:7–14), divine commands, and other types of messages from their specific deity. Since these individuals are not professional, prophetic figures and do not directly serve the king, the authors of these texts sometimes provide additional proofs, including a strand of their hair or an impression of the hem of their robe (A100). In this way, almost like taking an oath, the prophet's reputation and possibly their life are bound up with the truth of their message.

HEBREW PROPHETS AND THEIR MESSAGES

Having established an historical background for prophetic activity and prophetic speech in the literature of the ancient Near East, we can now turn to the major aspects of their messages in the biblical text and to an examination of the various types of prophets found in ancient Israel. Hebrew prophets, as both spokespersons for YHWH and champions of the covenant, focus on two binary themes: judgment oracles and salvation oracles. They interpret disasters in terms of calculated divine actions (theodicy), explaining that famine, disease, and military defeat are directly attributable to the failure of the people to live up to their obligation to worship only YHWH, uphold justice for every member of the community, and obey God's law as part of their covenant agreement.

Conversely, they also are able to proclaim a forgiving God, who is repeatedly willing to take the people back if they "amend their ways" (Jer 7:3) and "return and seek the Lord their God" (Hos 3:5). Even when the nation is utterly defeated and large numbers of the people are taken from their land into exile, the prophets continue to articulate the promise that a "righteous remnant" will see the demise of their oppressors and be allowed to return and restore the land and the community (Isa 10:20–27; Jer 50:20; Ezek 11:14–21).

The prophets in the biblical texts who had the most visibility among the people were either closely associated with the monarchy or the temple cult. Court prophets like Nathan, who like the *āpilum* are members of the royal court, sometimes speak for God upon request from the king (2 Sam 7:2–3) or take the initiative in the form of juridical parables when it becomes necessary to directly confront the king with his abuses of power (2 Sam 12:1–15). Those prophets who also functioned as priests (Isaiah and Ezekiel) already have that association as the basis of their authority and they tend to emphasize issues or settings related to the temple (Isa 6:1; Ezek 8–10), the priesthood (Ezek 44:15-1), or compliance with the legal stipulations of the covenant (Isa 24:5).

Prophets who operate independently of the priestly or royal establishment, such as Elijah/Elisha, Jeremiah, Amos, Micah, and Hosea, must establish their authority to speak for YHWH. As a result, their activities sometimes delight or outrage their audience by engaging in various types of "street theater" performance (Jer 27:2; 28:12–14), or by using broad imagery (Amos 4:1–3), transparent metaphor (Hos 1–3), mock trials (Micah 6:1–5), or staged contests with opponents (1 Kgs 18:17–40). In some cases, they are physically harassed or punished in an effort to lessen or eliminate their attempts at legitimation. Thus Elijah is forced to flee Jezebel's troops after his triumph on Mt. Carmel (1 Kgs 19:1–3), Amos is mocked and ordered to leave the "King's sanctuary" in Bethel (Amos 7:10–13), and Jeremiah is required to endure the indignity of being restrained in the public stocks (Jer 20:1–6).

The effort to obtain recognized authority also includes a recitation of their call to be a prophet, which gives them the right to speak and be taken seriously by the people and their leaders. Not all prophets have this event as part of their narrative. Possibly, the inclusion of an elaborate call narrative is the result of the writer(s) hand in distinguishing some of the prophets as particularly significant in Israelite tradition. Not surprisingly, Moses' call narrative/theophany at Mt. Sinai (Exod 3–4:17) is embedded into the fabric of the biblical narrative as the model for later call stories. It is echoed in the encounters with God by Isaiah (Isa 6), Jeremiah (Jer 1:4–19), and Ezekiel (Ezek 1–3:11). Adding to this legitimizing factor, the sixth-century BCE Deuteronomistic writer further solidifies who should be considered a true prophet, noting that the message must come true and that the prophet only speaks for YHWH (Deut 13:1–5; 18:15–22).

The need for such specific qualifications is made necessary by the appearance of prophetic figures who claim to speak for YHWH or even other gods while challenging the word of other prophets. The fact that there were contests between prophets is made evident in the conflicting messages of Micaiah and Ahab's 400 court prophets (1 Kgs 22:1–28) as well as Jeremiah's public conflict with Hananiah (Jer 28) and his reference to unreliable prophets in his Letter to the Exiles (Jer 29:8–9). Given the polytheistic culture within which the people of Israel and Judah lived, it was often a struggle and required the passage of many years to determine which prophet or diviner was telling the truth until circumstances proved one or the other to be correct.

Status as prophets in Israelite society, as spokespersons of a god, does not simply originate with their call from YHWH or their use of the god's name. To an extent, their authority is based on the public's recognition of the existence of prophetic figures in the ancient Near East. For many centuries, records were produced documenting the appearance and words spoken by prophets, and therefore when they emerge in ancient Israel they are simply part of a longstanding tradition of prophetic activity. However, in Israel the call of a prophet is not associated with having been born to a "family of prophets" (see Amos 7:14). Instead, they are said to speak at various times as was deemed necessary by YHWH. Their identification by civil and religious authorities as spokespersons for YHWH makes the Hebrew prophets a recognized class of persons in their society, but not as a guild or hereditary class of persons.

MAJOR THEMES AND MODES OF DELIVERING THE PROPHETIC MESSAGE

As they are described in the received text of the Bible, the Hebrew prophets are not standardized characters, nor are the narrative accounts or books that contain their words and actions. They all do not follow a set script or always recite their prophecies as set pieces in lockstep with each other. As we consider the manner in which the prophets delivered their messages, it is important to note that many of them may have even been semi-illiterate like the majority of those in their audience. In ancient Israel few persons other than members of the royal court and the scribal guild would own or read scrolls. Therefore, the oracles of the prophets would have been spoken and then later edited into the written form with which we are familiar. Of course, there are some instances in which a prophet cannot voice a message personally and therefore must resort to writing a letter that can be read to a distant audience (Jer 29). In some instances, the prophet is instructed by God to write down a message that can serve the needs of future generations (Isa 30:8; Jer 30:2–3). There are cases in which a prophet is required to dictate the oracle to a scribe, such as Baruch, who in turn will read it to a target audience (Jer 36:4).

Very often the prophets are focused on the injustices of their day as well as the heightened tensions brought on by an increasingly hostile international situation (see Hos 14:1–3; Amos 3:9–11; and Jer 25:1–14). Each of the prophets, while sharing a common purpose or theme as spokesperson for YHWH, gives a unique character to his or her prophetic utterances based on these specific social or political conditions. The differences or specific characteristics of particular prophets are due in part to their individual social background, the point in time that they represent (from ca. 1000 BCE to ca. 400 BCE), the events and social conditions of which they are a part (fall of the northern kingdom and the exile after the destruction of Jerusalem), and, to a certain extent, their reliance on ancient Near Eastern prophetic models and the words or actions of earlier Hebrew prophets.

Despite their differences and social circumstances, all of these prophetic figures, including those who are unnamed in the text (1 Kgs 13:1–32), share a common theme of calling the people back to obedience to the covenant and to YHWH. The fact that their message does contain some shared imagery (the good shepherd: Isa 40:11; Jer 31:10; Ezek 34:15) or shared themes ("Day of the Lord": Joel 2:1–2; Amos 5:18; Zeph 1:7–8) speaks both to their common cultural heritage and the likelihood that the prophets or the compilers of their materials are aware of a body of orally transmitted prophetic speech from different periods and places in Israel.

To express their concerns, the prophets make use of many different modes of speech and public displays. Among the modes of delivery that the prophets employed and that their audience readily understood were certain physical gestures, such as Ezekiel's laying on his side for many days (Ezek 4:4–8), or Isaiah stripping himself of his robe to portray himself as a prisoner or slave taken captive by the invading Assyrian army (Isa 20). Jeremiah enacts his prophecy of God's dissatisfaction with the people of Judah by going to watch a potter at work and then uses the spoiled object to remind his audience that God will not waste the clay, but start again reworking it into a proper creation (Jer 18:2–11).

The use of everyday analogies is common in prophetic speech. For example, Hosea compares Israel with an ungrateful child (Hos 11:1–4) and Amos uses a bricklayer's plumb line as an analogy with God's measurement of Israel's infidelity (Amos 7:7–9). Given the nature of their predictive speech, the prophets employ some common vocabulary or phrases, such as "on that day" (Isa 7:18; Amos 8:9; Zeph 1:9), or a reference to God's "outstretched hand" as the instrument of divine punishment (Isa 5:25; Jer 6:12; 15:6; Ezek 25:7).

Because idolatry is a common theme in the prophetic materials, there are numerous references to non-YHWH rituals and religious beliefs associated with other gods, including Asherah and Baal (Isa 57:5; Jer 2:20; 7:9). The worship of these other gods in violation of the covenant with YHWH is termed "playing the whore" (Jer 3:1; Ezek

16:15; Hos 2:5). The many references to idols of gold, silver, wood, and stone serve both to condemn the people (Isa 10:11) and as a sign of repentance when they are discarded with the trash (Isa 30:22; 31:7). In their effort to warn the people of imminent danger when they are unfaithful to YHWH, the prophets use graphic language to describe how the land given to them will be stripped of its abundance and the people will be taken away into exile (Jer 5:17; 51:2; Hos 9:1–3; Amos 4:9). Once the people return to proper worship of YHWH, they can celebrate the restoration of the land's abundance (Isa 30:23; Micah 4:4; Zech 8:12).

The prophets also made use of performance styles that had originated with prophetic figures at least a thousand years earlier and are recorded in Mesopotamian texts. For example, Jeremiah traverses the streets of Jerusalem carrying a pottery jar. When he comes to one of the city gates, he uses that strategic location to pronounce his condemnation of the city and its ruler (Jer 19:1–13). A similar performance is recorded about a *muḫḫûm* ecstatic prophet in a Mari text (ARM 26 206). This individual goes to the city gate of Saggaratum and publicly commands in the name of the god Dagan that he be given a lamb to eat. The effect of his culinary performance is to show how a plague would consume the city just as he had so graphically consumed the lamb. The way to prevent this calamity from happening is to return a group of consecrated objects that had been taken by other towns from the god's sanctuary.

Complaints about social injustice are also a reflection of a theme found in ancient Near Eastern wisdom literature, and are another influence on prophetic speech. For example, when Jeremiah describes everyone as "greedy for unjust gain" (Jer 6:13), or when Isaiah and Micah point to judges and rulers who eagerly take bribes (Isa 5:23; Micah 3:11), and Amos repeatedly condemns those who "trample the heads of the needy" for their own enrichment (Amos 2:7; 8:4), they are echoing the words of Mesopotamian and Egyptian sages, who decry a world marked by the oppression of the weak. Thus the "Babylonian Theodicy" (ca. 700 BCE) cries out against those who "harass and drive away the powerless,"[4] and the Middle Kingdom Egyptian (ca. 2000 BCE) "Tale of the Eloquent Peasant" includes in his recitation of civil injustices the inequitable distribution of grain and shorting of people by authorities using false scales.[5]

---

[4] Victor H. Matthews, and Don C. Benjamin, *Old Testament Parallels: Laws and Stories from the Ancient Near East*, 4th ed. (Mahwah, NJ, 2016), 258.

[5] Ibid., 250–51.

In examining these prophetic materials, attention needs to be given to the circumstances (social, political), the various physical settings in which their message is delivered, and the intended audience that they address or confront (king, court, or the general public). For example, Jeremiah's "Temple Sermon" plays on a number of factors to increase its visibility and effectiveness. It occurs in the doorway of the Jerusalem Temple, obstructing traffic and causing people to pause to hear and see what is happening. There is a crowd gathered in Jerusalem for a festival day and that insures an even larger audience when Jeremiah begins to harangue the people using the Temple as both a backdrop and a "character" in his condemnation of false worship, injustice, and indifference to the covenant (Jer 7:1–15).

Some prophetic orations are quite creative in their elaborately composed "oracles against nations" (Jer 46–51; Ezek 25–32), but it is unlikely that they were originally designed as public addresses. In comparison, Amos' "stump speech" in Bethel serves as a good example of public oratory. He begins by whipping up the crowd as he describes YHWH's punishment of their enemies (Amos 1:2–2:3). He then turns the occasion on its head by focusing attention on Judah's and Israel's own sins and reminding them that they will not escape divine retribution (Amos 2:4–16).

Some prophetic messages are quite succinct and hard hitting in their condemnations of social injustice (Hos 10:13; Amos 2:6–8) or empty expressions of worship by the Israelite people, the priesthood, and the king (Isa 1:13; Amos 4:4–5). In many cases, the prophets use examples of everyday activity to strengthen or illustrate their messages. Agricultural imagery, including plowing, sowing, and threshing (Isa 28:24–28; Jer 26:18; Micah 4:12), is a common feature, perhaps as a reflection of the culture's economy and lifestyle, and the general character of many in their audience. Typical commercial activity, such as the selling of grain, evokes false business practices, and complaints about the requirement to cease business during religious holidays highlight the merchants' greed (Amos 8:5). The use of false balances is a common charge made against grain dealers (Hos 12:7; Amos 8:5; Micah 6:11). The practice of forcing the poor into debt slavery paints a picture of a society with little compassion for those in dire straits (Jer 34:8–22; Amos 2:6; 8:6).

Since prophecy is not always constrained to follow a set pattern or to be subject to standardized ritual practice, the Hebrew prophets have the freedom to focus in their own way on fundamental issues such as the failure of their people to obey the word/command of YHWH or to maintain socially acceptable or right behavior within the community. The word *hesed*, commonly found in the Psalms (see Ps 17:7; 23:6; 32:10) and variously translated as everlasting love, mercy, or kindness, increasingly appears as a standard for YHWH's relationship with the chosen people (Jer 9:23–24), as the basis for their obedience (Hos 6:6), and a mandate that they care for each other (Micah 6:8; Zech 7:9).

While there is a predictive character to prophetic speech, there is also a sense in many of their pronouncements that the deity is express-ing immediate concern with specific events (Isa 7:3–9; 20:3–6; Jer 4:6; 21:1–10). As the demise of the nation may be drawing nearer, greater attention is given to improper or empty practices (Amos 5:12), or to giving explicit instructions that require specific actions to avoid God's wrath (Amos 5:4–6; Ezek 12:17–25). That is not to say that there is never any ambiguity in prophetic speech because warnings do not always bring immediate consequences or are explained to be tempered by divine mercy (Isa 30:18; Jer 31:20). In the midst of crisis there also is evidence of competition among prophetic figures, who voice diametric-ally different words (see Jer 23:16). The belief, however, in the conse-quences of ignoring a divine message often makes it necessary to take these prophetic figures and their words very seriously even when they provide contradictory messages (see 1 Kgs 22:13–28 and the cognitive dissonance created by the words of Hananiah and Jeremiah in Jer 28 over the fate of the city of Jerusalem).

The prophet's expectation or plea is that the audience will respond appropriately to their message. Their message is echoed by a succession of prophets, who appear over the course of several centuries (see 2 Kgs 17:13–18). That repetitive process in turn demonstrates just how often the audience has ignored divine warnings in the past as well as the persistence of the deity (Jer 7:25; Zech 1:4). Despite a history of dis-obedience, the prophet still proclaims YHWH's message (see a frus-trated and compelled Jeremiah in Jer 20:7–9) with the hope that this time the people will listen to the divine message's admonition (Hos 6:1–3; Micah 7:18–20).

The body of prophetic speech, whether in its original oral form or its later edited format, does not seem to serve as precedent for future action like those found in cuneiform tablets containing lists of omen interpretations. While a prophet or members of the community may quote or paraphrase the words of an earlier prophet as they do at Jeremiah's trial (Jer 26:16–19), there is nothing legally binding or ritually mandated by these references based on their cultural memory. The question then arises why this material survived or was preserved as part of ancient Israel's cultural heritage. Perhaps it is the destruction of Jerusalem and the exile that finally gained the attention of the people as they struggled to maintain their identity in a foreign land. The retained memory of these prophetic figures and their words in the canon of the Hebrew Bible are a testament to their ultimate value to later generations of Israelites, whether in the diasporic communities or in the restored Persian province of Yehud, centered on Jerusalem.

There is also a shift in the tone of prophetic speech during the exile and in the post-exilic period. With the unlikelihood that the Davidic monarchy would be restored, the people find it necessary to accommodate themselves to Persian and then Hellenistic rulers. Emphasis is then placed on restoring the sacrificial cult, the strictures of ritual purity, and the authority of the priestly community. Second, Isaiah's call to return to the Promised Land and to Zion (Isa 40:1–11; 43:14–21) is coupled with a reminder that the people must also return to the covenant to prevent further disaster. The value of the exile to the nation's purification is explained in an extended theodicy found in Second Isaiah's Servant Songs (Isa 40–55). With the Persian king Cyrus heralded as a messianic figure, who has freed the exiles to return after 535 BCE and provided them with funds to restore the Jerusalem Temple (Isa 44:24–45:13 and in the Cyrus Cylinder), the expectations for what might be accomplished by the returned community may have been high. However, the realities of rebuilding a ruined Jerusalem and restoring the land to production lead to delays and these in turn spark the appearance of new prophetic figures.

Haggai and Zechariah harangue the community in Jerusalem like the prophets of previous centuries and they draw on some of the same themes. For instance, Haggai's charge that the failed harvests and drought the people had experienced were because they had not rebuilt the Temple (Hag 1:2–6) recall the theodicy of agricultural calamity in Mic 6:15 and in Isaiah's oracle against Ethiopia (Isa 18:4–6). Zechariah's reminder (Zech 1:4–6) that God had previously sent prophets to warn the people to "return from your evil ways" quotes Jeremiah's similar statement (Jer 25:4–7). He notes that in earlier times the people did not heed these words and faced the consequences. When Third Isaiah (Isa 58:4) and Zechariah (7:1–7) condemn the self-serving priestly community, after the restoration of the Temple (post-515 BCE), for their extravagant fasting practices, they echo Jeremiah's call for true devotion to the Sabbath and proper regulation of religious behavior (Jer 17:19–27; compare Isa 56:2–6; 58:13).

Eventually, the sayings or oracles of these ancient prophets were compiled and edited together either within biblical narratives or as separate collections of sayings. This tabulation of prophetic speech during the late post-exilic and Hellenistic period may have been a reflection of the common practice of recording the interpretation of omens by Near Eastern divinatory priests. The result is that prophetic literature and the memory of prophetic speech continued to draw on their origin in divine revelation and retained their authority through repetition and quotation of the words of prophetic figures.

RECEPTION AND USE OF THE HEBREW PROPHETS IN THE NEW TESTAMENT

As time went on, it became the common practice to engage in "inner-biblical exegesis" in an effort to remind the people of their origins and identity, and in the case of prophetic speech to point to the ultimate, although delayed, fulfillment of their messages. By the New Testament period, that urge or desire for fulfillment contributes to Paul's and the Gospel writers' use of quotations from the prophets to bolster their case for identifying Jesus as the Messiah. In many instances, these quotations or references are preceded by phrases, such as: "As the prophet said" (John 1:23), or "what had been spoken by the prophet" (Matt 2:17), or "everything that is written about the Son of Man by the prophets" (Lk 18:31). In particular, when the Gospel writers specifically proclaim that these events or this person "fulfill what had been spoken through the prophet" (Matt 4:14; John 12:38), they address the long-held desire of the Jewish community to receive the Messiah figure in their time.

Drawing on traditions based on prophetic speech also adds an extra level of authority to the narrative, and drives characters to initiate the next step in the drama. This process is clear in a frightened Herod's questioning of the priests and elders about where the prophesied Messiah is to be born, and the answer that he receives directly quotes Mic 5:2, identifying Bethlehem as the location (Matt 2:1–6). It also provides an intellectual foundation for the failure of some to believe the message of the early Christian evangelists. For example, Paul, clearly frustrated but philosophical when his arguments meet stiff resistance by some of the Jewish leaders in Rome, quotes a portion of the Septuagint version of Isaiah's call narrative (Isa 6:9–10) that fits with the reality that not every listener will either comprehend or see the truth.

What makes the use of quotation from literary or oral traditions powerful, however, is the extent to which the intended or original audience is familiar with these traditional sayings. The impact is weakened or lost if the reference is unknown or so obscure that only the most learned catch its meaning. Presumably, when Matthew cites Isaiah's prophecies, as he does repeatedly (see among many references: Matt 3:3; 4:14; 8:17; 12:17), that is because they serve as solid proof texts for his description of Jesus' person and mission. However, if Isaiah's words were not readily available to be read in the synagogue (Lk 4:16–19), or were lost to memory for the general population, then there would be no point in recycling them.

Note also that direct quotation is not always the only means of drawing upon biblical literary traditions. When Matthew describes Judas' suicide and burial in a "potter's field" (Matt 27:3–10), he makes explicit reference to Jeremiah, but the parallel is based on a composite of several texts (Exod 9:12; Jer 32:6–15; Zech 11:12–13). Similarly, the apocalyptic vision described by its author in Rev 1:7 combines images from Zech 12:10 and Daniel 7:13 while couching them in the form of a composite quotation. For these texts to be accepted as a valid use of earlier prophetic works, the audience would have to be fairly sophisticated. They must be skilled at unravelling a literary puzzle, or familiar with layering traditions to create a new, but related, image. The difficulty in interpretation suggests these visions were not created for the general public or the majority of the early Christian community.

It is not surprising therefore that references to or quotations from the Hebrew prophets or other facets of Jewish tradition are largely missing in the later Christian writings such as the Pastoral Epistles. Since their audience was primarily Gentile, they would not share the Jewish heritage, and therefore Jesus' tie to the House of David, his efforts to fulfill the traditional messianic prophecies, and his adherence to Jewish law and custom are of little importance to the new churches founded in Greece and Cilicia. As Paul and his companions found new churches with a mixed membership of Jews and Gentiles, references to prophets shift to those in the Christian community who have been given the gift of prophesy by the Holy Spirit (1 Cor 12:28). Interestingly, and without reference to the Hebrew prophets (see Deut 18:22; Jer 27:15), cautions against false prophets do appear in the letters to these communities. Those who do not speak in the name of the Lord or uphold the words of the evangelists are condemned (1 Cor 14:37; 1 John 4:1; 2 Peter 2:1).

The cautionary attitude toward prophets lives on in modern literature. Reinhold Niebuhr warns anyone who would attempt to take on the role of prophet that he "stands under the judgment which he preaches. If he does not know that, he is a false prophet."[6] Horace Walpole takes up this theme, pointing out that the wisest prophets are those who "make sure of the event first" before speaking.[7] His remark is an extension of the logic found in Jeremiah's warning that the "prophet who prophesies peace, when the word of that prophet comes true, then ... the Lord has truly sent the prophet" (Jer 28:9; compare Jer 8:11). The difficulty for a prophet to obtain recognition or honor from the people of his hometown is illustrated by Jesus' visit to Nazareth after he began his ministry (Matt 13:57; Lk 4:24; John 4:44). That theme serves as a backdrop to Fëdor Dostoevski's remark that prophets are so often rejected and slain, but martyrs are revered.[8] Perhaps his conclusion was influenced by the reference in Matt 23:37 that Jerusalem "kills the prophets" (a reference in turn to the fate of Zechariah ben Jehoiada in 2 Chron 24:20–22).

Even though the level of general familiarity with the words of the Hebrew prophets outside academic and theological circles has diminished, the basic prophetic themes of social consciousness, concern for the needs of the poor and weak, and obligation to God remain a significant part of a large segment of Western society today. The use of Old Testament prophetic material by the New Testament authors has also contributed to the retention of at least some of the major speeches of the Hebrew prophets. Certainly, these authors made extensive use of Second Isaiah's message, including the "voice crying in the Wilderness" (Isa 40:3–5) coupled with John the Baptist's ministry (Matt 3:5; Lk 3:4–6), and his image of the "suffering servant" (Isa 52:13–53:12) that provided a prophetic foundation for the climax of Jesus' Passion story (Lk 22:37).

Like all forms of literary expression, the prophetic literature contained in the Old Testament served its original audience and continues to provide modern audiences with a window into the way in which these ancient people perceived their God and the spokespersons who transmitted divine messages to them. Of course, later generations may interpret this material in ways that are very different from its original context and purpose. Prophetic literature then becomes a part of the literary traditions upon which they draw as proof texts like the New

---

[6] Reinhold Niebuhr, *Beyond Tragedy: Essays on the Christian Interpretation of History* (New York, 1937), 110.

[7] Spencer Walpole, ed., "Letter to Thomas Walpole, February 19, 1785," *Some Unpublished Letters of Horace Walpole* (London, 1902), 90.

[8] Fëdor M. Dostoevsky, *The Brothers Karamazov*, Book VI, chapter 3.h (Garden City, NY, 1970), 298.

Testament writers or as useful speeches to quote or paraphrase in short stories, novels, and plays. The fact that prophetic literature continues to live on within the liturgy of the church, or even in modern literary reincarnations, reinforces its value. It is in the air waiting for us to contemplate its meaning, and continue to use in our own speech and writings.

Further Reading

Matthews, Victor H., *The Hebrew Prophets and Their Social World* (Grand Rapids, MI, 2012).

Nissinen, Martti, *Ancient Prophecy: Near Eastern, Biblical, and Greek Perspectives* (New York, 2017).

Nogalski, James D., *Interpreting Prophetic Literature: Historical and Exegetical Tools for Reading the Prophets* (Louisville, KY, 2015).

7 Wisdom Literature

JAMES CRENSHAW

The classification "wisdom literature" is a scholarly inference from the common interest of three books – Proverbs, Job, and Ecclesiastes (hereafter Qoheleth, the Hebrew name for the book). That interest is called *hokmah* (wisdom). In Proverbs, wisdom is personified as feminine and placed at the beginning of all things as a witness to creation. In Job, wisdom is unfathomable, known only to humans as rumor, yet more valuable than gold, and for Qoheleth, wisdom is bankrupt, like existence itself. Two additional books, Sirach (also called Ecclesiasticus) and Wisdom of Solomon, resemble these three but show developments that reflect the influence of Greek thought.

In its early form, this literature comments on the human condition and life's meaning. It promotes universal moral values and lacks anything that is specific to Israel. The main characters in the book of Job are not even Israelite, and Qoheleth uses only Elohim, the generic name for deity. With Sirach and Wisdom of Solomon, a change occurs, perhaps due to their Hellenistic environment. Now Israel's own traditions are used along with new ideas from Stoic philosophy such as a balance of good and evil in the universe, wisdom as the divine word (*logos*), the twenty-one divine attributes, and the four cardinal virtues.

Each of these books has a distinctive style. Proverbs consists of rare insights reached by closely observing people and nature. The sayings resemble sound bites, succinct summations for popular consumption. Over time, they are subjected to literary improvement and given religious underpinnings to enhance their practical and aesthetic appeal. In this way, wisdom and the fear of the Lord are integrated and human advice becomes tantamount to divine instruction. Because it is directed to offspring either in the home or in schools, it deals in absolutes to bolster their beliefs, and to hold the interest of young males, it often highlights the erotic. The voices of children are entirely missing, drowned out by parental authority.

The book of Job takes the form of a religious debate, in poetry, about the problem of innocent suffering. Its hero challenges traditional belief in reward for good behavior and punishment for bad conduct, but Job's friends vigorously defend views that had become dogma for them. The debate is a dramatized conflict that often reaches emotional intensity of raw feelings. The drama is slowed once by a reflective poem in chapter 28 about the impossibility of attaining wisdom, a reminder that the various opinions being voiced did not hold the full answer to the issue at hand. In the end, God appears and brings the debate to a resolution, although the epilogue complicates matters once more by restoring Job and his possessions as if rewarding him for faithful service and proving the provocateur correct. The poetry is rich in images from the beginning. Job's initial curse of the day of his birth and the night of his conception almost exhausts available vocabulary when he develops the image of darkness (shadow of death, cloudiness, gloom, murkiness). The poetry in the book of Job varies with the speakers, becoming more sublime when God finally appears. In the divine speeches, beauty and violence exist side by side, just as evil and good do in daily existence.

Qoheleth uses refrains to emphasize cyclic reality, an alternative to the biblical notion that the deity is guiding history toward a providential goal on earth. For him, life is empty, totally meaningless, even for the young who are encouraged to enjoy life if able to do so. His approach of observing reality and drawing conclusions based on his own experience resembles philosophy but without Greek emphases – ontology, epistemology, metaphysics. His style combines prose and poetry, leaving a haunting effect. It is as if he must tell readers the same thing over and over lest they miss the point that everything is futile, even absurd. In the closing poem on the onset of old age and its inevitable end in death, he uses complex images with double meanings that have given the impression of allegory. Only insiders grasp the deeper sense of ordinary language.

Sirach resembles Proverbs in its use of aphorisms but often links them together by means of thematic clusters. It also has refrains, hymns, prayers, and instructions. The praises are directed toward two subjects: wisdom and the beauty of nature, its balance of good and evil. Both Sirach and Wisdom of Solomon borrow elements of Stoic philosophy to address the presence of evil in a supposedly good universe. The dialog form makes a brief appearance in Wisdom of Solomon when the author tries to defend God's animosity toward Egyptians and Canaanites as reported in Israel's sacred writings.

In brief, both form and content contribute to make wisdom literature a treasure in the Bible. Few poems can match the beauty of Job, and
no other book surpasses Qoheleth in its understanding of the human
condition. As for moral instruction, the simplicity of Proverbs and
Sirach can hardly be surpassed, while Wisdom of Solomon comes close
to philosophical reflection.

PROSE

Wisdom literature in the Bible is predominantly poetry. The notable
exception sets the stage for the drama in the book of Job and brings it to
a close (Job 1–2, 42:7–17). In addition, Qoheleth's conversational style of
self-reflection resembles narrative, although he is capable of writing fine
poetry, as the poem about a time for everything in Eccl 3:2–8 illustrates.
Even the book of Proverbs mixes prose and poetry in a story about a
seductress who leads a young man to his ruin (Prov 7:6–23). The present
chapter will examine some larger texts in both prose and poetry before
examining short lines that are more or less semantically parallel. I begin
with an epic story.

In Job 1 and 2, the three main characters are God, who is called the
Lord, a celestial provocateur, and a human paragon of virtue. The term
for the villain (*satan* with an article) indicates a function like a CIA
agent. His duty is to determine genuine loyalty. This character initiates
the dramatic action by means of a philosophical dilemma that is
summed up in a question: "Will anyone revere God for nothing?" (In
this chapter all translations are the author's). In short, is virtue possible
apart from an anticipated reward or a dreaded punishment? The divine
response, "Have you thought about my servant Job," becomes the
structuring principle for the entire book. A question is followed by a
response.

Five series of texts make up the story that tugs at the human heart;
they begin in the warmth of the family circle and alternate between the
earth and heaven. Everything the narrator says about the hero suggests
completeness rather than perfection. He is both moral and religious; the
deity confirms that assessment twice. With God's permission, the provocateur brings an end to Job's bliss. First, he destroys Job's property,
then slays his ten children. Refrains have a haunting effect ("One day
when . . . "; "Where did you come from?"; "from wandering throughout
the earth"; "his sons and daughters were eating and drinking wine";
"While his messenger was speaking, another arrived and said"; "Only
I escaped to tell you"). In rapid succession they report four calamities

wrought by Sabean raiders, a celestial fire, Chaldeans, and a mighty wind. Suddenly, Job is bereft of everything except his wife.

Job comes through the first test with flying colors. Proof comes from his statement of fidelity: "Naked I came from my mother's womb, and naked will I return there [land of the dead, Sheol];[1] the Lord has given; the Lord has taken; bless the Lord's name" (Job 1:21). A refrain sets the stage for a second test. Question and answer repeat what is said in the first meeting between God and the provocateur. Once again the Lord acquiesces and allows the provocateur to harm Job, but this time sets a limit to his power. Again Job scores high marks, even when his wife irks him with the words, "Bless (or Curse) [given the blasphemous element in the statement] God and die." Job responds as follows: "Shall we receive good from God and not also receive bad?" This time, however, the narrator adds something to his earlier assessment: "In all this Job did not sin nor accuse God of wrongdoing" now reads "In all this Job did not sin with his lips." Does Job harbor an accusation against God in his heart? The poetic debate will answer that question.

Two thematic words link the prologue to the epilogue and to the poetry. The first, *barak*, occurs seven times (six in the prologue, once in the epilogue). Ordinarily, it means "to bless," but the poet stretches its sense to convey Job's upturned world. The provocateur uses it to mean "curse," and his use may be picked up by others, even by Job's wife. The other thematic word, *ḥinnam*, "for nothing," is spoken by the provocateur (Job 1:9), the deity (Job 2:3), Job (Job 9:17), and one of his friends (Job 22:6). Its initial meaning of goodness without thinking about a reward or retribution, the carrot or the stick, gives way to the idea of crushing someone without cause. It thus indicts both the Lord and the provocateur. These thematic words focus the two problems introduced by the unknown author: speaking correctly about God and the suffering of the innocent.

HEBREW POETRY

Normally, Hebrew poetry appears in two or three cola (or versets) and achieves parallel structure by contrast, synonymy, or climactic development. Its images are drawn from nature, daily life, and the imagination: weaving, agriculture, meteorology, crafts, cooking, warfare, seasonal cycles, myth, and much more. The images are kaleidoscopic;

---

[1] "There" refers to Sheol, the land of the dead, not to the mother's womb.

consistency is not an aesthetic norm, whereas emotional intensity in extended poems matches the rising intensity in the second half of parallel cola. Above all, the poetry strives for concision; often the brevity creates a sense of mystery.[2]

Job 3:1–26

Job's opening curse of his birthday and night of his conception in 3:1–26 is unsurpassed for raw emotion and graphic imagery, although it is matched by his later wish to die in 19:23–27. Because seven was considered a perfect number in the ancient world, the four references to day and three to night symbolize suffering to the fullest degree. Ironically, the first and last words, perish and trouble, express a sense of utter isolation from life itself. Darkness plays itself off against light, days against months, disease against rest, a closed womb against an infant sucking at its mother's breast, barrenness against conception, death against life, gloom against a joyful cry. Merisms (small and great, slave and master) universalize the misery while imagination reaches into the watery abyss for the mythic figure of Leviathan and into the land of the dead, Sheol, for supposed rest from oppressors. Language of proximity and distance, here and there, repeated twice in verse 17 along with *rogez* (trouble), focuses on the contrast between Job's misery and the restful state of the dead. Unfulfilled hope contrasts with the actualization of unspoken fears. Sighs for bread and groans for water justify Job's comparison of his eager search for death with that of persons looking for treasure and rejoicing when finding it. The bold personification of dawn implied in the expression "eyelids of the morning" is a striking image when set alongside the wish that its stars be dark and its hope for light be in vain.

The movement within the poem becomes increasingly more internal. Days and months of the calendar, celestial phenomena, skilled experts at cursing, and mythological beings fade as Job's bitter existence takes center stage. The first section, 3:1–10, focuses on the day of Job's birth and night of his conception. Part two, 3:11–26, argues that non-being is preferable to having been born and questions the gift of life for those in miserable circumstances. In this context the poet provides a verbal link with the prologue. The provocateur asks: "Did you not place

---

[2] On Hebrew poetry and narrative, see Robert Alter, *The Art of Biblical Narrative* (New York, 1985) and his "Afterword," in Ariel Bloch and Chana Bloch, *The Song of Songs* (Berkeley, 1995), 119–31. James L. Crenshaw, *Samson* (Atlanta, 1978) discusses stylistic characteristics of Hebrew narrative as seen in the story about Samson.

a hedge about him, his dwelling, and everything he owns?" (1:10) and Job asks: "Why is light given to a person whose way is hidden, whom God has fenced in?" (3:23). At the end, Job can only say: "I had no ease, quiet, or rest and trembling came" (3:26). His first word, "Perish," now applies to his whole being, not just to the time of his conception and birth. Trouble, the shaking brought on by the combination of fear and sickness, has become his companion, like a garment to be worn night and day.[3]

Ecclesiastes 1:4–11

Qoheleth's poem about the cyclical nature of reality lacks the emotional intensity of Job's curse but makes up for it by its broad sweep. Beginning with the sun, it mentions the wind and rivers before focusing on the human body (mouth, eyes, ear). Two Hebrew words, *holek* and *sobeb*, emphasize movement and circularity, respectively. Here the former has both its basic meaning, "to walk," and an extended sense of going to be with the dead. The latter sense of *holek* has precedence, for death is never far from Qoheleth's mind.

The poem begins with a twofold use of the word for generation: "A generation goes, and a generation comes." Departure trumps arrival; death trumps birth. If the reference is to humans, the sequel is sobering: "But the earth remains into the ages." The irony could hardly be greater. Those who came from the dirt, according to the account in Genesis, are destined to return to the earth, which alone endures. Human beings are, in Qoheleth's view, fleeting (*hebel*).

Turning to the sun, Qoheleth refers to its rising and setting, but now he uses the same verb for its setting that in verse 1 signifies birth, although the sequence is reversed. Rising (birth or rebirth) precedes setting (death). His further observations about the sun reflect the ancient myth of the solar deity standing in his chariot drawn by steeds that are panting from the strenuous task. Directional markers follow; south and north suggest a change in subject, for the sun's movement is from east to west. That subtle hint alone alerts readers to a shift but is soon accompanied by a word indicating circularity, *sobeb*, repeated for emphasis. The participle expressing movement occurs here for the third time. In verse 4 it indicates death but the two uses in the next verse resort to the verb's basic meaning, simple progress. The subject of this sentence is withheld until the second half of the verse, where it occurs

---

[3] When Job mentions the day-cursers who are skilled at rousing Leviathan, he may think of the Canaanite god of the sea, Yamm (*yam*, sea instead of *yom*, day).

twice. What moves southward, turns around to the north, and goes around and around? The answer: wind which turns as it will. To stress the circular motion, *sobeb* occurs three times, reinforced by another form of the word. Movement also takes place in the poem from the nonspecific "generation" to the celestial orb, then to the ubiquitous wind. In an abrupt move, the poet comes down to earth and focuses on streams that constantly flow toward the sea but the sea is never full. The overworked participle *holek* occurs two more times along with an infinitive of the verb. The result approximates an incantation.[4]

The next word is comprehensive (all), as in the case of the streams. The effect of every thing or word is tiring. Furthermore, they cannot be adequately expressed. With the dual sense of the word *dabar* (here in the plural), the poem has finally brought human beings into the picture. The attention on eye and ear, the instruments of learning, leads to the unexpected result: neither sight nor sound is ever satisfied.

The concentration of a word expressing movement (six times) and another signifying circularity (four times) explains how the poet can conclude that there is nothing new under the sun. Even repetition underscores the point (what, what, that, that), and the word "all" rules out any exception. Every claim to have discovered a new thing is labeled a falsehood. Why? Memory is fickle, whether ancient, contemporary, or future.

In this exquisite poem, Qoheleth throws the spotlight on movement that achieves nothing, like life if viewed absolutely. In doing so, he stands against the biblical notion of divine leadership toward an eschaton of peace and tranquility, at least for the righteous. He has asked whether there is any profit to living (1:3); this poem gives an answer, which Qoheleth later puts into a few words ("There was no profit under the sun," 2:11).

The two thematic summations in 1:2 and 1:3 insist that everything is futile and question the profit of all endeavors. They set a somber mood, which verse 4 continues by the initial position of death. That negative mood prevails. The sun's steeds pant from exhaustion, the wind's trajectory abruptly becomes circuitous, streams achieve nothing despite ceaseless motion. Both events and words are tiring, desire is never fulfilled, and memory leads to false conclusions.

---

[4] Robert Alter, *The Wisdom Books* (New York, 2010), 346, writes: "The constant use of repetition, from this initial verse onward, gives the rhythmic prose of Qoheleth's rhetoric an incantatory power."

Like much that Qoheleth says, the poem can be read two ways.[5] A positive spin on it is possible. Birth replaces death, the sun's steeds eagerly charge ahead, the wind brings respite without favoring any geographical area, the sea has the capacity to hold whatever flows its way, the quest for knowledge is insatiable, and failed recollection engenders a sense of novelty. Such ambiguity lends mystery even when the imagery appears to be unambiguous.[6]

Proverbs 8:22–31

The third example of poetry moves beyond either private or universal misery to sing the praises of a "greater than human" figure: personified wisdom. Antecedents for this bold move exist in Israel and in Egypt. Zion is personified, as are the divine name and face, but the tenderest personification of an abstract quality occurs in the affirmation that "Loving-kindness and truth have come together; righteousness and peace have kissed" (Ps 85:10). The Egyptian goddess Maat was the personification of order, hence life-giver. Woman wisdom in the Bible is probably modeled on her, with important differences. Maat does not address humans with prophetic warnings or with instructions like those of parents and teachers. Moreover, a rival, Woman Folly, excels in seductive speech aimed at restless young males. "Stolen water is sweet, and bread eaten furtively is pleasant" (Prov 9:17) appeals to youthful thirst for the forbidden. Wisdom's allure is directed at an equally powerful urge, the wish to acquire knowledge and ultimately wisdom. Although desirable in the erotic sense, she is preeminently cognitive, offering an understanding of how things work to make life successful and ethical.

Two versions of the origin of the universe, cosmogony, form the backdrop for Wisdom's self-description. The first version, Prov 8:22–26, establishes her honorable status as present in primordial times. She claims to have existed alongside the formless mass, the chaos from which God created heaven and earth, according to Genesis 1. She is older than the earth, its heights and depths, its fixed mountains and

[5] James L. Crenshaw, "A Rhetoric of Indecision: Reflections on God as Judge in Qoheleth," in Scott C. Jones and Christine Roy Yoder, eds., "When the Morning Stars Sang," *Essays in Honor of Choon Leong Seow on the Occasion of His Sixty-Fifth Birthday*, BZAW 500 (Berlin/Boston, 2018), 177–88.

[6] Edwin M. Good, "The Unfilled Sea: Style and Meaning in Ecclesiastes 1:2–11," in *Israelite Wisdom*, eds. John Gammie et al. (Missoula, 1978), 59–73, gives a compositional analysis of this text that emphasizes two stylistic techniques: delaying an expected consequent and using the interrogative.

meandering streams. In a society where seniority implied authority, her claim sets her apart as worthy of honor. The second cosmogony, Prov 8:27–31, emphasizes her special relationship with the creator, either as artisan or small child.[7] While the heavens were formed, the waters given fixed zones, and earth's foundations established, Wisdom played before God, delighting both heaven and earth. The ABBA form in verses 30–31 (delight; playing; playing; delight) approaches playfulness, a mood not found in her earlier speeches with their harsh warnings and threats.

The tenor of the last two verses may explain the further speculation about Wisdom in Prov 9:1–6. Here she presents herself as the builder of a palace and gracious host who extends an invitation to the simpleminded to come and eat her bread and drink her wine. In the early second century BCE Jesus Ben Sira develops this figure further in the direction of worship. Now she describes herself as the divine word like the Stoic philosophical concept expressing universality. Accordingly, Wisdom covers the earth like a mist and eventually takes up permanent abode in the holy tent at Jerusalem (Sir 24:1–29).

Because she was created in the beginning and issued from the mouth of the deity, Wisdom has the authority to minister in the Tabernacle where she flourishes. Cedar and palm tree, olive and rose imply majesty and beauty. An assortment of spices provides fragrance. Together, they cover three dimensions: sight, smell, and taste. The imagery vaguely recalls the poet's experience in the temple when incense was being burned. Ever the gracious host, Wisdom invites the young to eat, promising them that their hunger for knowledge will never dull.

The swerve[8] that occurs at this point in the poem is akin to that inaugurated by the modern scientific revolution. In a daring move, Ben Sira equates Wisdom and the Torah of Moses. The endless nature of its teaching reminds him of a primordial stream that flowed out of Eden and divided into four rivers: the Pishon, Gihon (another name for the Nile), the Tigris, and the Euphrates in Gen 2:10–14. Ben Sira adds the river Jordan, a subtle reminder that wisdom is Israel's heritage as claimed by Deut (4:6–8).

The thoroughly Hellenized author of Wisdom of Solomon takes the personification in an entirely different direction from that inaugurated

---

[7] The meaning of the unique 'amon is much debated. To date, no satisfactory solution has emerged from the discussion. The suggested meaning is based on ancient translations.

[8] The term "swerve" comes from Stephen Greenblatt, *The Swerve* (New York, 2011). For him, it involves the impact of the discovery of Lucretius' *De rerum natura* and how, he thinks, the world became modern.

by Ben Sira. Wisdom is viewed as an emanation of God, an earthly manifestation in the same way the rays of the sun participate in their source. It follows that she possesses all twenty-one divine attributes, seven times three, reflecting perfection (Wis 7:22–23). At the same time, Wisdom retains the erotic element from Proverbs and Sirach, but now as wife rather than just a lover.

Stylistic Features in Parallel Cola

Not only did the sages compose complex poems; they also excelled at writing short sayings in which striking stylistic devices abound. The striving for synonyms in ever-increasing intensity is best found in numerical sequences. The mystery of sex produced an unforgettable numerical saying about three things, indeed four, things too wonderful for comprehension: the way of an eagle in the sky, the way of a snake on a rock, the way of a ship in the heart of the sea, and the way of a young man with a young woman (Prov 30: 18–19). The fourfold use of the Hebrew word for "way" contrasts with the singularity of the final topic, sex. In this proverb, three instances of forward movement, progress without leaving a trace, are dwarfed by the mystery of Eros.

By a slight alteration, even this type of saying could yield a surprising result; emphasis falls on the first three things instead of the last one in the sequence. "Of three things my heart is afraid, and of a fourth I am frightened" in Sir 26:5a goes on to call slander, a mob, and false accusation worse than death. In his view, the eternal decree that all must die was not altogether bad. For him, leaves falling from a tree symbolized the termination of life.

For many readers, the most memorable feature of the poetry in wisdom literature is its use of similes. To an ancient poet, lazy people resembled the effect of vinegar on teeth or smoke on eyes (Prov 10:26) and a beautiful woman without discretion was as outrageous as a gold ring in a pig's snout (Prov 11:22). Possessing knowledge without being able to use it advantageously was like having legs but lacking the ability to walk (Prov 26:7). A man who strays from home was like a bird that strays from its nest (Prov 27:8). Ben Sira's disdain for merchants yields the following indictment of their profession: "As a stake is driven firmly into a fissure between rocks, so wickedness is wedged in between selling and buying" (Sir 27:2). His contempt for loose women approaches the obscene when he compares them to thirsty travelers who drink from any water source. Equally undiscriminating, such women, he says, sit anywhere and "open their quivers to the arrow" (Sir 26:12).

Metaphors coined by discerning poets accurately describe the existential situation. Marital fidelity is the topic of a beautiful proverb that encourages the husband to drink only from his own cistern (Prov 5:15–19). It then identifies the wife as that cistern and extends the metaphors to include a fountain, a lovely hind, and a graceful doe. Water imagery continues when the poet likens semen to springs and streams. Ben Sira envisions life as a tree (Sir 14:18) and Qoheleth depicts death as a failed lamp and broken pitcher (Eccl 12:6). Breath as a lamp is also used metaphorically for divine statutes (Prov 6:23) and for God's searching the human heart (Prov 20:27).

Sages were also capable of graphic images. Ben Sira describes frost and freezing as the earth donning thorns and bodies of water putting on ice like a breastplate (Sir 23:20). The author of Wisdom of Solomon calls reason a spark kindled by the rhythmic beating of the heart (Wis 2:2). Job compares the passing of time with the speed of a weaver's shuttle (Job 7:6) and the origin of life with the curdling of cheese (Job 10:10). By means of a striking personification of dawn, God imagines the eradication of evildoers when she takes hold of the skirts of the earth and shakes the wicked out of it (Job 38:13).

One of the most memorable examples of metonymy involves the organs of the body. In this instance, eyes stand for sight, ears for hearing, heart for life, and feet for movement (Prov 4:20–27). An ironic use of hyperbole indicates self-deprecation in Prov 30:2–3. "Surely I am the stupidest of men and do not have human understanding. I have not acquired wisdom, nor do I have knowledge of the Holy One." Paradox invariably defies human calculation, as in this instance: One person's generosity is rewarded with more wealth while another individual's stinginess only produces want (Prov 11:24).

Ancient teachers could wield a sharp pen when the occasion called for it. When Job asks, "What is man?" and adds "that you (God) visit him and test him daily," he treats a revered tradition in Psalm 8 cavalierly (Job 7:17–21). Job hardly thinks of humans as having an elevated status just below celestial beings. Similarly, when he tells his friends that wisdom will die with them, he has not changed his view that they are miserable comforters devoid of both wisdom and compassion. His words reek with sarcasm.

The common practice of worshiping the work of one's hands evokes bitter satire in Wis 13:18–14:1. The sage mocks those who hope to benefit from the veneration of idols as follows: They expect health from a weakling, life from a dead thing, help from an inexperienced object, success on a journey from weak hands. In Job 32:1–5, the narrator employs bluster to indicate a flawed character. Here Elihu is said to be angry four times in only five short verses. A rare instance of gallows humor robs death of its terror in Sir 38:22 ("Remember my doom, for yours is like it; mine yesterday, yours today"). The opposite occurs when a sage reflects on the angst deep within the psyche: "The heart knows its own bitterness, and no stranger enters into its happiness ... Even in laughter the heart may hurt, and the end of pleasure is sadness" (Prov 14:10,13). Occasionally, a touch of nostalgia can be detected, especially if it involves childhood (Prov 4:3–4). Even unexpressed thoughts, a form of imagined dialogue, open a window through which to understand others. "Let's swallow the living like the grave ... fill our houses with plunder ... share our money" (Prov 1:12–14).

Some thoughts should not even be entertained. Ben Sira hoped to discourage certain types of intellectual inquiry, especially speculation about the unknown and unknowable. For his purposes, the ancient formula, "Do not say" came in handy (Sir 5:3–6), along with an interdiction limiting attention to what had been assigned. Teachers understood that some questions could not be answered with a simple "yes" or "no." The reason: situations require different responses depending on the circumstances. The proverb, "Do not answer a fool according to his folly lest you be like him" and "Answer a fool according to his folly lest he be wise in his eyes" (Prov 26:4–5) calls upon readers to consider the circumstances and act accordingly.

That at least one teacher, Ben Sira, recognized the influence of social context can be inferred from his comments about death (welcome when sickness and poverty reign; unwelcome when the zest for life is strong) and about the essentials of life (water, bread, clothing, house in Sir 29:21 and water, fire, iron, salt, flour, milk, honey, wine, oil, and clothing in Sir 39:26). The contrast between village life and urban existence gives rise to ever-increasing desire.

Some sayings derive their power from hidden meanings. References to forbidden sex often take advantage of a word's double meaning. (This is the way of an adulteress. She eats, wipes her mouth, and exclaims, "I have done nothing wrong," Prov 30:20). Teachers may appeal to a mysterious aura. For example, Eliphaz employs images to describe a revelatory experience during semi-wakefulness that matches the mystery itself ("But a word sneaked up on me; my ears caught a hint of it ... a breeze swept by my face; the hair of my skin bristled. It stopped. I didn't recognize its visible form, although a figure was in front of my eyes. Silence ..." Job 4:12–16). What was the word? A blunt reminder in question form that no human can be more righteous than God.

Although mysterious, Eliphaz's dream can be understood. Job's encounter with God whom he no longer recognizes leaves him so perplexed that he responds to the barrage of questions with ambiguous grammar and syntax that amounts to equivocation. His admission that previous understanding, which he calls hearing, has been corrected by sight issues in a stammering reply: "Therefore I relent (or despise) and find comfort (or repent) on (or concerning) dust and ashes" (Job 42:6). The missing direct object and double sense of the verbs leave the matter open. Does Job really repent? If so, for what?

Judging from frequency of occurrence, rhetorical questions and refrains were much loved by sages. "Many a one is called a kind person, but who can find a truthful one?" (Prov 20:6) may not be gender specific, although it uses two different Hebrew words for man, but the following is: "Who can find a woman of substance?" (Prov 30:10). In both instances, the emphasis falls on rarity or even nonexistence. Such questions usually demand a negative response as in the following: "Who has gone up to heaven and come down; who has gathered the wind in his fist; who has wrapped the waters in a garment? Who has established all the ends of the earth? What is his name or his son's name? Surely you know" (Prov 30:4).[9] Behind these questions lies a myth about a primordial man ascending to heaven, something denied to mortals. The picture of someone clothing chaos with a diaper approaches the absurd. When Qoheleth uses the question, "Who knows?" he implies that nobody knows, as when he worries that the person who inherits his wealth may be a fool. "Who knows," he asks, "whether he will be wise or a fool?" (Eccl 2:19). A barrage of rhetorical questions aimed at Job by the deity exposes the poverty of his strength and knowledge when compared to God's (Job 38–39).

Sometimes a point needs to be made more than once to rouse the sleepy. The lack of comforters becomes truly poignant when repeated in Eccl 4:1 ("And they had no comforters," to which may be compared Lam 1:2, 21, a lament over the lack of comforters for Jerusalem in ruins). Qoheleth's teachings are sprinkled with catchy refrains ("utter futility, all is futile, chasing or shepherding, or even feeding on the wind, no one knows, he cannot find it, cannot know"). Ben Sira's expansive treatment of topics enables him to make full use of refrains, both introductory and concluding. In Sir 1:11–30 he incorporates twelve refrains about fearing

---

[9] James L. Crenshaw, "Clanging Symbols," in *Justice and the Holy*, eds. Douglas A. Knight and Peter J. Paris (Philadelphia, 1989), 51–64, reprinted in James L. Crenshaw, *Urgent Advice and Probing Questions* (Macon, GA, 1995), 371–82.

the Lord and seven about wisdom. The introductory refrain, "You who fear the Lord" is repeated three times, while the concluding refrain is varied to yield "Anyone who trusted in him, anyone who called upon him, and anyone who persevered" in Sir 2:7–9. A variant, alternating refrains, each one repeated, occurs in Sir 19:13–17 ("Question a friend" and "Question a neighbor").

True wisdom required sages to compare relative values. The result was expressed as a "better saying." A dinner of herbs is better than a fatted ox where hatred exists (Prov 15:17) and a dry morsel with quiet is better than a feast with strife (Prov 17:1). According to Qoheleth, a poor and wise youth is better than an old and foolish king (Eccl 4:13), doubly surprising, because wisdom increased with age and poverty was thought to be the result of laziness. Comparisons can be extended beyond two things. Qoheleth thinks that never having been born is better than both the living and the dead (Eccl 4:2–3). And yet, he says, two are better than one because a companion can help an individual in certain circumstances (Eccl 4:9). In Qoheleth's view, sorrow is better than laughter, the end of something than its beginning (Eccl 7:3, 8).

Here and there in the literature one comes across rarities such as puns, rhyme, ellipsis, and even a saying without a parallel colon. In Prov 6:29 the addition of the word for woman, *'ishah*, appears to be chosen as a play on the similar word for fire, *'esh*, and in Sir 6:22 Ben Sira emphasizes the hidden nature of wisdom by a play on her name and a homonym (*musar*). A rhyme occurs in Eccl 7:1 ("A good name, *shem*, is better than fine ointment, (*shemen*). In Eccl 9:3 Qoheleth's sentence breaks off as a subtle reminder of how death comes unexpectedly ("and then to the dead"). Both subject and verb ("they go") are missing. The lone saying without its own heightening or contrast reads as follows: "Whoever answers with honest words kisses the lips" (Prov 24:26).

The first epilogue in Ecclesiastes states that Qoheleth sought to find pleasing words, adding that what he taught was true (Eccl 12:10). The discussion thus far confirms the judgment about aesthetics and suggests that the same can be said of Israel's sages generally. Why else did they include such pleasantries as the playful reversal of consonants in Prov 14:4 (*bar/rab*), the ABAB scheme in Job 5:18 (he wounds: binds up: smites: heals), a single consonant, *'aleph*, at the beginning of fifteen verses out of twenty-three in Job 9:18–35, an alphabetic poem (acrostic) to describe the wife in Prov 31:10–31 by the almost hypnotic repetition of *'et we'et* (a time and a time) in the well-known poem that Peter Seeger set to music? (Eccl 3:2–8).

Ecclesiastes 11:7–12:7

If anyone doubts the validity of the claim in Eccl 12:10 that Qoheleth was interested in aesthetics, Qoheleth's final poem will set that disbelief to rest. As in 1:4–11, ancient Near Eastern solar worship lurks in the background of this poem with which Qoheleth concludes his teaching, except for the *inclusio* in 12:8. The warmth of the sun is pleasant, but the short lifespan of humans ushers in a never-ending darkness. That sad prospect prompts Qoheleth to exclaim: "Everything that comes is meaningless" (Eccl 11:8). Even pleasure, which he commends to the young, has at least two downsides; it does not last, and acting on secret desires subjects one to divine judgment (Eccl 11:8 and Num 15:39). Still, he urges youth to remove care and pain insofar as possible, since the dawn of life is short.

Qoheleth's last imperative calls on young people to remember their *bore'eyka* before the onset of old age. This unique Hebrew word plays on the similarities of three nouns (creator, cistern, and pit). The first one requires a reading of the plural as an indication of majesty; the second term is a metaphor for one's wife as in Prov 5:15; and the third expression suggests the tomb. Qoheleth may have all three possibilities in mind, although the first one is rather jarring, given his world view.

The second half of verse 1 begins with the first of three adverbial phrases meaning "before." Together they paint a dreary picture of old age and death. The response to the evil days is personalized: "When you will say, 'I have no pleasure in them.'" The second "before" introduces the image of a world overcome by darkness, an image that is common in apocalyptic literature. For the aged with diminishing visibility, the sources of light – sun, moon, and stars – fail, and clouds prevail following the rain.

The images that follow mix the literal with the allegorical; they describe a crumbling house, which symbolizes the human body. The guardians of the house (arms) tremble; strong men (legs) are bent; grinders (teeth) cease because they are few; those looking through the windows (eyes) are dimmed; the doors (lips) are shut; the sound of grinding (ears) is muted; the daughters of song (voice) are low; the almond tree (white hair) blossoms; the locust drags itself along (limited mobility); and the caper berry (a stimulant to appetite) has no effect.

Most of the images can be read literally. Managers of the collapsing estate are afraid; the maidens who grind grain are few; the shops are closed; the aged have difficulty sleeping; venturing outside imperils the old; and desire, sexual and otherwise, fails with the passing of years and cannot be restored. The contrast between humans and nature is powerful. Humans grow old and die but nature rejuvenates itself and flourishes. When the body gives out, humans go to their eternal home and mourners go about the street, the sole reminder of the dead. This verse links up with Qoheleth's initial poem about nature's cyclical movement in that the two theme words, *holek* and *sobeb*, occur once more, making a total of seven and five, respectively. The third "before" is followed by two exquisite images for death: the snapping of a silver cord holding a lamp and the breaking of a golden bowl and pitcher when the wheel gives way. Just as the oil and water flow out, the dust returns to the earth from which it came, and the breath returns to God who gave it.

CONCLUSION

The books of Proverbs, Ecclesiastes, and Job make no claim to convey a divine word. Instead, they offer a human perspective about everyday life, its joys and frustrations. These three are sufficiently alike in their pursuit of something called wisdom to be linked, but each one has its own distinctive features that set it apart from the others. A linear examination of them requires considerable speculation about the date of each text, making a synchronic approach a better alternative. Nevertheless, two books, Sirach and Wisdom of Solomon, invite a diachronic reading because of historical information in each one. Therefore one can speak of early and late texts, the earliest one, Proverbs, being the product of ordinary people in small villages, with the others deriving from learned teachers called *ḥakamin* (sages) who lived in urban settings during the late post-exilic and Hellenistic periods.

Still, a synchronic analysis best exposes the hidden treasures within wisdom literature: the art of storytelling and poetic imagery. The preceding discussion began with a narrative about a conflict like no other. The characters represent heaven and earth, with a villain functioning as a spy for the celestial realm. At issue is the profoundest question known to humans: Will anyone revere God for naught? This epic tale sets a stage for an analysis of Hebrew poetry by way of contrast with the learned prose. Three examples are investigated: Job's cursing the day of his birth, Qoheleth's description of nature's cyclical movement, and the praise of personified Wisdom. Together they paint a picture of Israel's poetic repertoire equal to anything in the rest of the Hebrew Bible.

From larger poems, the focus moves to stylistic features in parallel cola. The similes, metaphors, metonymy, numerical sequence, "better" sayings, puns, hyperbole, sarcasm, gallows humor, and more prove that sages were interested in delighting readers, as the epilogue in Ecclesiastes claims. It seemed appropriate to end with a poem that describes the moment awaiting everyone. In this case, it is preceded by poignant images of old age. After that, the lamp breaks, the oil flows out, life ebbs away, dust returns to the earth, and the divine breath returns to God who gave it.

Further Reading

Brown, William P., *Wisdom's Wonder* (Grand Rapids, MI, 2014).
Christianson, Eric S., *A Time to Tell* (Sheffield, 1998).
Collins, John J., *Wisdom in the Hellenistic Age* (Louisville, KY, 1997).
Crenshaw, James L., *Old Testament Wisdom*, 3rd ed. (Louisville, KY, 2010).
Crenshaw, James L., *Qoheleth* (Columbia, 2013).
Fox, Michael V., *A Time to Tear Down &. A Time to Build Up* (Grand Rapids, MI, 1999).
Fox, Michael V., *Proverbs 1–9* (New York, 2000).
Fox, Michael V., *Proverbs 10–31* (New Haven, CT, and London), 2009.
Rad, Gerhard von, *Wisdom in Israel* (Nashville, TN, 1972).
Schrorer, Silvia, *Wisdom Has Built Her House* (Collegeville, 2000).
Trible, Phyllis, "Wisdom Builds a Poem: The Architecture of Proverbs 1:20–33," *JBL* 94 (1975), 509–18.
Weiss, Meir, *The Story of Job's Beginning* (Jerusalem, 1983).

8 The Gospels

JEANNINE K. BROWN

The four canonical Gospels – Matthew, Mark, Luke, and John – are situated at the beginning of the New Testament and have enjoyed significant attention by interpreters of the Bible, given their subject matter – *the words and deeds of Jesus of Nazareth*. What has often been lost in the interpretive process is a view toward a Gospel as a story cut from whole cloth. The narrative contours of these four Gospels have often been obscured by a fairly exclusive attention to their details – a particular saying of Jesus or a specific account of something he did. Recent scholarship, however, has begun to reconnect with the Gospels as stories.

In this essay, we will explore what literary or narrative analysis offers to interpretation of the canonical Gospels. After a brief discussion of the historical tendencies to read these writings in a rather piecemeal fashion, we will introduce recent conversations about the genre of these works and certain methods that have given greater attention to their storied features (e.g. plotting, characterization, and thematic development). The rest of the essay will turn to analysis of two texts from the Gospels, extended sections from Matthew and John, with the goal of illustrating a storied interpretive method.

The tendency to focus on the smallest segments of a Gospel (often called "pericopes" by scholars) has a long history. And even a cursory look at the recent history of the church and the academy surfaces numerous examples of this tendency. In the church, catechesis around the Gospels has focused on individual stories about Jesus and shorter sayings of Jesus. From Sunday school lessons to lectionaries, we see the Gospels apportioned and delivered in "bite-size" pieces. This practice might be practical for teaching, but it has often obscured the storied contours of each individual Gospel. It might be assumed that academic scholarship on the Gospels would have followed a different model. Yet in spite of its more varied set of approaches, the academy, like the church, has tended to study the Gospels in ways that minimize or even set aside their overarching stories. Certainly, historical-critical study – prominent in the last few centuries – has often exhibited atomizing tendencies.

The recent trajectory of Gospels scholarship has involved the reclamation of their storied shape, especially as more attention has been given to the Bible as literature. This turn toward the literary is quite appropriate, since whatever else it is, the Bible is certainly a literary work, and as such becomes subject to literary criticism – the purpose of which is to bring into clearer focus the subtleties of language, style, and meaning that are the fabric of the text.[1] We can see this shift toward Gospels as wholes in recent discussions of genre and method.

THE GENRE AND INTERPRETATION OF THE GOSPELS

The four canonical Gospels most closely resemble Greco-Roman *bios*, or biography. The seminal work of Richard Burridge has demonstrated similarity with such biographies of both form and content.[2] Formally, the Gospels fit expectations for a *bios* in terms of length and topic (directed toward a single person), as well as their shape: an overarching chronological outline filled in with topically arranged episodes and sayings.[3] In terms of substance, the Gospels, like their *bios* counterparts, provide a kind of travelogue of the primary character (journeying from place to place), focus primarily on the events that follow versus precede the person's public debut, and spend significant space narrating the person's death.

One of the features of the canonical Gospels that is most distinct from the genre of Greco-Roman *bios* involves the question of audience. While *bioi* are intended for broader consumption, the four Gospels clearly have an ecclesial or church audience in view – that is, they are written in the late first century to provide encouragement and direction to communities of Jesus-followers, whether Jewish, Gentile, or mixed. Yet, even given this important distinction, the Gospels resemble ancient biography in key ways when viewed as whole narratives.

Earlier assessments of genre often focused on the smaller, episodic parts of a Gospel, as in form-critical methods, which had their heyday in

---

[1] Adele Berlin, "Characterization in Biblical Narrative: David's Wives," *JSOT* 23 (1982), 69–70.
[2] Richard A. Burridge, *What Are the Gospels? A Comparison with Graeco-Roman Biography*, 2nd ed. (Grand Rapids, MI, 2004), 185–212.
[3] Luke has more often been categorized as Greco-Roman historiography, given its companion volume, Acts.

the first half of the twentieth century. For form critics, individual pericopes were assessed and categorized by their specific genres: for example, pronouncement stories, miracle stories, or controversies, and parables, proverbs, aphorisms, or other kinds of sayings. For the most part, the interpretive value of the Gospels was found in their individual segments, likened to pearls on a string that could be let loose and rearranged without any great interpretive loss. A strength of form-critical work on the Gospels was the recognition of the significance of the oral transmission of the traditions about Jesus (what he was remembered to have said and did) along with assessment of the settings in which these traditions emerged and functioned. What was downplayed was the sense of the Gospel writers – the four evangelists – as authors in their own right. Within form criticism, the evangelists were viewed as little more than compilers or editors of the Jesus traditions.

Comparisons with ancient biographies, like that done by Burridge, have yielded a more holistic assessment of the genre of the Gospels.[4] This has invited or at least been accompanied by interpretive methods with a greater interest in reading Gospels holistically. For instance, redaction criticism, rhetorical criticism, and narrative criticism have each offered greater focus on the aims and interests of the evangelists as well as the shaping and plotting of the Gospels.

Seeing the evangelists as authors in their own right and not merely "cut and paste" editors was a hallmark of redaction criticism begun in the late 1950s and early 1960s. In redaction criticism, an evangelist's theological tendencies and particular writing context (or community) were studied by reference to the sources he used. For example, redaction critics analyzed Luke in close comparison with his source, the Gospel of Mark. While reliant on some form-critical categories and assumptions and, though not yet embracing a fully storied approach to a Gospel, redaction critics worked with individual Gospels in more holistic ways, as they sought to hear the unique interests and contexts of Matthew, Mark, Luke, or John.

Narrative criticism found fertile soil in this growing interest in the Gospel authors (or narrators). This literary method has developed and flourished from the early 1980s to the present and was adapted from the use of narratology in the study of literature. Although narrative

---

[4] As well as attention to the multifaceted purposes of such works, which include encouraging emulation (of virtuous characters) and historical interests (Burridge, *Gospels?* 64–65).

criticism originally tended toward a more ahistorical focus, over the last 30–40 years, it has expanded and become more versatile by including greater attention to historical and well as theological emphases.[5] Narrative critics have been at the forefront of attending to the storied shape of each of the canonical Gospels.

In recent years, Gospel scholarship has also made room for a wide variety of interpretive methods, including those that engage in more expressly "interested" (or located) exegesis.[6] These include feminist and womanist criticisms, post-colonial criticism, disability studies, expressly theological readings, and readings from a variety of cultural contexts that have historically been marginalized in biblical studies (e.g. African American criticism, Latinx criticism). As representatives of these criticisms have asserted, there is no "uninterested" exegesis and all interpreters come to the Gospels from particular vantage points, which inevitably impacts their readings.

NARRATIVE ANALYSIS: STORY AND DISCOURSE

There are a number of features to highlight for studying a narrative from a literary perspective. Basic *story* elements – setting, characters, and plot – are crucial elements for analysis. These are helpfully combined with attention to an author's way of telling the story, what is sometimes referred to as a narrative's *discourse*.

STORY FEATURES

Readers are initially drawn to the story features of a narrative. *Characters* – what they do and say – are central to the Gospels, especially the protagonist, Jesus, along with key groups like his disciples, the Jewish crowds who are drawn to him, and Roman and Jewish officials, who frequently serve as antagonists in the story. *Settings* are often used intentionally to signal literary or theological motifs. For example, mountains are used in Matthew to signal key moments of revelation (e.g., 5:1; 17:1; 28:16). The *plot* of any particular Gospel moves along via these interactions between characters, from conflict to resolution.

---

[5] Jeannine K. Brown, "Narrative Criticism," in *Dictionary of Jesus and the Gospels*, eds. Joel B. Green, Jeannine K. Brown, and Nicholas Perrin, rev. ed. (Downers Grove, IL, 2013), 619–24.
[6] Joel B. Green, *Practicing Theological Interpretation* (Grand Rapids, MI, 2011), 2.

The climactic moment in each of the Gospels centers on Jesus' crucifixion (e.g. Mark 15:33–39), which in each case is foreshadowed by Jesus' own testimony about his impending, representative death (Mark 8:31; 9:31; 10:33–34).

DISCOURSE FEATURES

Narrative analysis is helped along by attending to the way an author tells the story, what is referred to as the narrative's discourse or rhetoric. Discourse features include, but are not limited to, characterization, plotting, use of structural and rhetorical devices, and inclusion of citations and allusions to antecedent texts (particularly the Old Testament), what has been called "intertextuality." We will define and explore briefly these four categories in preparation for a narrative analysis of two Gospel texts.

CHARACTERIZATION

At their center, the four canonical Gospels are works of characterization of their central personage, Jesus of Nazareth. These ancient biographies are portraits of Jesus developed through narration of what he did and said, as well as through commentary the evangelists provide to accentuate these portraits. Each evangelist portrays Jesus in ways that overlap with the others. Jesus' Messianic identity, for instance, is highlighted by all four Gospels – Jesus as Israel's Messiah is a central affirmation for each of them (e.g., Matt 1:1; Mark 1:1; Luke 2:11; John 20:31). Yet there are also distinctive facets to each Gospel's Christology – that is, the specific portrait of Jesus being sketched. Matthew, for example, offers a Wisdom Christology by characterizing Jesus as the embodiment of Jewish Wisdom (e.g., 11:2, 19, 28–30).[7] While John does allude to Jesus as Wisdom in his prologue via the concept of the *logos* (John 1:1–18), Mark and Luke show little interest in this particular facet of Christology. Another example of distinctive Christology comes in John's Gospel. Although each of the evangelists communicate the importance of Passover in connection to the time of Jesus' death, only John portrays Jesus as Passover lamb ("Here is the Lamb of God"; 1:29, 36; cf. 19:33, 36).

---

[7] Jeannine K. Brown and Kyle Roberts, *The Gospel of Matthew* (Grand Rapids, MI, 2018), 388–91.

PLOTTING: NARRATIVE ARRANGEMENT

Even a cursory reading of the canonical Gospels reveals differences among them in the ordering of events within the life of Jesus. As noted previously, biographical writing contemporaneous to the canonical Gospels often followed the topical or thematic interests of an author, with only loose attention to chronology (moving from birth and early years to public debut, public life, and death). This topical interest fits the Gospels and their plotting strategies. As Graham Stanton explains, "Concern for chronological order was not characteristic of ancient biographical writing. As a stylistic technique, presentation of biographical material *per species* is much more common."[8]

This feature of *bios* encourages the reader to notice how each Gospel author shapes their story about Jesus – where the story begins and ends and how episodes along the way are plotted for literary and thematic effect. For example, the Gospel of Luke – which includes more references to the Jerusalem temple than its counterparts – highlights this setting by beginning and ending his Gospel at the temple (1:5, 8–9; 24:52–53). And given Matthew's interest in accenting the teachings of Jesus in five lengthy teaching discourses (chs. 5–7, 10, 13, 18, 24–25), it is not surprising that Jesus' first action in that Gospel on his public debut, after calling disciples, is to provide his followers with an extensive teaching on God's benevolent reign (5:1–2).

STRUCTURAL AND RHETORICAL DEVICES

The authors of the Gospels draw on a variety of structural, stylistic, and rhetorical devices to communicate with their audiences. These include various forms of repetition – from simple repetition of a word, phrase, or idea to *inclusio*, a linguistic bracket used at the beginning and end of a narrative or section of narrative. For example, fear is a theme linked with discipleship in Mark, and the evangelist communicates this motif through repetition across his Gospel (e.g., 4:41; 5:15, 33, 36; 6:50; 9:32; 10:32; 16:8). Yet an author may use repetition more sparingly and still emphasize a theme through *inclusio*: Matthew's motif of Jesus' presence with his people is accented by its placement at the beginning and the end of that Gospel (1:23; 28:20; cf. 18:20). This narrative bracket

---

[8] Graham Stanton, *Jesus of Nazareth in New Testament Preaching* (New York, 1974), 121.

places emphasis on Jesus as "God with us" (with his people) without having to repeat the theme in ongoing fashion.

Other structural devices used in the Gospels include narrative patterns, such as interchange (an alternating pattern; e.g. ABABABA) and intercalation (an ABA pattern).[9] An example of interchange is Luke's repeated alternation of vignettes about the births of Jesus and John the Baptist in Luke 1–2.[10] Intercalation (ABA) is common in Mark's Gospel and is sometimes referred to as a "Markan sandwich" because of that evangelist's affinity for this device. For example, Mark signals the account of Jesus' action in the temple as an act of judgment by tucking this episode within the framework story about Jesus' cursing of a fig tree (with the temple scene in Mark 12:15–19 "sandwiched" between the two-part fig tree pericope of 12:12–14 and 20–25).

INTERTEXTUALITY: SCRIPTURAL CITATIONS AND ALLUSIONS

A significant feature in each of the four Gospels is their reliance on Old Testament texts to authenticate and clarify their story about Jesus. These authors may use the Old Testament differently, with Matthew often citing texts and John using briefer, more sparing allusions much of the time. Yet they each weave into their narrative rich veins mined from the texts they understood to be Scripture. Exploring the why and how of this "intertextuality" can, therefore, prove insightful for interpretation, especially if we consider that an author might be referring to a precursor text for its storied potential.

In this way, study of intertextuality can contribute to narrative analysis by exploring and illuminating the layering of stories between two texts. Take, for example, the way in which a story in Genesis 4 is evoked and transposed in Matthew 18. We can recognize the layering of these two stories by their shared language: "seven times" and "seventy-seven times" (*heptakis* and *hebdomēkontakis hepta*, respectively, in the Greek translation of Gen 4:24 and in Matt 18:21–22).[11] In Genesis, Lamech, a descendant of Cain, claims that retribution against anyone

---

[9] For a more exhaustive list of structural devices with examples, see David R. Bauer, The Structure of Matthew's Gospel: A Study in Literary Design, *JSNTSup* 31 (1998), 13–19.

[10] Ibid., 18.

[11] The Septuagint is the Greek translation of the Old Testament and is often abbreviated "LXX."

harming Cain would be visited exponentially on anyone harming himself:

> Seven times vengeance has been taken by Cain, but by Lamech seventy-seven times. (Gen 4:24, LXX; cf. 4:15–16)

This story of human revenge is met in the Gospel of Matthew by an episode involving Peter and Jesus. Peter wonders how many times he is required to forgive a fellow believer and suggests "As many as seven times?" (Matt 18:21). Jesus raises the bar by teaching that forgiveness in the time of God's reign should be as much as "seventy-seven times" (18:22). While Genesis narrates an archetypal story of revenge spiraling out of control, Matthew transposes that story to offer a vision from Jesus of limitless forgiveness in the community of faith.

To illustrate how these various narrative features come together in particular Gospels texts, we explore next a passage from Matthew's Gospel and a series of texts from John on a particular theme. In line with the storied and literary focus of this discussion and to highlight the importance of a narrative approach, this exploration involves longer portions of text from both these Gospels.

THE FRAMING AND PLOTTING OF MATTHEW 4:23–9:38

The author of Matthew signals the literary structure of this part of his Gospel by framing chapters 5–9 with an *inclusio*. By repeating much of Matt 4:23 in 9:35, the evangelist indicates that these chapters are in some sense a unit within the whole structure of the Gospel.

> 4:23 And he *traveled* throughout all of Galilee *teaching in their synagogues, preaching the gospel of the kingdom, and healing every disease and sickness* among the people.

> 9:35 And Jesus *traveled* through all the towns and villages, *teaching in their synagogues, preaching the gospel of the kingdom, and healing every disease and sickness.*[12]

The material between these two markers delineates and expands on the activities mentioned in the summaries: Jesus teaches and preaches

---

[12] The Matthew texts in this section are my own translations derived from Brown and Roberts, *The Gospel of Matthew.*

(chs. 5–7); and he heals those who are sick (chs. 8–9).[13] In this way, Matthew begins the account of Jesus' public ministry with a concerted focus on the words and "the deeds of the Messiah" (see this language from 11:2 referring to Jesus' miraculous activity in chs. 8–9). Jesus' words – a summary of his teachings – come in the Sermon on the Mount (5:1–7:29). His deeds, focused primarily on his healing ministry on behalf of his Jewish compatriots who live in Galilee, are gathered together in 8:1–9:34 (with a transitional summary in 9:35–38).

8:1–17	(A) Three healing episodes
8:18–22	(B) Discipleship teachings on the priority of following Jesus
8:23–9:8	(A) Three miracle episodes
9:9–17	(B) Discipleship teachings on inclusive meals and fasting
9:18–34	(A) Three healing episodes

Already, we can see that the evangelist has carefully arranged this section of his Gospel to clarify his portrait of Jesus (his Christology) and other key themes. This attention to plotting is even more obvious when comparing Matthew and the two other Gospels it most closely resembles. (Mark and Luke, with these three being referred to as the Synoptic Gospels because of their similarities, in contrast to John's distinctiveness.) Such a comparison surfaces differences in arrangement of these sayings and episodes. For instance, the account of Jesus healing a man who is paralyzed comes early in Mark (2:1–12) but is included in Matthew (9:1–8) between an exorcism (Matt 8:28–34//Mark 5:1–20) and a pair of healings (Matt 9:18–26//Mark 5:21–43). If we recall the tendencies of Greco-Roman biographies toward arrangement by theme or topic, Matthew's narrative logic in chapters 8–9 emerges – to show Jesus as a merciful and powerful healer. An Old Testament citation (from Isaiah 53:4) at Matt 8:17, after the first trio of healing stories, confirms this portrayal of Jesus as healer:

> This fulfilled what was spoken by Isaiah the prophet: "He took our sicknesses, And carried our diseases."

We can see Matthew's attention to plotting and arrangement on a more granular level as well. For example, through intercalation (an ABA narrative pattern), the evangelist signals that the two healing stories woven together in 9:18–26 form a single unit and should be mutually interpreting:

---

[13] Although Matthew can distinguish preaching from teaching (e.g. 4:17; 5:2), especially in the ministry of the twelve apostles (see 10:7; 28:20), in 4:23–9:38 the distinction is not a significant one.

A—9:18–19   A father's plea to raise his daughter
B—9:20–22   A woman's plea to be healed from chronic illness/Jesus heals her
A—9:23–26   Jesus brings the daughter back to life

Themes of Jesus' Messianic authority and the importance of human faith in response to Jesus surface in the A parts of the account, accenting these same themes in the B section.

Another example of the interpretive importance of Matthew's arrangement of material can be seen in the Beatitudes (5:3–12), which are the first words of Jesus in the Sermon on the Mount. While much of the Sermon will turn to exhortations or commands (e.g. 5:20, 21–48; 6:1–34; 7:1–27), Matthew decidedly does not begin this Sermon with Jesus' commands. Instead, he places blessings at the front of the Sermon to announce what God has begun to do among all people to reverse the fortunes of those who are most disadvantaged and who lack societal privileges. Matthew's Jesus begins the Sermon on the Mount with the blessings of God's reign – what "is" occurring – before turning to what his disciples "ought" to be doing. For Matthew, indicative precedes imperative.

MATTHEW'S CHARACTERIZATION OF JESUS

The way in which Matthew has plotted 4:23–9:38 contributes in significant ways to his characterization of Jesus (his Christology). By arranging the episodes as he has, Matthew has accentuated Jesus as Israel's consummate teacher (5:1–7:29) and healer (8:1–9:38). Moreover, Jesus is portrayed by Matthew as authoritative in both his teaching and his healing ministries. The crowds notice and are amazed that Jesus teaches "as one who had authority and not as their scribes" (7:29). This assessment is not surprising to the reader, since Matthew has already characterized Jesus as teaching with authority in 5:21–48, where he comments directly on the Old Testament and provides his authoritative teachings on it for his followers with his refrain, "You have heard it was said ... But I say to you" (e.g., 5:21). Jesus also heals with authority; he is able to heal with a word even from a distance (8:13; cf. 15:28).

Jesus' compassion is also a crucial part of his identity as portrayed by Matthew; and compassion is frequently attributed to Jesus as he heals people. When a man with leprosy desires healing ("Lord if you are willing, you can make me clean"), Jesus affirms that he desires to heal him: "I am willing; be clean" (8:2–3; see also 9:9–13, 27). And immediately following the summary statement of 9:35, Matthew accents the compassion of Jesus for the crowds that have come to him for healing: "And when he saw the crowds, he had compassion on them, because they were distressed and discarded, like sheep without a shepherd" (9:36). Jesus' love for people mirrors that of the God he represents (5:43–48).

SCRIPTURE AND THEMES ACROSS MATTHEW 4:23–9:38

Matthew uses Scriptural (Old Testament) citations quite liberally across his Gospel and this passage is no exception (e.g., 5:21, 27, 31, 33, 38, 43; 8:17; 9:13). By doing so, he can accent and give Scriptural support for themes and ideas being developed. The citations in Matthew 5 center on interpretation of the Jewish Law (the Torah). Jesus draws on these Torah texts and, in the process, presses his followers to a higher ethic or greater righteousness (5:20). The need for applying a merciful lens to Torah interpretation and application is highlighted by Jesus' use of Hos 6:6 (at Matt 9:13; also 12:7): "I desire mercy not sacrifice." What begins to emerge in Matthew 5–9 and becomes clearer later in the Gospel is that Jesus fulfills the Torah (5:20) and calls those who follow him to a life characterized by "the weightier matters of the Torah: justice and mercy and loyalty" (23:23).

A central theme that emerges across Matt 4:23–9:38 is the arriving reign of God ("the kingdom of heaven;" e.g. 5:3, 10, 19–20; 8:11), which is, paradoxically, both now arriving and still to come (or, already and not yet; see 4:17; 5:3–10). Matthew ties the present arrival of the kingdom to Jesus' ministry of healing, preaching, and teaching. This "kingdom" ministry focuses on compassionate care for the Jewish people (4:23; 9:35), while also hinting at God's wider purposes for full inclusion of those who are Gentiles (8:5–13).

The surprising reversals accompanying God's reign are also apparent in this early part of Matthew's story. The kingdom unexpectedly belongs to those who are most destitute – those who are spiritually impoverished (5:3), those who are grief-stricken (5:4), people on the lowest rungs of society (5:5), and "those who hunger and thirst for justice" because they have been deprived of it (5:6).[14] Correspondingly, people who determine to stand in solidarity with those who are most destitute show that they belong to God's benevolent reign; these are the

[14] Brown and Roberts, *The Gospel of Matthew*, 56–58.

merciful ones (5:7), people full of integrity (5:8), those who enact peace (5:9), and people who suffer because they stand up for justice (5:10).[15]

Later in the Sermon on the Mount, Jesus calls his followers to prioritize God's reign by longing for and praying for its arrival (6:9–13). The Lord's Prayer is at its heart a kingdom prayer, with three parallel petitions requesting that God bring about restoration of all that is good:

> May your name be recognized as holy,
> May your kingdom come,
> May your will be done, as in heaven so also on earth
>   (6:9b–10)

The call to prioritizing the kingdom is reaffirmed at 6:33: "pursue above all else [God's] kingdom and promised redemption." Here, God's reign is, in part, defined by the redemption that God will bring in fullness at "the end of the age" (24:3; 28:20).

A motif in this section of Matthew that corresponds closely to the reign of God follows the Greek word, *dikaiosynē*, traditionally translated "righteousness." This word occurs seven times in Matthew, and five of these occurrences come in the Sermon on the Mount (5:6, 10, 20; 6:1, 33). This thematic clustering highlights the importance of loyalty to God and others in a section of Matthew devoted to Jesus' teachings on Torah and kingdom (5:1–7:29). Specifically, the evangelist narrates Jesus teaching his followers the importance of living out faithfulness to the commands of the Torah in the time of the arriving reign of God.

While *dikaiosynē* in Matthew has overtones with God's covenant with Israel, its specific sense in any particular use arises from the directionality of the loyalty being expressed – to God, from God, or between people. In the Beatitudes – blessings Jesus announces on those who live to see the kingdom's arrival and live in light of it – the emphasis is on restoration of "justice" (5:6, 10), communal covenant loyalty that is shown between and among people. In the body of the Sermon, Jesus' expectation that his followers exhibit a "covenant loyalty" that exceeds that of Pharisees and scribes (5:20) emphasizes Israel's loyalty to God's covenantal obligations in the Torah. The warning to avoid ostentatious obedience at 6:1 has a similar focus: "Be careful not to practice your covenant loyalty [*dikaiosynē*] in front

---

[15] Brown, "Justice, Righteousness," in *Dictionary of Jesus and the Gospels*, 464–65.

of people to be seen by them." Finally, in Jesus' call to prioritize [God's] kingdom and *dikaiosynē*, the focus rests on divine covenant loyalty – God's own covenant promises to restore the people of God. In this case, it is God's "promised redemption" that is linked to the arriving kingdom.

Another significant theme in this section of Matthew, especially apparent in the Sermon on the Mount, is that of integrity. In the Beatitudes, Jesus announces divine blessing on "those whose hearts are undivided" (5:8; traditionally "the pure in heart"). This is an image of integrity – the whole person living out consistently an ethic in line with God's benevolent reign. Jesus provides specific expressions of integrity in 5:21–48 (these verses being traditionally referred to as the "Antitheses"), in which Jesus calls for a unity of intention and action, motive and behavior. The goal is to be like God: to "be complete and whole as your Father in heaven is complete and whole" (5:48). In context, this is defined by loving others consistently and without partiality (5:45–47; cf. 9:9–13). Then Jesus turns to critique those he calls "hypocrites," whose behavior and motives are precisely not in alignment (6:1–18). In the end, ethical actions matter (7:24–27) and motivations are to be consistent with those actions.

READING THE BEGINNING AND ENDING OF JOHN AS CONVERSATION WITH GENESIS 1–2

In turning to John, we encounter a quite different way of telling the story of Jesus. While Matthew's Jesus speaks in parables and spends significant time traveling the Galilean countryside healing and preaching about God's kingdom, the Johannine Jesus never uses the specific form of parable, though he often teaches allegorically ("I am the gate for the sheep and "I am the good shepherd"; 10:7, 11), and his teachings routinely confound those who hear him. This Jesus also spends significant time in Jerusalem across his public ministry and performs just seven miracles, or "signs" as John refers to them (2:11; 4:54), only three of which are healings (4:46–54; 5:1–15; 9:1–41).

Differences also emerge from a comparison of how the two evangelists use their Scriptures. While Matthew cites the Old Testament more than fifty times, John does so only a little over a dozen times. Nevertheless, allusions are common across both Gospels. In other words, both authors layer their stories with a textual tapestry from the Old Testament. We can observe this Scriptural reliance in John through the prominent placement of early Genesis allusions at the beginning and ending of his story as well as in the central theme of life in the Fourth Gospel.[16]

WHERE JOHN BEGINS: GENESIS ECHOES IN JOHN 1:1–5

The first words of John's Gospel echo the first words of the first book of the Bible. The Septuagint of Genesis begins with the phrase, *en archē*, as does John's Gospel: "in the beginning" (Gen 1:1 [LXX]; John 1:1). It is evident that the author of John wants the reader to connect his account of the story of Jesus with God's creation of the cosmos. The first lines of John's Gospel (1:1–5) reflect this connection through a number of allusions to Genesis 1:

> [1] In the beginning was the Word, and the Word was with God, and the Word was God. [2] He was in the beginning with God. [3] All things came into being through him, and without him not one thing came into being. What has come into being [4] in him was life, and the life was the light of all people. [5] The light shines in the darkness, and the darkness did not overcome it.

There are multiple points of resonance between this first stanza of John's prologue and Genesis 1. In Genesis, God creates by speaking the world into existence (e.g., Gen 1:3, 6, 9, 11). In John, that divine speech is identified as the *logos*, the "Word" (John 1:1), a Greek term that can do double duty in terms of communication. This word not only fosters a connection with Genesis, within Greek philosophy *logos* refers to the rational principle underlying all things.

Both Genesis and John emphasize the contrast of light with darkness, showing God (and the Word) to be the source of light (or to be light itself). In Gen 1:2, darkness covers the earth until God speaks light into existence (1:3). In John, the *logos* is virtually identified with light (1:4–5), and the author uses a wordplay to show that light is greater than darkness. The darkness neither overcomes the light nor understands it (with the Greek *katalambanō* allowing for either sense). John communicates both realities in his Gospel: Jesus as the light is often misunderstood (e.g., John 3 and 4); and, even when crucified, Jesus has not been forever overcome – he will be raised again to life (John 20).

---

[16] For an extended look at this intertextual connection, see Jeannine K. Brown, "Creation's Renewal in the Gospel of John," *CBQ* 72 (2010), 275–90.

WHERE JOHN ENDS: REBREATHING THE BREATH OF LIFE (JOHN 20:22)

These initial allusions to Genesis find their counterparts in the final chapters of John; allusions to Genesis form a bracket or *inclusio* in John that connects this story of Jesus with the story of creation (Genesis 1–2). The clearest of these later allusions comes at John 20:22, where the narrator portrays Jesus *breathing* on his disciples and granting them the Holy Spirit. John uses a fairly unusual term here (*emphusaō*) for the act of breathing (i.e. conferring). It is the same term used for God *breathing* life into the first human (Gen 2:7) and the divine breath bringing Israel to life after their time in exile (Ezek 37:9). The associations are rich: For the evangelist, a kind of renewal of creation is occurring in the experience of Jesus' disciples as he imparts the Holy Spirit to them. Jesus, whom John refers to as life itself (John 1:4–5; 6:35; 11:25), now gives eternal life to his disciples (3:16; 20:30–31). Edith Humphrey suggests, "The climax of the Fourth Gospel presents Jesus as 'breathing' upon the apostles after the pattern of the creating God who breathed upon the Edenic couple; now they receive the Spirit, and not simply the gift of life."[17]

OTHER GENESIS ALLUSIONS IN JOHN 18–20

While John 1:1–5 and 20:22 provide the clearest allusions to the creation stories of Genesis, other echoes are also recognizable, especially when these various possible echoes are viewed within a narrative whole. Richard Hays, who has developed a set of criteria for determining biblical echoes, identifies recurrence as a criterion. Recurrence is the use of echoes from the same precursor text (in this case, Genesis) in more than one place in the text being analyzed (here, John).[18] Potential additional echoes to Genesis in John's passion narrative include the setting of Jesus' resurrection in a "garden" and Mary's reference to Jesus as "gardener" (19:41; 20:15); Pilate's exclamation to the crowds referring to Jesus as "the man" (19:5); and John's language of "the first day of the week" (20:1, 19).

John sets Jesus' crucifixion and resurrection in a garden: "Now there was a garden in the place where he was crucified, and in the garden there

---

[17] Edith M. Humphrey, "New Creation," in *Dictionary for Theological Interpretation of the Bible*, ed. Kevin J. Vanhoozer (Grand Rapids, 2005), 536–37.
[18] Richard B. Hays, *Echoes of Scripture in the Letters of Paul* (New Haven, CT, 1989), 30.

was a new tomb in which no one had been laid" (19:41). John routinely repeats this physical setting across his narrative of Jesus' death and resurrection (18:1, 26; 19:41; 20:15). This identification gains further significance since John is the only one of the four Gospel writers to locate Jesus' death and resurrection in a garden.

Through this setting, John reminds the reader of humanity's original garden setting as portrayed in Gen 2:8–10.[19] Through this correlation, the author seems to suggest that Jesus' death and resurrection set in motion a renewal of creation (or "new creation," which is Paul's language in 2 Cor 5:17; Gal 6:15). The connection is strengthened further by Mary Magdalene's notion that Jesus is the gardener (20:15). While on the story level of John, Mary is clearly mistaken in her identification, the author on the discourse level may very well want readers to recognize the connection to Genesis. "Mary thinks that Jesus is the gardener. The real question is, is she right or wrong?"[20] If this moment of identification is meant to echo Genesis 2, what might be its significance? It is quite possible that John may be reminding his reader of Adam – the first gardener (Gen 2:15) – whose role at the origin of humanity prefigures Jesus, who now represents a renewed and restored humanity.

Another narrative moment that would confirm this Adam Christology – Jesus as a kind of second Adam – comes during Jesus' trial before Pilate, the Roman governor or prefect in Jerusalem (John 18:28–19:16b). As Pilate brings Jesus out to the crowd after he has been flogged and demeaned by the Roman soldiers, Pilate says, "Here is the man!" (19:5). Like Mary's words, which seem to have more to say than Mary intends, Pilate's words might be used by the evangelist to highlight Jesus' role as "second Adam" and his inauguration of creation's renewal.

Not only is the resurrection set in a garden, it is also set on "the first day of the week" – a temporal setting that is mentioned twice by John for emphasis (20:1, 19). In this way, the evangelist stresses that Jesus is raised at the beginning of a new week, another likely signal of the renewal of creation. If we return to Genesis, we hear that after six days of creation, God rests on the seventh day (2:2–3). In John, Jesus' death and resurrection functions to complete that first creative week; we might even hear this intimated in Jesus' final words, "It is finished" (19:30). In his new resurrected life, Jesus inaugurates a new week of creation. Additionally, the phrase in John 20:26, "a week later,"

---

[19] For a discussion of the two distinct Greek words for garden used by the Septuagint of Genesis and in John's Gospel, see Brown, "Creation's Renewal," 280.

[20] Edwyn C. Hoskyns, "Genesis I–III and St. John's Gospel," *JTS* 21 (1920), 214.

translates the Greek phrase, *meth' hēmeras oktō,* which can be more formally rendered, "after eight days." John's use of this language of *an eighth day* finds expression in later Christian writers, including the author of the Epistle of Barnabas, who refers to "the beginning of an eighth day, which is the beginning of a different world" (*Barn.* 15.8).

JOHN AND THE MOTIF OF LIFE

It is no secret that the theme of life features prominently in John's Gospel. In addition to the way the author has "front-ended" this theme (John 1:1–5), the reader will catch its importance through sheer repetition: The word "life" (Greek, *zōē*) occurs almost fifty times across the Fourth Gospel. This motif culminates in the expressed purpose statement of John's Gospel (20:30–31):

> [30] Now Jesus did many other signs in the presence of his disciples, which are not written in this book. [31] But these are written so that you may come to believe that Jesus is the Messiah, the Son of God, and that through believing you may have life in his name.

The highest goal for humanity is identified as life, which arises from faith (another key theme in John's Gospel). And this (eternal) life comes from Jesus, with "life in his name" meaning something like "life in him" (i.e. life in his very person). This purpose statement invites the reader to understand life as coming from Jesus and shared with those who trust in him. For John, Jesus is the giver of life and his followers receive life from him.

We see these twin motifs across the Gospel. First, John identifies Jesus himself as life (see 5:26). Jesus is "the bread of life" (6:35, 48, 51), "the resurrection and the life" (11:25), and "the way, and the truth, and the life" (14:6). John also invites people to receive this life – that is Jesus – from Jesus. Those who believe in him receive eternal life (3:15–16, 36; 6:40, 47); Jesus gives a living water that sustains those who drink it (4:14); and Jesus grants abundant life (10:10).

Given the way John begins and ends his Gospel echoing Genesis themes of creation and life, it is important to link what we hear across his Gospel about this motif of life with the renewal of creation. Life in John is not so much a philosophical or a private concept; instead, it is a communal and embodied one. John perceives in Jesus restoration of life – indeed, restoration of creation itself. And these themes are best heard by a careful and close reading of John's Gospel as story.

CONCLUSION

In this essay, we have explored the Gospels of the New Testament for their genre and storied features. We suggested a narrative approach to interpreting the Gospels that capitalizes on these storied features. This approach was then employed on Matthew and John. In Matthew, we looked at an extended section of the Gospel – Jesus' early Galilean ministry of teaching and healing narrated in 4:23–9:38. In John, we analyzed the author's use of Genesis 1–2 and some of its themes at the beginning and the end of that Gospel. The goal in each case has been to attend to the storied contours of Gospels, thereby providing an additional window into their unique literary qualities.

Further Reading

Bauer, David R., The Structure of Matthew's Gospel: A Study in Literary Design, *JSNT Supp.* 31 (1998).

Burridge, Richard A., *What Are the Gospels? A Comparison with Graeco-Roman Biography*, 2nd ed. (Grand Rapids, MI, 2004).

Green, Joel B., *Practicing Theological Interpretation* (Grand Rapids, MI, 2011).

Green, Joel B., Jeannine K. Brown, and Nicholas Perrin, eds., *Dictionary of Jesus and the Gospels*, rev. ed. (Downers Grove, IL, 2013).

Hays, Richard B., *Echoes of Scripture in the Letters of Paul* (New Haven, CT, 1989).

Stanton, Graham. *Jesus of Nazareth in New Testament Preaching* (New York, 1974).

Vanhoozer, Kevin J., ed. *Dictionary for Theological Interpretation of the Bible* (Grand Rapids, MI, 2005).

9 Paul's Letters

TODD D. STILL

INTRODUCTION

Paul of Tarsus, who was also known in certain circles as Saul (see Acts 9:11; 13:9), was by any measure a complex character. By virtue of a life-changing encounter with the risen Jesus en route to Damascus, a one-time zealous Pharisee, who sought to destroy the nascent church, became a demonstrably successful, frequently controversial apostle of the gospel to the Gentiles (see esp. Gal 1:11–24).

As an apostle, he traveled extensively throughout the Eastern Mediterranean world, making converts and founding fledgling fellowships of Christ-followers. In order to be able to preach the gospel to people free of charge (1 Cor 9:18), Paul labored as a leather-worker (Acts 18:3; 1 Thess 2:9). Partly due to his sense of his apostolic vocation and partly due to his capacity to stir up controversy, Paul was unable to remain indefinitely in any of the strategic, largely urban centers where he proclaimed the gospel and established churches.

This created for Paul a double bind. On the one hand, he could only be physically present with one church at a time. On the other hand, he felt a deep spiritual affinity with and responsibility for all churches, not least those he founded (2 Cor 11:28). This conundrum gave rise to Paul's invention of the pastoral letter. As a substitute and surrogate for his personal presence, Paul composed and sent letters to both congregations and persons. Indeed, there is evidence suggesting that certain of Paul's letters may even have circulated among congregations during his lifetime (Col 4:16). A number of letters written by Paul remain extant.

Pauline interpreters differ in their thinking regarding which surviving letter Paul first wrote (the leading candidates are 1 Thessalonians and Galatians). They also disagree as to how many of the thirteen New Testament letters bearing Paul's name can rightly be attributed to him (views range from as few as seven to all thirteen). About this, however, there is little to no scholarly debate – Paul was the genesis and genius of the letter *genre* that dominates the New Testament literary landscape (twenty-one of the twenty-seven New Testament documents are letters/epistles).

As it happens, during his own life (roughly 5–65 CE) and ministry (ca. 35–65 CE), Paul developed a reputation as a formidable letter writer, even among his apostolic opponents. Although Paul's critics regarded both his appearance and his speech to be unimpressive, they conceded that his letters were "weighty and forceful" (2 Cor 10:10), if sometimes difficult to comprehend (2 Pet 3:16). Given the valuable Christian instruction contained within Paul's letters, the New Testament document known as 2 Peter (thought by most New Testament scholars to have been written by one other than Peter in the early to mid-second century CE) describes certain, unnamed Pauline letters as Scripture (2 Pet 3:15–16).

In due time, believers the world over would come to regard no less than thirteen letters attributed to Paul as Scripture. The purpose of this essay is to introduce readers to the letters of Paul in their original historical context with the hope of fostering a greater understanding of, appreciation for, and conversation about his literary work and legacy.

GALATIANS AND ROMANS

With respect to certain portions of Galatians and Romans in particular, it is easy to appreciate why some people have regarded certain things in Paul's letters as hard to understand. In Galatians, which by all academic accounts was written prior to Romans (be it in the late 40s or early to mid-50s), Paul is at pains to impress on Galatian congregations (be they in South or North Galatia), comprising Gentiles (see 4:8) who came to believe through Paul's ministry in their midst, *not* to be circumcised (so, e.g. 5:2). Paul was deeply disturbed by the prospect that his Gentile male converts in Galatia would be persuaded by his Jewish-Christian missionary competitors to receive circumcision and to live according to various other strictures set forth in the Jewish law. Indeed, Paul was so concerned that he fashioned a fiery communiqué to dissuade the Galatians from turning to what the apostle viewed to be a categorically different gospel – one lived according to the law and not according to Christ.

At the outset of a letter, whose strength eclipses its length, Paul dispenses with spiritual pleasantries and forcefully denounces those who are preaching a gospel other than the one that he first proclaimed to the Galatians and that they readily received. The apostle's agitation with the agitators or troublers, which is apparent at various places within the letter, not least in his pronouncing *anathemas* on them and wishing that they might emasculate themselves (see 1:8–9; 5:12), is not due only, or even primarily, to his opponents' seeming disparagement of his apostolic call and credentials (note 1:10–12). Rather, Paul's passion is ignited by his Jewish-Christian opponents calling into question whether his Gentile converts could be God's children without following the works of the Mosaic law, especially circumcision (see 2:16). That is to say, Paul's ire is stoked by the agitators' casting aspersions on the gospel that he received from and preached regarding Christ.

Building on the personal examples he sets forth in chapters 1–2, in chapters 3–4 Paul appeals to both the Galatians' experience in the faith as well as to Scripture (i.e. the Old Testament) in an effort to persuade his converts to stay the spiritual course and to counter his competitors. In contrast to the agitators' claims regarding the ongoing validity of the works of the law for Gentile Christians, particularly circumcision, Paul declares that their (and by way of extension, other Gentiles') experience of the Spirit when coupled with the teaching Scripture – not least regarding Abraham – establishes that right standing before God through Christ is predicated on and determined by faith and not the law.

If this line of theological reasoning seems cogent, coherent, and even convincing, it would not have been immediately compelling for those who contested Paul's reading and appropriation of Scripture. Appealing to Abraham's belief in God and God's promise to him as paradigmatic and applicable for Gentiles, Paul maintains through the selective citing and creative interpreting of Scripture that Christ redeems those who believe in him from the curse of the law, which was both necessary and temporary (see, e.g., 3:7–14; 3:15–22; 4:21–31). Throughout Galatians, including the often dense, sometimes difficult, but never boring chapters 3–4 (note esp. Paul's allegory in 4:21–31), Paul's conviction that God sent Christ to redeem sinful people from the curse of the law through Christ's faithful death drives Paul's biblical interpretation and shapes his conclusions.

Furthermore, Paul seeks to demonstrate in chapters 5–6 that Christ's faithful death and subsequent resurrection, along with the empowerment of the promised now palpable Spirit of God's Son, makes it possible for believers to live out the law's demand to love one's neighbor as oneself (note Gal 5:14 citing Lev 19:18), not least within the church (6:10). If Christ's freedom and the Spirit's fruit are to be made manifest within and among the churches of God in Galatia, however, they must eschew the burden of the law and its enslavement and embrace a life of faith working through love (see esp. 5:1–6, 22–23).

Paul's longer, later letter to the Romans (written ca. 57 CE from Corinth) shares a number of themes in common with Galatians (to mention but seven – sin, faith, justification, Abraham, the law, the Holy Spirit, and Israel) and has proven to be every bit as demanding, if not confounding, for readers and would-be interpreters. As it happens, no preserved Pauline letter has commended itself more or commanded (and demanded) more interpretive attention than Romans. Across the centuries, it has been particularly influential in informing and shaping Christian thought and doctrine, not least through the writings of Augustine (354–430), Martin Luther (1483–1546), and, more recently, Karl Barth (1886–1968).

It was neither for posterity nor for matters of theological inquiry, however, that Paul wrote Romans. Rather, the apostle composed his most expansive, extant letter in order to introduce the gospel he preached to and to garner support from Christ-followers living in Rome. Having proclaimed the gospel from Jerusalem to Illyricum (located on the eastern shore of the Adriatic Sea), Paul indicates that there was no further place for him to preach in those regions (i.e. urban centers in the Eastern Mediterranean; note Rom 15:19–23). As a result, he had set his sights on Spain. He was hopeful, however, that en route to Spain he might at long last visit Rome and proclaim the gospel there too. Before traveling westward, however, he was preparing to journey eastward to Jerusalem to deliver a collection from Grecian congregations to impoverished believers in the holy city (see Rom 1:10–15; 15:22–31; cf. 2 Cor 8–9).

In advance, then, of a long-awaited and much-anticipated visit to Rome, Paul wrote to Christians living in Rome, not a few of whom he already knew (so Rom 16:3–16). Given that his reputation for teaching both to good and ill effect preceded him (see Rom 3:8) and that he was hopeful that Roman congregations would support his announced Spanish mission (Rom 15:24), Paul seemingly regarded it as prudent, if not necessary, to pave the way for his coming by writing a letter. And write a letter he did – one some 7,111 Greek words in length! In Galatians, Paul reports that he presented to the Jerusalem pillars (i.e. James, Cephas [Peter], and John) the gospel that he preached among the Gentiles (Gal 2:2); in Romans, Paul arguably sets forth his gospel in terms and tone akin to what he might have preached were he to have been present in Rome (note Rom 1:15). Of the gospel – empowered by and revealing of God – Paul was not ashamed and believed that it brought salvation to all who would believe, be they Jew or Greek (Rom 1:16).

In the first three chapters of Romans, Paul seeks to establish that all people are sinful and are, moreover, culpable before and accountable to a righteous God (see, e.g., 3:9, 19–20). Having painted a black backdrop, declaring that "all have sinned and have fallen short of the glory of God" (Rom 3:23), the apostle propounds that God's grace and redemption are made possible by and may be found in Christ Jesus through faith and apart from the works of the law (Rom 3:28). To illustrate justification before God by faith, Paul appeals to Abraham. As with Abraham, the apostle maintains that those who entrust themselves to God – now through the crucified, resurrected Christ – are rectified, redeemed, and reconciled (see Rom 4).

In the next panel of the epistle, namely Romans 5–8, Paul considers the impact of having been justified by faith in the lives of believers. Peace, grace, hope, and love abound for those who embrace and rejoice in Christ's justifying, reconciling death and resurrection (Rom 5:1–11). Furthermore, Paul contends that even as sin, death, and condemnation entered the human race through the disobedience of Adam, grace, life, and righteousness came through the obedience of Jesus Christ (Rom 5:12–21). "Where sin had abounded [in Adam]," Paul declares, "grace super-abounded [in Christ]" (Rom 5:20).

Given the surplus of God's grace in the midst of human sin, one might well reason that one would do well to sin all the more. To conclude as much, however, would reveal a clear misapprehension of what it means to be Christian, according to Paul. Having been buried with Christ through the ritual of baptism, it is incumbent on believers to lead lives of righteousness leading to life and not lives of sin leading to death. If Christ-followers were formerly slaves to sin resulting in wickedness, they were now to be enslaved to righteousness resulting in holiness (Rom 6:1–23). "For the wages of sin is death, but the grace-gift of God is eternal life in Jesus Christ our Lord" (Rom 6:23).

Paul continues in Romans 7–8 to reflect on what it means for believers to live not under the law, but under grace (Rom 6:14). Having died to the old way of the law that once bound them, they are now released to serve in the new way of the Spirit. By way of analogy, Paul propounds that those who live by the Spirit are no more bound by the law than a widow is to her deceased husband (7:1–6). Whereas those who live by the law are enslaved to the law, which both identifies and exacerbates sin (7:7–25; N.B. The "I" in this section of Romans, which has been variously interpreted and hotly debated, appears to be both autobiographical and paradigmatic for one living life under the law), those who are in Christ live by the law of the Spirit that frees one from the law of sin and death (8:1). By associating the law with sin and death, Paul seeks to dissuade Roman believers from living under its sway.

Instead, the apostle appeals to them to live in the realm of the Spirit (8:5–13), for "those who are led by the Spirit of God are the children of God" (8:14). As God's adopted children and by virtue of the presence and empowerment of the Spirit, they can cry out to God as Father (8:15).

Present sufferings notwithstanding, God's children – along with creation – can live in hope of redemption (8:18–25). The Spirit's intercession coupled with God's good intention to conform believers into the image of his Son emboldens the people of God to live as more than conquerors. In drawing this section of Romans (i.e. chs. 5–8) to a conclusion, Paul assures his beleaguered recipients that no force from any place can separate them from God's love in the Lord Jesus Christ (8:26–39).

Turning to Romans 9–11, the interpretative sledding gets tougher still. As Paul puzzles over the spiritual plight of his fellow Israelites, he is greatly grieved. Despite decided spiritual advantages, taken together, Paul's Jewish kith and kin were not responding positively to the gospel (9:1–5). Unwilling to countenance the possibility that God's word had failed or that God is unjust (9:6, 14), Paul seeks to establish on the basis of select Scriptures – including texts drawn from Genesis, Malachi, Exodus, Isaiah, and Hosea – that God's mercy is not limited to Israel alone any more than being an Israelite according to the flesh in and of itself ensures one's status as a child of God (so Rom 9).

At the outset of Romans 10, Paul reiterates his hope and prayer that his fellow Israelites might embrace God's grace given through Christ – the *telos* (meaning end, aim, or perhaps both) of the law for all who believe (10:1–4). Additionally, by appealing to various verses from Leviticus, Deuteronomy, Isaiah, and Joel, the apostle reinforces his claim that God will save all people – both Jew and Gentile – who declare that Jesus is Lord and believe that God resurrected him (10:5–13). Textual citations from Isaiah, Psalms, and Deuteronomy also shape Paul's understanding that although the gospel must be proclaimed not all (Israelites) will accept it (10:14–21).

That being said, hope springs eternal in the apostle's breast. Insisting that God is not rejecting but is still electing his people by grace, as in the days of Elijah (quoting from 1 Kgs 19:10, 14, 18 in 11:4–5) – though to be sure, some, as of old, are not spiritually capable of seeing or hearing (11:7–10 citing portions of Deut 29:4; Isa 29:10; and Ps 69:22–23) – Paul maintains that Israel has not stumbled so as to fall. Rather, Paul remains resolute in his hope that through God's inclusion of and his mission to the Gentiles that his fellow Israelites will also embrace God's grace through Christ (11:11–16). Meanwhile, the apostle reminds Gentiles who have been grafted in that they have no grounds for boasting (11:17–24) and that God is able to save the whole of Israel (see 11:25–27; Isa 59:20–21; Jer 31:33–34). Convinced that God's gifts and calling are unalterable, Paul anticipates a great reversal on the part of Israel, akin to what had taken place among the Gentiles, wherein the disobedient become obedient and God's mercy rains down on all (11:28–32). Thus, Paul praises God for his wisdom and knowledge and lauds the LORD as creator, sustainer, and savior (11:33–36 citing Isa 40:13 and Job 41:11).

On the heels of his dense, demanding, Scripture-saturated reflections on his mission and proclamation to the Gentiles and the place of Israel therein in chapters 9–11, Paul devotes the final portion of Romans (i.e. chapters 12–15) to instructing believers as to how they might live so as to please God. According to Paul, transformed living (note 12:1–2) entails, among other things, humble service to God and others in the context of a loving, caring community (12:3–21; 13:8–10), (a highly contextualized call of) submitting to governing authorities (13:1–7), and an understanding that the soon-return of Christ requires upright moral behavior (13:11–14).

Paul draws his lengthy letter to a close with matters of pressing concern as well as personal greetings in 15:14–16:27 (N.B. Scholars have sometimes thought that chapter 16 was not a part of the original letter, a view that now seldom commands attention). Before doing so, however, he instructs Roman believers who consider themselves strong with respect to whether certain foods should or should not be eaten and whether certain days should or should not be observed to bear with the so-called weak, who have scruples regarding diet and days (14:1–15:6). In a word, in keeping with Scripture (note 2 Sam 22:50; Ps 18:49; Deut 32:43; Ps 117:1; Isa 11:10 in 15:9–12), Paul envisions communities of Christ-followers, comprising both Jews and Gentiles in Rome and elsewhere, who "accept one another … just as Christ accepted [them], in order to bring praise to God" (15:7).

THE CORINTHIAN CORRESPONDENCE

Paul's passion for congregational unity, maturity, and purity also animates the large Pauline letter known to us as 1 Corinthians. As it happens, the pastoral missive called 1 Corinthians is but one of many contacts that the apostle had with that Grecian assembly. Following Paul's first visit to Corinth around 50 CE, at which time he founded the church (see Acts 18:1–18), he composed a now-lost letter to the assembly that included instructions as to how believers should relate to others engaged in sexual immorality (so 1 Cor 5:9). Sometime thereafter (likely in the early to mid-50s CE from Ephesus), Paul fashioned 1 Corinthians in response to reported divisions and disorders in Corinth on the one hand (note 1 Cor 1:10–12; 16:17–18) and raised questions and concerns from the Corinthians on the other (1 Cor 7:1).

At the outset of the letter, Paul calls a fractured fellowship to concord in Christ and challenges them to fix their focus on Jesus Christ and him crucified, the very message the apostle proclaimed in their midst (1:10–2:5). This foolish proclamation, which flies in the face of conventional wisdom, is to serve as the foundation of any Christian congregation, including the one in Corinth (so 2:6–3:23). Paul insisted on as much amid different, competing visions that had developed within the congregation as to what the Christian existence and experience was meant to be (note 3:1–4:21).

Identifiable forms of tension between Paul and various Corinthians included how best to respond to a case of incest (5:1–13) and how best to adjudicate disagreements between believers (6:1–11), not to mention Paul's disbelief that any number of the assembly continued to frequent prostitutes (6:12–20). While some within the Corinthian congregation were actively engaged in what Paul unequivocally regarded to be sexual immorality, others within the assembly were rejecting sexual relations altogether and advocating that other believers do likewise, seemingly even within the bonds of marriage (7:1–5). As it happens, Paul was single – at least when he composed 1 Corinthians – and wished that others might also be celibate (7:7). As 1 Corinthians 7 reveals, for reasons both theological and practical, Paul thought the single life to be preferable. That being said, Paul's habit of heart and mind at that given time was for Christ-followers to remain as they were – whether married or unmarried, circumcised or uncircumcised, slave or free – believing that the time was short and that the world as it was passing away (7:29, 31).

Various views and palpable tensions also existed between Paul and the Corinthians (and among the Corinthians themselves) regarding whether or not to eat meat that had been sacrificed to idols (in idols' temples) (8:1–11:1) and how best to observe the Lord's Supper (11:17–34). Paul was particularly troubled that those who were comparatively strong and successful were treating the weak and vulnerable within the church with disrespect and as dispensable. There was also conflict and competition in Corinth regarding how (and if) women/wives were meant to participate in worship (11:2–16; 14:34–36) and how prominent a place was to be accorded to *glossolalia* (or speaking in tongues, i.e. ecstatic spiritual utterances) among the *charismata* (i.e., spiritual gifts) as well as when the church gathered for worship (12:1–14:40). Most problematic for Paul, however, was the fact that some Corinthians were for some reason(s) contending that there is no such thing as resurrection from the dead. For Paul, this was tantamount to a denial of and a desertion from the very faith that he had proclaimed to them and that they had received from him. The apostle responds to this deleterious development in some detail in chapter 15, by declaring that Christ has indeed been resurrected (15:20) and by assuring believers that they will also be raised at the time of Christ's coming so that death might be swallowed up in resurrection victory (15:23; 54–57 [citing Isa 25:8 and Hos 13:14]).

Difficulties and discord notwithstanding, Paul was resolute in his commitment to stay in contact with the Corinthians. Indeed, even as 1 Corinthians concludes by outlining Paul's hoped-for plans for continued interaction with the congregation (see chapter 16), 2 Corinthians commences with Paul referring to a painful, second visit (2:1) and to a tearful letter (2:4). When writing 2 Corinthians (likely from Macedonia in the mid-50s CE [note 2:13; 7:5]), which is at least the fourth letter that he wrote to the church and may itself be a composite document (comprising, according to scholars, anywhere from two to five letters), Paul is anticipating his third visit to Corinth (13:1), which seemingly was his last (see Rom 16:21–23).

As it comes to us, 2 Corinthians begins with a benediction, where Paul blesses the "God of all consolation" who had recently delivered him from a deadly peril (seemingly in Ephesus) (1:3–11). Thereafter, Paul turns his attention to repairing his imperiled, fractious relationship with the Corinthian fellowship. Assuring them of both his integrity and his forgiveness of a now-unknown person for an unspecified act (1:12–2:11), Paul reflects on the nature and character of his apostolic ministry with special respect to the Corinthians (2:12–7:15), whom he describes as a living letter of Christ (3:1–6). Weakness and frailty notwithstanding (4:1–5:10), Paul espouses a ministry of the Spirit (3:8), proclaiming Jesus as Lord (4:5), and a ministry of reconciliation (5:18), imploring people – including the Corinthians – to be reconciled to God (5:20). Furthermore, Paul pleads the Corinthians to embrace him even as he has them (6:11–13), maintaining that he would live or die with them (7:2–4). If the coming of Titus (a Pauline coworker) to Paul in Macedonia (that is, northern Greece) from Corinth (in southern Greece) with a (largely) positive report regarding the church and its relationship to its missioners was a source of encouragement to Paul (7:5–16), the rest of the letter indicates that significant relational and ministerial obstacles remained.

The so-called Jerusalem Collection, addressed in chapters 8–9, was one such identifiable challenge. Even as Paul was actively engaged in soliciting and preparing for the delivery of a gift from his largely Gentile congregations in the eastern Mediterranean to impoverished believers in Jerusalem, the apostle was clearly anxious about the Corinthians' commitment to and participation in the offering. Thus, he seeks to cajole and counsel them, as it were, to put their money where their mouths were. Holding up Macedonian assemblies as exemplary (8:1–5) and appealing to the grace of Christ (8:9) and the generosity of God (9:6–11), Paul implores the Corinthians to make good on their commitment to contribute to the Collection, to finish what they had started and thus spare all involved embarrassment (8:6–7, 10–12; 9:1–5). The apostle states that he does not want to burden the Corinthians (8:13–15). Neither does he desire for them to grudgingly or under compulsion (9:5, 7). He clearly wants them, however, to give cheerfully and bountifully to the Collection (9:12–15). (If Rom 15:26 –27 is any indication, then it would appear that this was what eventually happened.)

Meanwhile, 2 Corinthians 10–13 reveal an acute conflict between Paul and those he sarcastically and derisively dubs "super-apostles" (11:5; 12:11). Given the fact that we only know of these people through Paul's occasional, polemical remarks, our knowledge of this group is partial. It does appear, however, that when speaking of the super-apostles Paul has in view a group of Jewish-Christian competitors who were actively, if belatedly, engaged in ministry in Corinth (10:15–16; 11:12–15, 22). Additionally, it would appear that these people were casting aspersions on both Paul's person and approach to ministry (e.g., 11:5–11; 12:11–21). To combat these opponents, Paul appeals to weakness and hardship, including a now unidentifiable thorn or stake in the flesh (11:16–12:10). The epistolary library that comes to us in the form of 1–2 Corinthians concludes with a Trinitarian benediction (13:14).

THE THESSALONIAN CORRESPONDENCE

If Paul's relationship with the Corinthians was characterized by conflict, his interactions with the Thessalonians were marked by concord. Not long after Paul was forced to depart from Thessalonica (note 1 Thess 2:2, 15; cf. Acts 17:1–10a), he composed, apparently from Corinth, what may well be his earliest surviving letter, namely, 1 Thessalonians (written ca. 50 CE). In this missive, Paul reminisces on his initial ministry in that ancient seaport city. He fondly recalls the Thessalonians' reception of the gospel amid affliction and employs familial metaphors (see 2:7, 11, 17) to describe their life together (1:1–2:16). The apostle heaps praise on the Thessalonians, describing them as his joy, glory, and crown and referring to them as beloved (2:8, 19–20). Furthermore, he assures them of his ongoing care for and commitment to them, made manifest by his sending of Timothy in his stead to strengthen and encourage them in their faith (2:17–3:13).

Though absent, through written communication Paul was able to continue to instruct the Thessalonians. In 1 Thessalonians, he exhorts the assembly to sexual purity (4:3–8), "brotherly love" (4:9–11), and productive, respectable living (4:11–12). He also encourages them in the midst of their mourning over deceased loved ones in Christ to recall the promise of Christ's coming (Greek – *parousia*) and resurrection hope (4:13–18). Until Christ comes like a thief in the night (5:2), Paul calls the assembly to live as "children of the light ... and day" (5:5), putting on spiritual armor (5:8), building each other up (5:11), and living together in peace, patience, sympathy, purity, joy, and gratitude, striving "to do good for one another and for all people" as they are guided and undergirded by the Spirit (5:12–22).

Contemporary scholars differ as to whether Paul actually wrote 2 Thessalonians. If he did not, then it is probable that a Pauline disciple took up the apostle's mantle to address various concerns facing (Pauline) congregations near the close of the first century CE, not least how believers ought to comport themselves in the troubled time between Christ's resurrection and return. If he did, then it is likely that not long after composing 1 Thessalonians Paul felt it necessary, likely due to reports that had come to him in Corinth regarding the church in Thessalonica, to offer the congregation further encouragement and instruction in their newfound faith.

Regardless, the three-chapter letter named 2 Thessalonians focuses primarily on three matters. At the outset of the letter, the author – be it Paul or another – seeks to comfort the beleaguered recipients by assuring them that the affliction that is theirs will ultimately give way to rest, even as God will hold their opponents accountable (see 1:3–12). Furthermore, 2 Thessalonians is at pains to impress on its audience that the day of the Lord has yet to come, despite claims to the contrary. Indeed, the writer insists that day will not come until various end-time events occur, most notably the revelation and destruction of the man of lawlessness (2:1–12). Meanwhile, the congregation is called to stand firm and hold fast to the traditions entrusted to them (2:13–17), including teaching regarding working and eating (3:6–15). Avoiding idleness and unruliness, they were to "settle down and earn the food they [were to] eat" (3:12).

PHILIPPIANS AND PHILEMON

Paul also experienced a rich, reciprocal relationship and partnership (Greek – *koinōnia*) in the gospel with the Philippian congregation. Seemingly the first assembly the apostle founded on Grecian/European soil in the late 40s CE (see Acts 16:11–40), over the years and the miles Paul and the Philippians were able to stay in close contact with one another (note Phil 1:5–6; 4:15–16). In fact, Paul's well-known, well-loved letter to the Philippians was spawned by a gift that the fellowship had sent to him through one Epaphroditus while he was in chains, probably in Rome but possibly in Ephesus (so 1:7, 13; 2:25–30; 4:10, 14, 18, 22). If Paul wrote to the Philippians from Ephesus, then the letter would date to the mid-50s CE; if written from Rome, then the letter is best dated to the early 60s CE.

Place and date of writing notwithstanding, Paul composed Philippians to express his gratitude to a congregation who had been with him through thick and thin. Other identifiable reasons for the apostle's composition of Philippians – punctuated with some of the most memorable lines ever penned by Paul (so, e.g., 1:6, 21; 2:1–13; 3:7–11; 4:4–13, 19) – include: 1. A personal update from an upbeat apostle with special reference to the gospel (1:12–26); 2. Encouragement for the church to stand fast and to hold firm as a unified fellowship (1:27-2:18; 4:1–3); 3. Affirmation of Timothy and Epaphroditus, respectively (2:18–30); and 4. A warning against (potential) opponents (3:1–6, 17–21).

Paul also wrote the comparatively brief, 335-word letter to Philemon while in chains (vv. 1, 9, 12), whether in Ephesus or in Rome (see previously). This semi-private letter is unique among the preserved Pauline letters, wherein Paul appeals to a slave-owner (Philemon) on behalf of his slave (Onesimus). For some unknown reason the latter – whose name means useful (note the pun in v. 11) – had a falling out with his master and somehow came into contact with Paul thereafter (likely by intentionally seeking him out and/or by being directed to him by [a] believer[s]).

Through Paul's influence, Onesimus became a believer (v. 10) and subsequently agreed to return to his master – who seems to have resided in the town of Colossae in the Lycus River Valley (some 100 miles to the east of Ephesus) (note Col 4:9) – with the letter now known as Philemon in hand (v. 12). In this masterful little epistle, Paul praises Philemon, also led to faith through Paul, for his partnership in the faith and his support of fellow believers (vv. 1–2, 4–7, 19, 23–24).

Paul's purpose in crafting the letter is not simply to glad-hand or to ingratiate Philemon; rather, he hoped to secure a warm welcome for Onesimus as a fellow believer on his return home (see esp. vv. 15–17). What remains less than clear is the reason for the conflict between the two in the first place and precisely what Paul wanted Philemon to do on Onesimus' return (vv. 14, 17, 20–21). One gathers that had Paul his druthers, Philemon would have sent Onesimus back to the apostle's shackled side (vv. 12–13). It is often thought that the very preservation of the letter signals a positive response by Philemon to Paul's request, whatever its precise nature.

COLOSSIANS AND EPHESIANS

Colossians is a third letter that Paul, if it was he, wrote from captivity (note 4:3, 10, 18). Along with 2 Thessalonians, Ephesians, and the Pastoral Epistles (see above and below), a majority of contemporary Pauline scholars regard Colossians to be pseudonymous (i.e. written in Paul's name by one other than he). Whether Paul wrote Colossians from Ephesian or Roman captivity in the mid-50s to early 60s CE or another composed the letter in his name in the latter part of the first century CE, from beginning to end Colossians extols and exalts Christ as the be-all and end-all (so, e.g., Col 1:19; 2:9; 3:11). Indeed, Colossians may be rightly regarded and referred to as a Christological epistle.

The ostensible reason for the writing of Colossians was to combat a movement afoot in Colossae that was thought to deprecate Christ by adding various restrictions and observances to life in faith (note esp. 2:4, 8–9, 16–23). Colossians attempts to counter this influence, which it describes as a "philosophy and empty deceit" centered on "human traditions according to the elemental principles (or powers) of the world" (2:8), by lauding Christ as Lord of creation and of the Church (1:15–20), by reminding the recipients of the transformative work that had been wrought in their lives through the cross of Christ and their being raised to new life in him (see 1:19, 22; 2:11–15; 3:1–4), and by calling believers in Colossae to "live a life worthy of the Lord and to please him in every way" (1:10; cf. 2:6: "As you received Christ Jesus as Lord, walk [that is, live] in him.").

On the one hand, given that their lives were "now hidden with Christ in God" (3:3), the Colossians were to put to death various vices that marked and marred their old way of living (3:5–11). On the other hand, they were to clothe themselves with Christ-like virtues (3:12–14) and to do all things with gratitude as unto the Lord (3:17). In church and family life, as well as in their interaction with outsiders (3:15–4:6), they were to offer a winsome witness, realizing that they were being "renewed in knowledge in the image of the Creator," where there is neither "Gentile or Jew, circumcised or uncircumcised, Barbarian, Scythian, slave, [or] free" (3:10–11).

Colossians concludes with various greetings from given individuals (4:7–18), some of which form a (literary) connection with Philemon (see, e.g. the naming of Onesimus, Aristarchus, Mark, Luke, Demas, and Archippus). At the conclusion of Colossians, mention is also made of a letter from Laodicea (4:16). Over time, some commentators have sought to link this letter with the letter we now know as Ephesians. Given that Ephesians is a cyclical letter, akin to 1 Peter and Revelation, this is a tantalizing suggestion. (N.B. The words "in Ephesus," which appear in English translations of Eph 1:1, are missing from some of the earliest and best manuscripts of Ephesians and were probably not original to the epistle.) A one-for-one correlation, however, is not possible. Neither is it possible to know with certitude whether Paul or a disciple writing in his name composed the epistle in the mid-50s to early 60s CE from Ephesian or Roman captivity (note 3:1; 6:20) or from an unknown location near the end of the first century CE. It is possible, however, to trace the thought-lines of this highly influential letter.

Ephesians begins with a benediction, praising God for the glorious grace lavished on believers in and through Christ (1:3–14; cf. 2 Corinthians and 1 Peter). A prayer follows for believers to know God better, especially the hope and power of God given and displayed through the resurrected, reigning Lord Jesus Christ (1:15–23). Because God through his love, mercy, grace, and kindness has saved believers through faith, they are to do good works for God (2:1–10). Once uncircumcised Gentiles, estranged from God and the good, they have now been reconciled to God through the blood of Christ and thus can live in peace with God and God's people as a holy temple by the Spirit (2:11–22).

In chapter 3, the letter's recipients are reminded of the mystery of Christ entrusted to Paul, namely, that through the glorious gospel Gentiles are now heirs with Israel. Although previously hidden, the manifold wisdom of God made manifest in Christ is being made known through the church (3:1–12). The first major division of Ephesians concludes with Paul praying that God will strengthen the Ephesians and that they will be rooted and grounded in Christ's vast, unfathomable love (3:13–21).

Chapters 4–6 of the letter focus on how the Ephesians are meant to live as Christ's beloved children. They are urged to live in unity (4:1–13) and to attain maturity in Christ (4:14–16). Furthermore, in terms akin to Colossians, they are instructed not to lead lives of futility and impurity. Instead, they are to put off who they were and are to put on who they are becoming. Renouncing unwholesome speaking and living, they are to live in love and light as wise, grateful people in concert with God's example (4:17–5:20). Also in keeping with Colossians, on which a number of scholars think Ephesians is dependent, instructions are given to those living in Christian households (5:21–6:9). To be sure, these directives have been roundly criticized by contemporary interpreters and are clearly out of sync with patterns of thought and practice in much of the Western world today. It should not go unnoticed, however, that in Ephesians there is a call to mutual submission (so 5:21) and that all people – wives/husbands, children/parents, and slaves/ masters – are ultimately accountable to God (note 6:8). Ephesians concludes by calling recipients to be strong in the Lord, to put on the full armor of God, and to pray in the Spirit and by offering believers a wish for peace, love, and grace (6:10–24).

THE PASTORAL EPISTLES (1–2 TIMOTHY, TITUS)

An introduction to and overview of Pauline letters would be incomplete without mention of and comment on the so-called Pastoral Epistles, despite there being widespread agreement among Paul's recent interpreters that he did not write these letters. (Such reservations are based on a number of considerations, including the style, substance, and provenance of these letters.) In the course of Paul's apostolic ministry, Timothy and Titus were among his most trusted and erstwhile associates (see, e.g. Phil 2:19–24; 2 Cor 8:16–24).

In the letter addressed to Titus, who is on the Mediterranean island of Crete, he is instructed to put the Cretans spiritual house in order by appointing trustworthy elders in every town and by teaching sound doctrine and good works to the believers there. Woven into these instructions are memorable confessions regarding the Christian faith and life (note 2:11–14; 3:3–7). In 1 Timothy, Paul's "son" is in Ephesus, where he is meant to instruct people how to "conduct themselves in God's household" (3:15). As with Titus, this entails offering sound teaching and requires exemplary living (note 4:6, 16). As with Titus, substantive doctrinal and ethical statements recur throughout the letter (e.g., 2:3–6; 3:16; 4:4–5, 8–9; 6:6–10). This is not to say that either Titus or 1 Timothy is void of sayings now hard to understand (so, e.g. 1 Tim 2:11–15; Titus 2:12–14).

Second Timothy differs from its siblings, as it is a letter given over to theological reflection on Paul's life and ministry as well as to pastoral instructions for Timothy. In keeping with 1 Timothy and Titus, however, it is also laced with meaningful, memorable lines (note 2:8, 11–13; 3:16). Particularly poignant are the words regarding Paul's pending death, where having "fought the good fight, finished the race, and kept the faith," the apostle anticipates a crown of righteousness, which the Lord will reward him and others who have longed for his appearing (4:6–8). Given the distinct nature of 2 Timothy and the biographical materials contained therein, some scholars are inclined to think that Paul at least wrote it, if not the other two Pastoral Epistles.

CONCLUSION

The Welsh poet and Anglican priest, R. S. Thomas (1913–2000), once likened Paul to a mountain that theologians have unsuccessfully sought to scale ("Covenanters," in *Later Poems: A Selection 1972–1982* [London, 1984], 170–73). True though this may be, the place where one may begin to ascend "Mt. St. Paul" is with his preserved letters. This essay has sought to introduce and orient readers to the Pauline Letters, but it is, of course, no substitute for reading, reflecting on, and responding to the documents themselves.

The climax of St. Augustine's conversion to the Christian faith began in a garden in Milan, Italy, when he heard a playing child chant, "Take up and read" (Augustine, *Confessions* 7.1). This is valuable advice with respect to the thirteen letters of Paul that now comprise a goodly portion of the New Testament.

Further Reading

Barclay, John M. G., *Paul: A Very Brief History* (London, 2018).

Dunn, James D. G., ed., *The Cambridge Companion to St. Paul* (Cambridge, 2003).

Gray, Patrick, *Paul as a Problem in History and Culture: The Apostle and His Critics through the Centuries* (Grand Rapids, 2016).

Horrell, David G., *An Introduction to the Study of Paul*, 3rd ed. (London, 2015).

Longenecker, Bruce W. and Todd D. Still, *Thinking through Paul: An Introduction to His Life, Letters, and Theology* (Grand Rapids, 2014).

Meeks, Wayne A., *The First Urban Christians: The Social World of the Apostle Paul*, 2nd ed. (New Haven, CT, 2003).

Roetzel, Calvin J., *The Letters of Paul: Conversations in Context*, 6th ed. (Louisville, 2015).

Weima, Jeffrey A. D., *Paul the Ancient Letter Writer: An Introduction to Epistolary Analysis* (Grand Rapids, MI, 2016).

Witherington, Ben, *The Paul Quest: The Renewed Search for the Jew of Tarsus* (Grand Rapids, MI, 2001).

Wright, N. T., *Paul: A Biography* (San Francisco, 2018).

10 Apocalyptic Literature

MEGHAN HENNING

When the writers of the immensely popular television show, *Supernatural*, wrote the story arc for season five of the show around the major figures of the book of Revelation, they hoped that audiences would connect to the familiar images of the Apocalypse that were updated for the twenty-first century. This season of *Supernatural* drew on broad apocalyptic themes like cosmic battles, final judgment, angels, and demons. Even beyond these themes that would be recognizable from many ancient apocalypses, the show specifically connected its story to the narrative of the Biblical apocalypse, the book of Revelation, citing specific passages, and recasting the four horsemen from Rev 6:2–8 as a thirty-something businessman in a red convertible (war), an emaciated old man driving a black escalade (famine), a doctor driving a dilapidated green car (pestilence), and a gaunt older man dressed in black, driving a white 1950s Cadillac (death).

Apart from dramatic storytelling, this choice in plotlines is an interesting one. Why use a two-thousand-year-old Biblical story to frame a contemporary television show about two demon-hunting brothers? What is it about apocalypses and their distinctive style of storytelling that has allowed their popularity to endure to today? This essay will attempt to answer those questions by looking closer at the ancient stories that we call apocalypses, and the foundational literary elements of those stories, like genre, audience, and style. After we look at the fundamental literary elements of apocalypses, we will turn to the three apocalypses that are found in the Bible: Daniel 7–12, Mark 13, and the book of Revelation, looking at the distinctive way that each of the Biblical authors uses the apocalyptic storytelling techniques. We will also look at why these three Biblical authors told the story in this way, and what effects it might have had on each audience's political, economic, and social outlook. Finally, we will think about how these Biblical apocalypses have been used in art, contemporary literature, media, politics, and even religious pilgrimage sites. We will see that when we read the apocalypses as a particular kind of story we are not only able to better understand the Biblical texts themselves but we can also answer pressing questions about how and why the apocalypses themselves and their distinctive style of storytelling have endured in our own world.

GENRE: HOW DO WE RECOGNIZE AN APOCALYPTIC STORY?

We typically define a genre by identifying elements of the story that are distinctive to that type of story. While apocalyptic literature appears to be rather unstructured, or to follow an undiscernible course, the story-line does share features and strategies for communicating a message. Scholars began to isolate these features for the apocalyptic genre in 1979, identifying four distinctive features of an apocalypse, based on their reading of the earliest ancient Jewish and Christian apocalypses.[1] The four features of apocalypses that they highlighted in this definition were a revelatory story with a narrative framework, a revelation told to a human by an otherworldly being (like an angel), a reality that transcends time (tells us about future salvation), and a reality that transcends space (tells us about a supernatural world).

While this definition might seem broad, it is specific and flexible enough to apply to the eleven Jewish apocalypses. This definition is also carefully structured to account for the form of the apocalypses (narrative revelation, mediated by otherworldly being) and the content of apocalypses (reality that transcends time and space). As we look at apocalypses, I will argue that this definition should be emended to add a stylistic feature to take into account the ancient rhetorical techniques that apocalyptic authors used, namely vivid visual rhetoric.

AUDIENCE: WHO READS APOCALYPTIC STORIES?

A short answer to "who reads apocalyptic stories?" is "everyone." The number of texts that remain and the extent to which they were copied in the ancient world tells us that apocalypses were very popular in the ancient world. Some apocalypses were used in worship for centuries, like the Apocalypse of Peter, an early Christian apocalypse that describes hell and heaven, or the apocalyptic tours of hell that occur

---

[1] John J. Collins, ed., *Apocalypse: The Morphology of a Genre, Semeia* 14 (Missoula, MT, 1979).

in the stories of Mary's Dormition (when Mary "falls asleep" and is carried off to heaven). Like the apocalyptic sections of the stories of Mary's ascent to heaven, some apocalypses are imbedded in other texts that were read very widely, like the apocalypses in Dan 7–12, and Mark 13. The fact that apocalypses likely appealed to a general audience was used for many years as a way to discount them as unimportant or peripheral literature for the study of the Bible because they were seen as "popular literature" and not serious theological reflection.

The much more complex answer to "who reads apocalyptic stories" is that apocalypses and apocalyptic thinking have appealed to different types of audiences throughout history. Apocalypses as a genre all critique some element of the author's present reality, but the nature of that critique varies. The intended audience of each apocalypse depends on the type of critique that is imbedded in the apocalypse's narrative. Some are written in response to a particular historical moment of crisis. Part of the book of 1 Enoch, for example (the "animal apocalypse" in chapters 85–91), is written during the crisis leading up to the Maccabean revolt, exhorting readers to participate in the militant overthrow of Gentile rulers. For this type of apocalypse, the audience is made up of readers who find consolation in a vision of the future that counters the most troubling aspects of their historical moment. Some scholars have argued that this type of apocalypse was so effective at consoling the audience that they did not revolt, but responded passively because they believed that their enemies would be punished at a future time or in an otherworldly place.

Other apocalypses are written to a broader audience, attempting to make readers aware of a crisis that they do not yet perceive. In this type of apocalypse, the author hopes to use an alternative vision of the future to raise consciousness about an issue. The book of Revelation can be read as this type of apocalypse, encouraging readers to respond strongly to the rise of the emperor cult that the author perceives to be a threat to Christianity. In this interpretation the apocalyptic imagery of Revelation is meant to persuade readers of a crisis that they did not yet perceive.[2]

Yet another possible audience for apocalypses is simply a community that already values the apocalyptic perspective. In this type of community, apocalypses could be used as a mechanism for internal political critique. For instance, in the early Christian Apocalypse of

---

[2] Adela Yarbro Collins, *Crisis and Catharsis: The Power of the Apocalypse* (Philadelphia, 1984).

Paul bishops, lectors, and deacons are punished in hell for sins of hypocrisy, using the apocalypse to critique activities that were internal to the Christian community.

STYLE: WHAT ARE SOME OF THE MOST DISTINCTIVE FEATURES OF APOCALYPTIC STORIES?

Although previous definitions of the genre apocalypse have generally looked at the rhetoric or style of argumentation of an apocalypse as a function of each text's "social ideology," I argue here that apocalyptic rhetoric is a defining feature of apocalypses. Adela Yarbro Collins and John J. Collins laid the foundation for focusing on *how* apocalypses tell their stories, by isolating persuasive imagery and "imagination" as key elements. Greg Carey has argued that apocalyptic stories should be viewed as *rhetoric*. If we think about apocalyptic stories as rhetoric, then we also need to think about how apocalyptic stories work to persuade their audiences. As I have argued, one of the key features of apocalyptic rhetoric was drawn from ancient rhetorical techniques for using vivid imagery to emotionally move an audience. These techniques were outlined by Aristotle and Cicero as language familiar enough to an audience to trigger emotional responses. Visual rhetoric was able to elicit emotions by using descriptions so vivid that the readers felt as though they were present at the events described or could see the images as if they were before them.

Take, for instance, the lake of fire that is mentioned six times in the book of Rev 19–22 as a space of eschatological punishment. A fiery lake, the Acherusian Lake, was the entrance to the underworld in Greek mythology. In Greek myth this lake was also called the Lake of Avernus (or "without birds") because legend had it that poisonous vapors rising from the lake would kill birds mid-flight. In recent times, archeologists have found gates to the Acherusian Lake at temples devoted to Hades, usually in places where underground gases escape (https://news.nationalgeographic.com/news/2013/04/130414-hell-underworld-archaeology-mount-olympus-greece/). In addition to the Greek legends testifying to the danger of such a fiery lake, Strabo the ancient geographer also described the Dead Sea as smoky and full of asphalt that bubbles up underneath with fire and sulfur (16.42–44). Strabo goes on to explain that the Dead Sea is fiery because it used to be the metropolis of Sodom, connecting a familiar feature of Syrian geography with a story of Divine judgment. For readers of the book of Revelation, the "lake of fire" would not only be familiar but it would allow readers to imagine such a lake as if it were right in front of them. The act of imagining a lake of fire in turn would evoke emotions of fear by reminding readers of these other fiery lakes that were associated with death and judgment.[3]

In sum, I am proposing that in addition to the definition of an apocalypse that addressed both form and content we also add a functional element. Apocalypses then not only offer revelation in the form of a narrative that is mediated by an otherworldly being and describe a reality that transcends time and space, but they do so via ancient visual rhetoric, containing vivid imagery that is meant to have an impact on an audience. This definition does not change which texts are within the genre apocalypse, but helps us better understand how the genre worked in the ancient world. If we think about apocalyptic rhetoric as a defining feature of apocalypses, we are also better able to appreciate the malleability of the genre, which includes texts that were very different from one another but work in similar ways.

APOCALYPTIC STORYTELLING IN DAN 7–12

Chapters seven through twelve of the book of Daniel tell a story that has all the characteristics of an apocalypse that we have discussed so far. Although it tells a story that is set in sixth-century BCE Babylon, Daniel was probably completed during or around the Maccabean Revolt (167–164 BCE). The apocalyptic review of history in chapter 11 is the primary evidence for this dating, which reports the events of Antiochus's reign up to foretelling his death (11:45), suggesting that Daniel was written sometime before Antiochus died in 164 BCE. In this context, Daniel's earliest audience would have understood the visions as an invitation to resist the imperial rule of Antiochus IV. The apocalypse in the book of Daniel is a response to an identifiable crisis, offering readers consolation and suggestions for responding to the pressures of their present historical moment. As Greg Carey has argued, Daniel's relationship to its ancient audience is its most identifiable literary feature: "The book speaks to the eschatological present from the ancient past."[4]

The first six chapters of the book of Daniel are stories told in the third person, about Daniel, an exiled Jew, and his friends in the Babylonian court. Chapter seven shifts perspective, offering a first-person account of the visions that were revealed to Daniel. This revelation

[3] Meghan Henning, *Educating Early Christians through the Rhetoric of Hell*, 2nd series (Tübingen, 2014), 134–35.
[4] Carey, *Ultimate Things*, 47.

begins with a vision of four beasts which frighten Daniel, leading him to ask for an interpretation from a heavenly being (7:15–16). The fourth beast is the scariest, but is destroyed at the final judgment of the enthroned Ancient One. The fourth beast is ultimately supplanted by "one like a Son of Man" who arrives on the clouds and is granted everlasting dominion over the earth. The vision of the four beasts introduces the idea of political overthrow in the present (during the reign of the "fourth beast") by imagining it as a continuation of past upheavals. Daniel has a second vision (8), in which a Ram and a Goat represent Median, Persian, and Greek empires. This vision, like the first, ends with reassurance that the present imperial reign will end, and "not by human hands" (8:25). Daniel's final vision (10–12) is conveyed by "one in human form" (an angel), and offers another review of history in which Antiochus IV rises to power and persecutes the faithful, ultimately culminating in a vision of the death of Antiochus IV as a time of eschatological resurrection and judgment (11:45–12:3).

Within these visions, Daniel uses apocalyptic rhetoric to convey a future salvation and describe otherworldly spaces. The first vision of Daniel 7 reveals future salvation in the form of the overthrow of the present evil empire and the establishment of the eternal reign of God that is ushered in by the "one like a Son of Man." The futuristic element of this story is not simply an exercise in imagination, but a future that impinges on the audience's present world. The revelation of Daniel 7 is also spatial because it depicts the transcendent arrival of the Ancient One and his judgment from an otherworldly throne:

> As I watched in the night visions,
> I saw one like a Son of Man
> coming with the clouds of heaven.
> And he came to the Ancient One
> and was presented before him.
> To him was given dominion
> and glory and kingship,
> that all peoples, nations, and languages
> should serve him.
> His dominion is an everlasting dominion
> that shall not pass away,
> and his kingship is one
> that shall never be destroyed
>
> (Dan 7:13–14)

The transcendent, or otherworldly, elements of Daniel's vision are not a means of escapism, but instead are meant to be a powerful response to the worldly powers of the empire that seem to Daniel's audience as though they will go unchecked forever.

The apocalyptic visions in Dan 7–12 also offer excellent examples of the way in which apocalypses use visual rhetoric in order to tell a compelling story. Several visually stunning images occur in succession in Daniel's visions, all meant to tell a story that is persuasive for his Jewish audience that is feeling the pressures of imperial rule under Antiochus IV. Perhaps the most jarring images are the ones in the first vision, providing a review of history through successive depictions of startling beasts that rise from the sea. The first beast, a lion that stands on two legs and has eagle's wings, symbolizes Babylon. This beast is followed by a bear that has three tusks, and devours many bodies, representing the kingdom of Media. A third beast is like a leopard but with three heads and four wings and symbolizes Persia. Finally, the fourth beast emerges from the sea, representing the terrifying rule of Greece, and Daniel describes the beast as particularly frightening:

> After this I saw in the visions by night a fourth beast, terrifying and dreadful and exceedingly strong. It had great iron teeth and was devouring, breaking in pieces, and stamping what was left with its feet. It was different from all the beasts that preceded it, and it had ten horns. I was considering the horns, when another horn appeared, a little one coming up among them; to make room for it, three of the earlier horns were plucked up by the roots. There were eyes like human eyes in this horn, and a mouth speaking arrogantly. (Dan 7:7–9)

Daniel goes on to recount the things that the little horn says, the judgment of the Ancient of Days, and the triumphant reign of the one like a Son of Man.

But even after the destruction of the beasts and establishment of the sovereignty of the one like a Son of Man, Daniel remains afraid, saying "As for me, Daniel, my spirit was troubled within me, and the visions of my head terrified me" (Dan 7:15). The angel responds by offering Daniel an interpretation of his vision. Daniel's own emotional response is instructive for the book's ancient audience.[5] They too should be troubled by the visions Daniel recounts, and Daniel's emotional

---

[5] For discussion of Daniel's emotional response here and in 7:28, see Carol Newsom, *Daniel: A Commentary* (Louisville, KY, 2014), 236, 242.

response to these beastly empires offers his audience a template for their own response. In particular, the imagery of Daniel's vision invites his audience to view the reign of Antiochus IV as evanescent, but to be suspicious and even fearful of Greek rule.

At the end of these visions, Daniel is told that his people will be delivered, particularly those whose names are written in the "book of life" (Dan 12:1–4). In his prayer in chapter 9, Daniel repents of the sins of his people, specifically those who violated the covenant, calling the Judeans who are reading the text to renew their faithfulness to God as part of their response to Antiochene rule (Dan 9:15–25). The vivid imagery of Daniel's visions is not simply there to frighten readers, or even to offer hope for the future (though they do that too), but to galvanize them into action. The visions of Daniel demand that the audience take notice of the pride, arrogance, and excessive force of Antiochus IV, that they turn from apostasy and resist this empire as a sign of faithfulness to their God.

APOCALYPTIC STORYTELLING IN MARK 13

In the Synoptic gospels, apocalyptic storytelling is featured most prominently in the narrative about the future judgment of a heavenly being (Mark 13; Matt 24; Luke 21). Since Matthew and Luke used the story from Mark as a source, we will focus our attention on Mark as the earliest available version of it. Within the gospel of Mark, the story occurs in Jerusalem outside of the Temple after Jesus has predicted the death of the "Son of Man" three times (8:31; 9:31–32; 10:33–34). The passion narrative, or the story of Jesus' suffering and death, immediately follows (14–16). For the reader, the literary context situates the story of the Son of Man coming on the clouds in glory as the final teaching of Jesus.

Mark's gospel was written after the outbreak of the Jewish war with Rome but before the destruction of the Jerusalem temple (66–70 CE). For the audience then, Jesus' statement that "Not one stone will be left here upon another; all will be thrown down" (Mark 13:2) is still in the future, an unfulfilled prophecy, one that associates the destruction of the Jerusalem Temple with cosmic upheaval. What is more, the statement connects the destruction of the Jerusalem Temple to the restoration of Israel in the last days of time. The apocalyptic message of Mark's gospel is a political message that is enmeshed in the conflicts of the era in which it was written. Living in a time just after the outbreak of the war, the admonition to flee when the "desolating sacrilege" (Mark 13:14) is erected where it should not be serves as a warning to be distrustful of Roman occupation. In addition to the critique of the Roman occupation of Jerusalem, the apocalypse in the synoptic gospels also contains an admonition to thoroughly vet those who would claim to be members of the Judean community. During the Jewish war, there was a proliferation of messianic pretenders, so the warnings to avoid false messiahs and false prophets (Mark 13:21–22) serve as an internal check against inauthentic leadership. If we return to our discussion about the types of people who read apocalypses, the synoptic gospels seem to use apocalyptic rhetoric either as a response to a crisis (in the case of Matthew and Luke, it is a response to the destruction of the Jerusalem Temple in 70 CE), or in the case of Mark, it is a means of internal critique calling other Judeans to resist the allure of messianic pretenders.

The synoptic apocalypse is a revelation told to humans, but the "otherworldly being" who mediates the apocalypse is Jesus. This invites the question, is Jesus an "otherworldly being" in Mark? The identity of Jesus is a gap in the text and invites readers to speculate. There are multiple occasions in Mark in which someone reveals Jesus' identity and Jesus tells them to keep it a secret (as in Mark 8:29–30). In Mark 13, Jesus talks about the Son of Man in the third person, distancing himself from the otherworldly being that comes "in clouds with great power and glory" (13:26). Despite this intentional ambiguity in the text, the readers are already "in" on the secret and, having witnessed the transfiguration scene in Mark 9:1–8, constitute part of the elect group that understands Jesus' identity as otherworldly. So from the perspective of Mark's audience, Jesus is already identifiable as an otherworldly being. The questions around his identity in the gospel draw attention to it and require the reader to answer the questions for themselves.

The apocalyptic scene that Jesus reveals in his teaching also uses visual rhetoric to depict a reality that transcends time and space. The future that Jesus describes is one of eschatological upheaval that requires endurance on the part of the faithful who wish to be saved:

> Brother will betray brother to death, and a father his child, and children will rise against parents and have them put to death; and you will be hated by all because of my name. But the one who endures to the end will be saved. (13:12–13)

These violent scenes of fratricide and parricide not only evoke an image of a world in tumult but one that has fallen to wickedness, betraying the commands of God.[6] This imagery signals to followers that they need to be vigilant and particularly strong in the face of the pressures of war. Salvation not only comes to those who endure the tumult of war righteously but to a particular group of "the elect" (13:20).

By far the most vivid scene of the whole revelation is the arrival of the Son of Man, which serves to connect the supernatural world and the earthly world:

> But in those days, after that suffering,
> the sun will be darkened,
> and the moon will not give its light,
> and the stars will be falling from heaven,
> and the powers in the heavens will be shaken.
> Then they will see 'the Son of Man coming in clouds' with great power and glory. Then he will send out the angels, and gather his elect from the four winds, from the ends of the earth to the ends of heaven.
>
> (13:24–27)

Following the divine judgment of Jerusalem (Mark 13:14–23), this section of the narrative draws on Dan 7:13–14 in which the one like a son of man appears directly after the judgment of the four beasts. In Mark, the "Son of Man" is understood by the disciples (and the audience) to be equivalent to the "messiah," re-interpreting the majestic eternal king of Dan 7:13–14 as one who will be rejected, suffer, and die.[7] In its social context during the Jewish war, the visual rhetoric of cosmic upheaval paves the way for the instructions to stay vigilant in Mark 13:28–37. Readers are urged to endure the present pressures of war by being ever ready for the day when the moon will go dark, the stars will fall from heaven, and the Son of Man will arrive to gather the elect.

APOCALYPTIC STORYTELLING IN REVELATION

When people think of Biblical apocalypses, they usually think of the book of Revelation (sometimes called John's Apocalypse). This is probably because it is the longest apocalypse in the Bible and contains some

---

[6] Fratricide is the "first crime" in Gen 4:8 and occurs again in Judg 9:5; 2 Sam 13:28–29; 1 Kgs 2:23–25; 2 Chron 21:4. For other instances of parricide in the Bible, see 2 Kgs 19:37; Isa 37:38.

[7] Adela Yarbro Collins and John J. Collins, *King and Messiah as Son of God: Divine, Human, and Angelic Messianic Figures in Biblical and Related Literature* (Grand Rapids, MI, 2008), 150.

of the most striking imagery – no one can forget the four horsemen, the woman clothed with the sun, the battle between the beast and the lamb, the lake of fire, or the new Jerusalem emerging from heaven.

But the odd thing is that the most memorable of the Biblical apocalypses almost did not make it into the Bible. Although the book was widely accepted in the second century CE, it was not included in all of the fourth-century canon lists. Those who rejected the book of Revelation were often reacting to the way that others interpreted the book. In the second century CE, the Alogi (a third-century group of Christians in Asia Minor) rejected the Apocalypse entirely, mostly because they were worried that the Montanists (another late second-century group of Christians in Asia Minor who followed Montanus and emphasized the Holy Spirit) were using it to support their "new prophecy."[8] In the third century CE, Dionysius of Alexandria critiqued the book of Revelation, arguing that it was not written by John but by his opponents the Millenarians who took issue with the literal interpretations of the Apocalypse.[9] By the end of the fourth century CE, the arguments of Dionysius seemed to have influenced Christians in Asia Minor, where Revelation was outright rejected by some as appropriate reading material for Christians, or in other cases was simply excluded from canon lists (but was still understood as appropriate for edification).

Recent study of the history of interpretation of the book of Revelation has demonstrated that its interpretation oscillates between individuals who wish to "decode" the message in its own context, and those who see their own situation in the text, reenacting the drama.[10] Tina Pippen argues that the book of Revelation's imaginative project allows for it to be reinterpreted in new situations of colonial oppression tracing the way that it has been read and re-read by early Christians enduring oppression under Roman imperial rule. Pippen says that she wants to "enter boldly into these mythical and fictional worlds," harnessing the power of apocalyptic imagery for change in the contemporary world.[11] Jacqueline Hidalgo has examined the book of Revelation in relation to US Chicanx movement texts, demonstrating that the imaginative elements of apocalyptic literature can offer communities an opportunity to "remake the world into a better inhabitable place for dislocated

---

[8] Epiphanius, *Haer.* 51.3, 51.33.

[9] Eusebius, *Hist. Eccl.* 7.25.4.

[10] Judith Kovacs and Christopher Rowland, *Revelation: The Apocalypse of Jesus Christ* (Malden, MA, 2004), 7–11.

[11] Tina Pippen, *Death and Desire: The Rhetoric of Gender in the Apocalypse of John* (Louisville, KY, 1992), 105.

peoples," by inviting "social dreaming," the ability to critique and transform social spaces.[12] The interpretive viscosity one witnesses with the Apocalypse of John in these contemporary interpretations derives from the genre as we have defined it here. The visual rhetoric of an apocalypse lends itself to both prescriptive and polyvalent readings of the text.

In its earliest context, the book of Revelation was written by John around 95 CE from the island of Patmos, to seven churches throughout the Diaspora. Although researchers previously thought that the book of Revelation was written as a result of persecution in the reign of the emperor Domitian, that hypothesis has been revised. Since there is no evidence for the official persecution of Christians during that time period, the book of Revelation seems to have a different purpose for its earliest readers. As Adela Collins has argued, John is instead encouraging listeners to express their fears more fully about the rising popularity of the ruler cult. The apocalyptic images and cosmic battle do not reflect a readily observable battle or crisis in the present world, but a perceived crisis. The apocalypse, then, is a mechanism for making John's audience aware of mounting social anxiety over potential threat to Christian monotheism that was posed by the ruler cult's worship of the emperor. The bold imagery that Revelation uses to motivate early Christians in this late first-century historical situation of Roman oppression lends itself to transformative work in other social spaces of colonial oppression in the contemporary world as viewed by Pippen.

Like Daniel and the Synoptic apocalypse, the book of Revelation tells a story using all of the key features of the apocalyptic genre. The story is told to John but mediated by "one like the Son of Man," who has white hair, flaming eyes, and a voice like many waters (Rev 1:14–15). Elsewhere, John says that he was shown these things by an angel (Rev 1:1; 22:8).[13] In John's vision, the reader learns about a future salvation, "what is to take place after this" (Rev 1:19), in a vision that tells about the judgment of the dead. In this judgment, names are recorded in the book of life based on each person's "works" (Rev 20:12; 20:15; 21:27). This future culminates with a description of the new heaven and the new earth, and the New Jerusalem, an otherworldly space that is "coming down out of heaven from God" (Rev 21:1–2). The spaces that

---

[12] Jacqueline M. Hidalgo, *Revelation in Aztlán, Scriptures, Utopias, and the Chicano Movement* (New York, 2016), 5–6, 14, 238–48.
[13] Collins and Collins, *King and Messiah as Son of God*, 189–98, argue that the risen Christ is identified in Revelation as the Son of Man and is an angelic figure.

John describes throughout the apocalypse transcend the worldly
realm, providing early Christians with the beginnings of their ideas
about heaven and hell as separate spaces for afterlife rewards and
punishments. A loud voice from the throne describes this new otherworldly space, saying:

> See the home of God is among mortals. He will dwell with them as
> their God; they will be his people(s), and God himself with be with
> them; he will wipe every tear from their eyes. Death will be no
> more, mourning and crying and pain will be no more, for the first
> things have passed away. (Rev 21:3–4)

Similarly, this vision is followed by a promise that "those who conquer
will inherit these things," offering consolation to the audience who are
invited to imagine their resistance to the Roman ruler cult as part of a
cosmic battle (Rev 21:7). Likewise, those who capitulate to Roman
cultic practices are thrown into the lake of fire, including "the cow-
ardly, the faithless, the polluted, the murderers, the fornicators, the
sorcerers, the idolaters, and all liars" (Rev 21:8).

The primary way that Revelation has captured the attention of
readers is through its visual rhetoric. The imagery of the cosmic battle
and the otherworldly spaces draws on images that would be familiar to
its audience. These familiar images work to move the emotions of the
readers of the apocalypse, using the imagination of the listening audience to persuade people to resist the pressures of Roman enculturation.
As readers imagine the seven-headed Beast who has blasphemous
names on his heads and is worshipped (Rev 13:1–4), they are reminded
of the spectacle of the Roman ruler cult, and compelled to side with the
Lamb by actively resisting idolatry as they await the final judgment and
the arrival of the new heaven and the new earth.

EVERYDAY APOCALYPSES: APOCALYPTIC
STORYTELLING IN THE WORLD AROUND US TODAY

In each of the Biblical apocalypses we have looked at here, the techniques of apocalyptic storytelling were used to deliver a specific message about the present reality in which the audience was living. These
techniques were used to motivate the audience to change either their
political outlook or their behaviors. In Daniel, a retelling of history and
a vision of the future offer readers hope that the reign of Antiochus IV
would end soon, compelling them to resist Greek rule. Mark uses
apocalyptic storytelling to offer political commentary on the Roman

occupation of Jerusalem during the Jewish war, whereas Revelation made a strong case against the Roman imperial cult.

As effective rhetoric, apocalyptic storytelling has stood the test of time. Today, we find apocalyptic storytellers all around us. Politicians routinely paint pictures of a grim future in order to motivate voters to go to the polls and vote for change. In the *Left Behind* Series of books, authors depict a future in which eschatological judgment is based not on ethical deeds (as in Revelation) but on conversion to Christianity. For the authors of this series, the hope is to persuade readers to convert to Christianity by painting a grim eschatological future. Following the book of Revelation more closely, *Good Omens* offers a comedic retelling of the book of Revelation, but one that nevertheless offers critiques of modern economic and political excesses, depicting the four horsemen as a business tycoon (Famine), an arms dealer (War), a corporate executive whose goal is to pollute the globe (Pollution), and the assistant head of purchasing (Death). Television shows movies like *The Walking Dead and Star Wars* that offer viewers visions of a future time and space that critique the present world. Like the ancient authors, apocalyptic storytellers in the contemporary world use creative images of the future or otherworldly spaces in order to convince their audiences that there are alternatives to the present.

Apocalyptic storytelling has not only endured as a way of offering critique and hope for the present but it has borrowed heavily from some of the images of the ancient apocalypses themselves. In March of 2018, the internet was abuzz with claims that Pope Francis had denied the existence of hell, claims which were ultimately refuted. Later, in May of 2018, the presence of a sink hole on the White House lawn led people to speculate that a hell mouth had opened up in this conspicuous location as a result of Donald Trump's politics. In both of these examples, people were eager to draw on the ancient imagery of hell, not simply borrowing the apocalyptic rhetoric around it, but drawing on the specifics of an ancient apocalyptic description of an otherworldly space.

Even beyond the specific imagery of the ancient apocalypses, the broader concept of an otherworldly space that is used for judgment based on ethical deeds has also stood the test of time. The Irish Pilgrimage site, St. Patrick's Purgatory, on Station Island in County Donegal, offers pilgrims the opportunity to fast and pray for three days on an island where Patrick himself is said to have discovered a gate to purgatory where one could see both heaven and hell. Here, in times of both economic distress and flourishing, this ritual has maintained its popularity, offering pilgrims the promise of a connection to otherworldly spaces through prayer and fasting. Similarly, *The Good Place* is a television show that is set in the afterlife, offering the audience a critique of each character's questionable morals through flashbacks to his or her life. These personalized ethical critiques, however, are designed to resonate with a contemporary audience, offering lessons in moral philosophy for the casual viewer. In the real space of Saint Patrick's Purgatory on Station Island, and in the imagined spaces of *The Good Place*, the "otherworld" is leveraged as a space that influences earthly behavior.

These are but a few examples of our culture's overwhelming desire to imagine the otherworld in a way that is directly tied to the millennia-old traditions of the apocalypses. When we so connect, we become apocalyptic storytellers and harness the power of visual imagery.

Further Reading

Carey, Greg, *Ultimate Things: An Introduction to Jewish and Christian Apocalyptic Literature* (St. Louis, MO, 2005).

Collins, Adela Yarbro, *Crisis and Catharsis: The Power of the Apocalypse* (Philadelphia, 1984).

Engstrom, Erika and Joseph M. Valenzano III, *Television, Religion, and Supernatural: Hunting Monsters, Finding Gods* (Lanham, MD, 2014).

Henning, Meghan R., "Narrating the Future," in *Religion: Narrating Religion*, ed. Sarah Iles Johnston (Farmington Hills, MI, 2017), 191–206.

Moss, Candida, "Welcome to Hell: A History of Portals to Underworld," *The Daily Beast* (May, 2018). www.thedailybeast.com/welcome-to-hell-a-history-of-portals-to-the-underworld.

Murphy, Kelly J., "The End Is (Still) All Around: The Zombie and Contemporary Apocalyptic Thought," in *Apocalypses in Context: Apocalyptic Currents through History*, ed. Kelly J. Murphy and Justin Jeffcoat Schedtler (Minneapolis, 2016), 469–96.

Pippen, Tina. *Death and Desire: The Rhetoric of Gender in the Apocalypse of John* (Louisville, KY, 1992).

11 Shakespeare's *King Lear* and the Bible

WILLIAM J. KENNEDY

One inescapable fact about William Shakespeare (1564–1616) is that his life spanned a period of heightened activity among biblical scholars in the English church to consolidate gains of the Protestant Reformation. Upon her accession to the throne in 1558, Queen Elizabeth I revitalized the Reformation in England begun when her father King Henry VIII disavowed Pope Clement VII's authority in 1531. By 1562 England's bishops had agreed on a Reformed list of Thirty-Nine Articles of Religion. One consequential effect was to eliminate from its canon of sacraments the ritual of penance as an act of oral confession to a priest whose words of absolution affirm God's forgiveness of sin (Article XXV). The bishops relied on arguments by Luther, Calvin, and others that scripture offers no basis to warrant the institution of penance as a sacrament.

Shakespeare's friend and rival dramatist Ben Jonson famously declared that the author of *King Lear* and of forty or so other plays, in whole or in part, had learned "small Latin and less Greek" at his grammar school in Stratford. This low-grade accusation might have had little bearing on Shakespeare's understanding of the Bible and his references to it, were it not for debates about the meaning of Biblical texts crucial to Reformation theology at the time. Nearly a half century before his birth, Martin Luther and other Reformers undertook a return to Scriptural study in its original languages – Masoretic Hebrew for the Old Testament, but accessed largely through the third-to-second century BCE Septuagint Greek translation of it; and Koine Greek for the New Testament – supplanting St. Jerome's Latin Vulgate translation of the Bible, which had dominated the Western European understanding of Scripture throughout the middle ages. Their return to Greek texts offered a corrective to many misconceptions of terms associated with the sacrament of penance, the reception of grace, and the practice of charity. Shakespeare was admittedly no theologian or scriptural scholar, but even little Latin and less Greek would have enabled him to grasp the import of religious debate that had roiled the English Reformation. In what follows, I will examine the bearing of Biblical concepts of repentance on the action of perhaps Shakespeare's greatest tragedy, *King Lear*.

VECTORS OF ANALYSIS: BIBLES, TESTAMENTS, LITERATURES

The plural nouns in my subheading call for explanation. The word "Bibles" reflects the many translations of all or part of the Hebrew and Christian Scriptures available with various degrees of critical approval or disapproval by both clergy and laity in Shakespeare's time (see Shaheen 1999, 17–50 and Hamlin 2012, 9–42). Arguably the most influential of these was the so-called Geneva Bible (1560; see Berry 1969, 1–28). Begun during the reign of Mary Tudor, whose parliament in 1553 had reinstated Catholic doctrine and ritual, it was the work of Protestant exiles from England who had fled to John Calvin's Geneva. Rejecting earlier English renditions of the Latin Vulgate Bible, they applied themselves directly to the Hebrew and Septuagint Old Testament and the Greek New Testament. They also annotated their translation with chapter headings and commentaries that echoed Calvinist doctrine and theology. Perhaps most importantly, they aimed at a broad readership of England's laity. Earlier translations – notably William Tyndale's 1525 rendition of the Greek New Testament and his 1530–31 partial rendition of the Septuagint Old Testament, and Myles Coverdale's 1535 rendition of the Latin Vulgate Bible with his 1538 revision, which incorporated some of Tyndale's work into what was called the "Great Bible" – and the English clergy's 1568 composite translation, authorized for church services as the "Bishops' Bible," had all been planned for use by clergy. With a wider market, sales of the Geneva Bible superseded those of the Bishops' Bible (over 120 editions as opposed to 22 for the latter). Only the 1611 King James Authorized Version of the Bible, carefully cross-referenced with the Hebrew and Greek texts, supplanted the appeal of the Geneva Bible. The upshot is that Shakespeare would have heard the Bishops' Bible in church services, but could have had access to reading his own or another's personal copy of the Geneva Bible. This is not to say that he absorbed its Calvinist theology. More often than not, he went out of his way to offer a counter-interpretation.

The plural "Testaments" refers to ancient distinctions between the Hebrew and Christian Scriptures as "Old" and "New" Testaments. St. Augustine attributed to Hebrew Scripture the power of a "promise" to which Christian Scripture supplied its "fulfilment." Drawing on the meaning of the Latin noun *testamentum* as a legal "testament" or will that promises one's heirs the inheritance of a specific patrimony, Augustine reasons that as God's children we are granted the patrimony of divine love. The Hebrew noun at stake is *berith* which, with its Septuagint equivalent *diatheke*, means a covenant or agreement binding one side or sometimes both to a mutual understanding. Through this covenant, God and humankind agree to acknowledge their obligations and commitments to one another. While the idea of "testament" as "promise" conveys futurity, that of "covenant" focuses on the present state of things. A tension between futurity and the present governs these terms in Reformation bibles. Luther, for example, translates the Septuagint *diatheke* variously as *Bund* "a union or alliance of diverse parties" (as in Gen 17:9–14) or as *Testament* "a legal will or promise of patrimony" (as in Paul's Gal 3:17–18), while Calvinist translators render these terms consistently as "covenant" or "alliance" in their French Bible and in the English Geneva Bible. These issues may contribute to the action of *King Lear*, which is after all a tragedy about the misbestowal of political patrimony and the familial alliance of evil progeny against their father to protect their own interests. Many of these matters of ecclesiastical patrimony and covenant debated at the Hampton Court Conference of bishops in 1604 resonated with the concerns of his *King Lear* composed a year or two later.

From a related perspective, the noun "Literatures" raises a broad range of issues and concerns. Just as the "Bible" and its "Testaments" project a surplus of literary modes, styles, and genres over long periods of historical development, so does "Literatures" as a body of ancient and contemporary forms of written expression. From the fourteenth to the late eighteenth century, the term encompassed most kinds of writing composed for public readership. In the sixteenth century it referred widely to historical, philosophical, religious, and scientific writing as well as to ancient classical texts in general and to current experiments in mixed genres and unconventional forms.

One such innovation was the commercial publication of theatrical scripts as "Literature" for a public readership. The publication of Shakespeare's plays, as well as of those by less distinguished authors, exemplifies the broadening of this term. One example is an anonymous *True Chronicle History of King Leir*, performed in 1594 and published in 1605. Based on Holinshed's *Chronicles of England, Scotland, and Ireland* (1577), this play depicts the misfortunes of a legendary eighth-century BCE king of Britain who divided his kingdom between two scheming daughters after heeding their advice to exclude his youngest daughter from consideration. You'd never know from its flagrant anachronisms that the action takes place in a pre-Christian, non-Biblical culture. The envious sisters, for example, demean their junior sibling with the taunting remark that "She were right fit to make a Parson's wife ... [except that] she is far too stately for the Church" (sig. B4^{r-v}). In a happy ending, Cordella saves Leir from the treachery of Gonorill and Ragan. The king – in a further anachronism – attributes the successful outcome to God and those who serve him: "The thanks be his, and these kind courteous folk, / By whose humanity we are preserved" (sig. H2^v). Their reward is "as pleasant as the blessed Manna, / That rained from heaven" (sig. H2^v). Mediocre as this play is, it likely prompted Shakespeare to begin writing his own tragedy about Lear later that year (Shapiro 2015, 47–64).

Pride of place for literary merit at the time would have gone to ancient classical texts in Latin and Greek. During the preceding century, humanist discoveries of hitherto lost or obscured texts expanded the classical canon in a variety of genres and modes. For Shakespeare's generation, one such beneficiary was a long didactic poem by the ancient Roman polymathic writer Titus Lucretius Carus (99–55 BCE). With the title *De rerum natura*, "On the nature of things," its revival made a deep impact upon philosophical and scientific writing at the end of the sixteenth century (see Passannante 2011, 154–97). In opposition to the doctrines and outlook of Stoic philosophy, which asserted the primacy of divine will over the universe and human activity, Lucretius espoused the early third-century BCE teachings of Epicurus. Drawing upon the latter, Lucretius aimed to synthesize the tenets of ancient materialist thought that regarded the universe as composed of atoms in constant motion and fortuitous combination that determine the shape of things and their indifference to human concerns. Like Epicurus, he declared himself an enemy of superstition and tyranny while granting human beings the power of free will to control their passions and desires, and thereby – for better or for worse – to fulfill their own ambitions.

The Stoicism of Cicero and Seneca had long appealed to medieval writers who assimilated to Christian ideals its emphasis upon the rationality of a moral order, the pursuit of virtue as a key to happiness, and an indifference to inevitable fate as an empowering choice. The Epicurism of Lucretius now offered a countervailing view that equated rationality with an elimination of anxiety, the pursuit of virtue with an acceptance of responsibility, and the attainment of equanimity with a rejection of determinist necessity. Though no known translation of Lucretius's poem existed in Shakespeare's time, accounts of it and extensive quotation from it were available. Paraphrases of its tenets and translations of important passages appeared in the second of Edmund Spenser's *Four Hymnes* (1596) and in his mixed epic-romance-allegory *The Faerie Queene* (1590–96), notably in its Legend of Chastity (book 3, canto 6, stanzas 30–47); its Legend of Friendship (book 4, canto 10, stanzas 44–47); and, before the poet's death in 1599, its second Canto of Mutability. The French writer Michel de Montaigne quoted extensively from it in his *Essays* (published in 1580–94), which Shakespeare's friend John Florio had translated into English and published in 1603. From the perspectives of Spenser and Montaigne, one could say that the skepticism of Epicurus and Lucretius competes with received beliefs of Hebrew and Christian scripture in the matter of repentance, revision of one's moral attitude, and turning points in the course of one's moral life.

BIBLICAL CONCEPTS OF REPENTANCE

What kinds of moral misconduct would have called for repentance? Infractions against the Decalogue or Ten Commandments in Exod 20 certainly demanded it. Both the Hebrew and the Christian Testaments used several words to convey more general ideas of wrongdoing. The Septuagint Old Testament names them in Greek near-equivalents of the Masoretic Hebrew text. The Greek *adikia*, literally "injustice," renders the sense of "departing from God's justice" in the Hebrew noun *ra'ah*. Greek *anomia*, "lawlessness," confers the sense of "crookedness, twistedness" in Hebrew *awon*. Greek *parabasis*, "transgression, rebellion," captures the sense of "rebellion against the deity" in Hebrew *sarah*. As it turns out, the last of these Greek nouns finds literary currency in the performance of old Attic comedy, which concludes with a *parabasis* or song that rebels against the dramatic action that precedes it.

A noun more commonly used than any of these, and dominant because of narrowness of subject matter in the Greek New Testament, is *hamartia*. Derived from the verb *hamartano* "to miss the target, make a mistake, sin," it translates the meaning of the Hebrew *hata'* , "sin." As it happens, this noun likewise has a prominent literary application. It occurs in Aristotle's *Poetics* 13.4 (1453a15), where it designates an error of judgment that leads to a tragic conclusion. Some modern translators have misleadingly rendered the word as "tragic flaw," which would have been incomprehensible to Shakespeare and his contemporaries. Rather than a moral defect, *hamartia* registers a cognitive error, a mistake that embroils an individual in a series of consequences beyond one's control, often implicating a larger community in his or her downfall.

Even with just a little Greek, Shakespeare would have been able to comprehend the resonance of these words used in the Septuagint Old Testament and the Greek New Testament to convey the idea of repentance. The verb *epistrepho*, "to turn back, turn away," used mostly in the Old Testament to translate Hebrew *shub*, "to turn to righteousness," commonly "to turn to God," conveys the departure from a former pattern of behavior toward a new or renewed sense of one's conscience. The noun *metanoia*, used mostly in the New Testament to convey a "change of one's mind or a revision of attitude," translates the Hebrew *niham*, "remorse" concerning one's pattern of behavior. A different verb, *metamelomai*, corresponding to Hebrew *niham*, "to repent," "to regret," is commonly claimed to be weaker than *epistrepho*, Hebrew *shub*, "to return." There is, however, no evidence for such an overall ranking. The Hebrew *niham*, strictly, is more concerned with motivation, unhappiness about wrong, *shub* with result, re-adherence to right. Hence, the former tends to be more specific, alluding to the peculiar flaws renounced, the latter to concentrate on the general, positive outcome. In addition to their biblical applications, *epistrepho* and *metanoia* in Attic Greek have literary and rhetorical applications. In classical poetics, *epistrephein* refers to the turning of a metrical cadence from one line of verse to another and from it is derived the Greek noun *strophe*, "stanza of poetry." In classical rhetoric, *metanoia* refers to the literary act of redaction or revision.

In the Old Testament, the greatest concentration of these terms occurs in the Prophetic books, where the trauma of Babylonian captivity induced a sense that the Judean community was being punished for earlier transgressions and needed to repent. Hence Isa 55:7 exhorts the wicked to return (*epistraphete*) to the Lord, and Ezek 18:30 urges them to turn away (*epistrephein*) from their transgressions. The Geneva Bible's commentary on the latter passage implies that these acts require an interior change of heart that remains unspoken: "Man cannot forsake his wickedness till his heart be changed." In this context, the meaning of repentance as *metanoein*, "to change one's heart or mind," occurs in Jer 8:6.

Greek New Testament texts combine the sentiments of remorse and a moral turn or return as in Acts 3:19, "Repent (*metanoesate*) therefore and turn (*epistrepsate*) to God," while other texts focus on the hope of repentance as in Rom 2:4 or on the effects of it as in Matt 3:2 and Mark 1:4, which proclaim a "baptism of repentance (*baptisma metanoias*)." The reformers based their rejection of sacramental penance on these passages, prompted by Erasmus's discovery that the translation of *metanoia* in the Latin Vulgate had introduced a distortion into religious practice. Rendering the Greek noun by the Latin *poenitentia*, "penitence" (related to the adverb *penitus*, "inward, internal," but manifested by outward signs of rehabilitation) and rendering the Greek verb *metanoeo* by the Latin verb-object phrase *poenitentiam agere*, "to do penance," the words imply a performance of some physical act or acts that display repentance. In short, the original Greek conveys a wholly internal act of moral cognition without the intervention of a priest or minister and without the external ministration of confession, contrition, absolution, and atonement.

The result of the Reformers' denial of sacramental status to penance was to undo the assurance of a Christian that his or her sins had been forgiven through the words of a priest and to invite in its place a host of epistemological uncertainties about the thoroughness and sincerity of one's repentance, about whether God or collaterally offended human parties accepted it, and about whether the social and communal body wounded by sin might be healed through the sinner's private atonement (Beckwith 2011, 34–56). In dealing with these issues, the bishops' Hampton Court Conference left a precise doctrine of penance unresolved. Dramatic consequences of this irresolution in Shakespeare's plays before and after the conference shape the action of his history plays (*Richard II, Henry IV* 1 and 2), mid-career comedies (*As You Like It, Twelfth Night, Much Ado about Nothing*), mature tragedies (*Hamlet, Othello, King Lear, Macbeth*), and late romances (*Cymbeline, Winter's Tale, Tempest*).

Among them, *King Lear* represents Shakespeare's most sustained engagement with the problem and his most probing encounter with its biblical representations. Its protagonist makes a terrible mistake at the beginning of the play when he alienates Cordelia and divides his kingdom between Goneril and Regan. His recognition of this mistake generates the play's dramatic crisis and his efforts to repent dominate the ensuing action. Echoes from both Testaments inflect this action. Acts 1 and 2 draw chiefly on Hebrew scripture to set the terms of Lear's repentance as an act of *metanoia*, "change of mind or attitude," and as a movement of *epistrephein*, "turn or return," to repair his alienation from Cordelia. Act 3 dramatizes his recognition that repentance entails something more than regret and a return to the *status quo ante.*

It requires a wholly transformative internal change and moral recovery. Acts 4 and 5 focus on the processes of *metanoia* and *epistrephein* in Christian Scripture that enable such change and recovery, while challenging them with Stoic and Epicurean forces of determination and blind chance that crush the protagonists.

As it turns out, too, the play reflects something of the literary meaning of *metanoia* as a product of authorial redaction and revision. Within the Shakespearean canon, *King Lear* offers striking evidence of the author's habits of original composition and later revision (John Jones 1995; Halio 2005, 65–96). Variant copies of its first 1608 Quarto publication (referring to the size of the volume as a medium-range hand-held book) differ from each other, and they in turn differ from its first 1623 Folio publication (referring to its size as a deluxe volume for an elite readership). The play itself might be viewed as an instance and example of literary *metanoia* in which multiple revisions inflect different versions of the author's work. I'll call attention to a couple of passages deleted from its Folio publication and to the significance of their deletion for interpreting the text in relation to the Bible. Most of the omissions in the Folio version mitigate Lear's descent into madness as a consequence of his daughters' abandonment of him. They have the effect of suggesting that the change of temperament associated with madness is a feature of repentance and that Lear's repentance is the result of a clear-headed but understandably agonized examination of conscience.

Acts 1 and 2: Foreclosed Promises and Strained Alliances

The play's first scene addresses competing claims about the meaning and efficacy of the term "Testament" as "a legal will or promise" (Latin *testamentum*), "a covenant" (Hebrew *berith*), or "an alliance" (Greek *diatheké*). Confusions among these terms jump-start the action. Lear decides to foreclose the "promise" of his legal will by dividing his kingdom among his daughters before his death. The arrangement boxes him into a "covenant" with his daughters to respect his independence and *de facto* rights as a retired monarch. Though Goneril professes to love her father "as much as child e'er loved" (1.1.54) and Regan proclaims "my very deed of love" (1.1.66), neither agrees to an "alliance" with her father. Cordelia asserts that she loves her father "according to my bond, no more nor less" (1.1.88). The "bond" that she evokes is neither a covenant, alliance, nor sworn promise, but rather a nod to the Biblical injunction to love and honor one's parents (Exod 20:12; Deut 5:16), qualified by the further injunction of Gen 2:24 that a man shall "leave his father and his mother, and shall cleave to his wife, and they shall be one flesh" (quoted from the Geneva Bible with modernized spelling). The qualification implies that Cordelia's primary alliance will be with her future husband, to whom she will owe greater loyalty than to her father. The Geneva commentary on this scriptural verse underscores the implication, "that marriage requires a greater duty of us toward our wives, than otherwise we are bound to show to our parents." It posits a problem for – and potential conflict in – any alliance with Cordelia's promised husband, the king of France.

In general, during the first two acts, biblical references echo Septuagint and Christian translations of Hebrew scriptures, likely to strengthen a sense of remote antiquity in the play's historical setting. Lear's thundering rebuke of his youngest daughter, "Now, by Apollo," anchors the action in its ancient pagan milieu, further enforced by Kent's cautionary "Now, by Apollo, King, / Thou swear'st thy gods in vain" (1.1.159–61). Cordelia in turn defends herself by rebuking Goneril: "Time shall unfold what plighted cunning hides, / Who covers faults, at last with shame derides" (1.1.274–75), echoing Prov 28:13 about the disclosure of one's transgressions (*asebeian*, "wickedness"). She pointedly omits the suggestion of confession, contrition, and repentance in the second half of this biblical verse: "But one who confesses (*exegoumenos* 'one who declares') and forsakes them, will obtain mercy." This foreclosure of admitting one's guilt, evoking a choice passage in the Septuagint Bible about disclosing one's errors to others, will come to shape the play's treatment of repentance as a process.

In contrast to the world of the Old Testament, the play's second scene plunges us into the Roman world of pagan antiquity. Edmund's announcement that "Thou, Nature, art my goddess" (1.2.1) proclaims his allegiance to Lucretius's Epicurean tenets about the random and non-purposive order of nature, the gods' indifference to human beings, and the repudiation of social, cultural, and religious customs as products of superstition and coercion. "Wherefore should I / Stand in the plague of custom" (1.2.2–3), he reasons about his status as the Earl of Gloucester's illegitimate son. Echoing Montaigne's dismissal of reverence owed by sons to their fathers in *Essay* 2.8 ("On the Affection of Fathers for their Children") and slyly indicating the playwright's own source in describing his character's contempt as an "*essay* or taste of my virtue" (1.2.44), Edmund aligns the patriarchal justice of the Old Testament with hypocrisy, Goneril's and Regan's Mosaic attribution of affection due to parents with hyperbole, and Cordelia's expression of New Testament love with folly and weakness of character. His Epicurean skepticism puts him on a collision course not only with the Stoicism of his father's generation but also with the Biblical pronouncements at stake in Reformation theology.

So too do the declarations of Lear's rebellious daughters. In 1.4 Goneril confronts her father with the apparent voice of reason and common sense as she rebukes his pleasure-seeking retainers. Their licentious behavior infects her court with "Epicurism and lust," making it seem "more like a tavern or brothel / Than a grac'd palace" (1.4.199–200). Goneril's superficial equation of "Epicurism" with debauchery hides her own deep investment in Epicurean philosophy as a vehicle to justify her royal ambition. Like Edmund she champions Epicurean self-determination and overthrows conventional ideals of filial respect. Lear's response, "Hear, Nature, hear! Dear Goddess, hear!" (1.2.230) incongruously echoes Edmund's "Thou, Nature, art my Goddess" as he curses Goneril's succession to the throne: "Into her womb convey sterility" (1.4.233). Like a disease, Epicurism has imperiled the royal family in both senses, as licentious behavior in its reductive sense and as an anti-Stoic philosophy in its moral sense.

In 2.4 Regan too rebukes the behavior of her father's retinue and she elicits his terrible curse. In this instance, the daughter frames her accusation in terms that evoke the bargaining of Abraham with God to spare Sodom from destruction in Gen 18:22–30. When Lear proposes a retreat to Regan's court after reducing his followers to a hundred, she halves the number to fifty: "What should you need of more?" (2.4.231). After Goneril demands further reductions, Regan stoops to rock bottom, "What need one?" (2.4.256). In moral terms, the analogy of Abraham's bargaining situates Lear's self-seeking daughters (who haggle to humiliate him) in inverse relation to the Biblical patriarch (who negotiates against the rank injustice of the deity to save the inhabitants of Sodom). At the same time, it situates Lear in inverse relationship to the Old Testament Lord. The king becomes a powerless suppliant whose wishes, like Abraham's, the deity finally denies.

At this point, the play's argument takes a radical turn. Lear's response to his daughters' quantitative assessment of his retainers and their pleasures drives him to exclaim "O reason not the need" (2.4.257), arguing that something more than the basic necessities of survival is fundamental to human needs ("Our basest beggars / Are in the poorest thing superfluous," 2.4.257–58) and that to think otherwise is to demean human nature: "Allow not nature more than nature needs, / Man's life is cheap as beasts" (2.4.259–60). His reasoning aligns with that of Jesus in the gospel account of his anointing at Bethany

(John 12:1–8). When Judas objects to the expenditure of money for perfume and oil, Jesus defends it on grounds that the cost can be kept on deposit until his burial anointing (12:8). The contrast between Judas's petulant complaint and Jesus's prophetic response deepens with Lear's increasing agitation, registered in his broken sentence fragments and disrupted train of thought, culminating in his dramatic exit line addressed to the court jester: "O fool! I shall go mad" (2.4.279).

Act 3: Recognition and Charity

Modern actors have gambled many a critical reputation on acting scenes of Lear's purported madness. The play's Biblical resonances might put their success into question. In the Hebrew Bible, Deut 28:28 identifies madness as a curse or punishment for disobeying the Lord's command-ments, while Eccl 9:3 associates it with a heart full of evil. Depictions of madness in Matt 17:10, Mark 5:1–15, and Luke 4:33 refer to demonic possession. In John 10:19–21, Jesus' followers support him by arguing that he speaks not as "one who has a demon." Elizabethan and Jacobean England accepted these definitions, and Edgar's disguised impersonation of "Tom o' Bedlam" exploits their attributes. But Lear's behavior does not display them. The king alludes to his distress as *"hysterica passio"* (2.4.53), an emotional response to stress that causes a tightening of the throat and chest and brings on a sense of suffocation. A naturalistic account of these symptoms might relate them to emotional turmoil, lack of sleep, and mental and physical exhaustion, all of them behavior-ally and physiologically accountable, without assigning them to psych-osis. Lear's reaction to the storm in act 3 – "I tax you not, you elements, with unkindness. / I never gave you kingdom, call'd you children" (3.2.15–16) – assesses its fury as a fact of nature, not of divine judgment.

A different response takes place two scenes later when Lear sees himself no longer as a king but as a human being who, taking cogni-zance of other human beings, shares their travail. He experiences an interval of recognition during which he reframes, reassesses, and liter-ally *re-cognizes* his place in the world. Groping toward a reconstructed sense of himself, he ponders the condition of "Poor naked wretches, whereso'er you are / That bide the pelting of this pitiless storm" (3.4.28–29). With dissolving self-regard he comprehends that, as a former monarch answerable to the well-being of his people, he has neglected his charge – "O I have ta'en / Too little care of this" – and can only now dispose himself "to feel what wretches feel" (3.4.32–34). At this exact moment, Edgar intrudes on the king's party in disguise as "Tom." Role-playing the conventional figure of a madman, he readily impersonates demonic possession: "Away, the foul fiend follows me!" (3.4.44). And as part of his role-playing, he begs the conventional generosity and oblation extended toward madmen for basic survival: "Do Poor Tom some charity" (3.4.56). The insertion of the Biblical notion of "charity" into the action directs the scene of recognition beyond Lear to the broader community that he serves.

In its restricted sense, the idea of "charity" derives from the Latin noun *caritas* as a work of beneficence toward the poor and the disadvantaged. The word is used in the Latin Vulgate Bible to translate the Greek noun *agape*, "love," derived from the verb *agapaein*, "to love with affection in a non-sexual sense." In the Septuagint Old Testament and Greek New Testament the noun *agape* implies acts of consideration for others. It occurs in the Septuagint where it renders the Hebrew verb *'ahab*, "love." in such examples as Deut 4:37, with God's love for his people; Deut 6:5, with the love of God's people for him; Ruth 4:15, with one's love of family; and the Song of Solomon 2:4, with the bridegroom's encompassing love (noun *'ahaba*) for his bride.

The verb and its noun occur more frequently in the Greek New Testament in such examples as Matt 5:44, with its injunction to love (*agapate*) one's enemies; John 3:16, where God so loved (*egapesen*) the world; John 13:34, where Jesus's love should prompt us to love (*agapate*) one another; 1 Cor 13:13 where faith and hope abide with love (*agape*); and 1 John 4:8, where "God is love (*agape*)." In English the noun *charity* conveys an idea of considerateness for others through the practice of almsgiving and other kinds of assistance to the poor, the helpless, and the downtrodden, based upon examples in Matt 25:31–40, "for I was hungry and you gave me food": A cornerstone of Christianity when, from the start, *caritas*, "charity," signified "affectionate dealing" before it more narrowly signified "relief." Such benefaction had been consolidated during the middle ages and institutionalized in clergy-governed alms houses. Tom's "Bedlam" itself is a contraction for London's church-sponsored asylum, St. Mary's of Bethlehem.

Throughout Europe the Reformation had shifted the control of such institutions by the clergy toward communal supervision of them by the laity, with new mandates for acts of personal conscience and collective responsibility. From Lear's perspective, Tom's call for "charity" speaks to a complex recognition of social responsibilities that the king had neglected, including consideration toward others and tolerance for their human weaknesses. Such charitable allowance might be traced to 1 Cor 13:4–7, where love (*agape*) bears all and believes all. This allowance proves relevant to Lear's recognition of his administrative responsibilities and his turn toward repentance. As "Tom," Edgar identifies himself as a former "servingman" at court, "proud in heart and mind," who lost his moral balance amid palace intrigue, "light of ear, bloody of hand" (3.4.77–83). Lear responds to "Tom's" role-playing descent into madness with an interjection, "Is man no more than this?" (3.4.92), at once echoing the Old and New Testaments in Ps 8:4–6 and Heb 2:6. For Lear, the verses from Psalms and Paul's quotation of them in Hebrews question human superiority over lower forms of creation as opposed to God's infinite superiority over human beings, leading him to affirm Job's negative assessment of the human individual as a worm (Job 25.6).

Gloucester alone perceives that Lear's reactions, construed by others as "mad," are within normal range. To Kent's remark that Lear's "wits begin t' unsettle," the earl comments, "Canst thou blame him? / His daughters seek his death" (3.4.146–47). Refusing to identify Lear's behavior with divine displeasure or demonic possession, he attributes it to profound grief and emotional distress, to which we can add his physical depletion after journeying from Albany in northern Scotland (act 1) to Cornwall in southwest England (act 2) to southeast England and Dover (acts 3 and 4). Perhaps most telling is the truncation of lines from Lear's subsequent "mad" scene, act 3, scene 6, excised from the early Quarto format (1608), when the play is republished in Folio format (1623). The latter eliminates from the scene thirty-six lines that detail Lear's psychotic hallucination of Goneril and Regan and his arraignment of them in a mock trial (starting after 3.6.14; see Halio 2005, 270 and 297–300). The removal of these lines has the positive advantage of situating Lear's discovery of charity in a clear and rational light, as one that spurs his movement toward repentance as well as tragedy in the play's ensuing acts.

Acts 4 and 5: Repentance and Tragedy

By the beginning of act 4, the earl of Gloucester has been charged with treason by Regan's husband, the duke of Cornwall, and has been blinded by him. Gloucester's fortuitous meeting with his banished son Edgar imbues act 4, scene 1, with a series of echoes from Job's lamentations in the Hebrew Testament (see Hamlin 2012, 305–33; Boitani 2013, 25–39). On discovering his father's blindness, Edgar exclaims, "Who is't can say 'I am at the worst'? / I am worse than e'er I was" (4.1.25–26), capturing the lesson of Job epitomized in the Geneva Bible: "For Job held that God did not always punish men according to their sins, but that he had secret judgments, whereof man knew not the cause" (222^v).

Gloucester responds by recalling his encounter with Edgar-as-"Tom o' Bedlam": "I such a fellow saw, / Which made me think a man a worm" (4.1.32-33), echoing Lear's reference to Job 25:6. And Gloucester folds into the biblical echo a terse paraphrase of Lucretius's Epicurean position on divine indifference toward human suffering: "As flies to wanton boys, are we to th' gods; / They kill us for their sport" (4.1.36-37). Gloucester hardly comprehends that Edgar stands nearby, ready to help him. The good son's appearance belies the father's pessimism.

From the audience's perspective, another recognition occurs on Cordelia's arrival in England to help her father. Countering rumors in act 3 that France is preparing to attack England, the following act establishes that Cordelia has mobilized a French army to restore Lear to his throne. She apostrophizes her absent father with a recall of the New Testament that leaves no doubt about her intent: "O dear father, / It is thy business that I go about" (4.3.23–24). This echo of Luke 2:49 points to a higher obligation than filial respect to one's parents. The Geneva gloss on this verse ("Our duty to God is to be preferred before father and mother") broadens the scope of "my father's business" in Luke's gospel to include the supreme injunction in Matt 22:37–40 to love (*agapeseis*) God and love one's neighbor as oneself, epitomizing the concept of *agape* in the New Testament. They in turn underwrite Cordelia's claim that she will defend her father against Goneril and Regan: "No blown ambition doth our arms incite, / But love, dear love, and our ag'd father's right" (4.3.27–28).

The play's most powerful enactments of recognition and repentance unfold in act 4, scene 5, which begins with Gloucester's aborted suicide leap from Dover cliff. Edgar orchestrates the event by pretending that his father has actually fallen but somehow survived. "Thy life's a miracle" (4.5.55), he exclaims, while relinquishing his voice as "Tom" and adopting the new voice of a witnessing bystander. Adverting to Stoic – and, for Shakespeare's era, Reformationist – tenets of divine will, providence, and foreordination, Edgar anticipates Luke 18:27 when he argues that the gods bring honor to themselves by performing deeds that are impossible for human beings: "Think that the clearest gods, who made them honors / Of men's impossibilities, hath preserved thee" (4.5.73–74). What partially undercuts his claim is the audience's understanding that Edgar has fabricated this "miracle" out of whole cloth and that Gloucester's recovery is an inertly passive act based on an incomplete recognition.

At this point Lear enters with the modern stage direction "fantastically dressed with wild flowers," implied by his contrastive references to luxury apparel in the ensuing 4.5.155–56 and by Cordelia's reference to his garments "of worser hours" as "weeds" in 4.6.7. He appears to be in flight from public officials as he exclaims, "No, they cannot catch me for coining; I am the king himself" (4.5.83). Imagining that authorities have charged him with minting coins, he insists on his right to do so as a royal prerogative. Derangement is less an issue than fatigue and mental confusion. Lear is exhausted and emotionally fragile, but he senses that his composure has been challenged. His resort to decorating himself with wild flowers evokes Matt 6:28–29 about the lilies of the field as more splendid than the clothing of Solomon in all his glory. In their context, these verses follow Jesus' instruction about the nature of piety (*dikaiosune*, literally "a righteous deed"), to which he contrasts hypocritical displays of public charity (Matt 6:1). The Greek noun is translated in the Geneva Bible as "alms," meaning "a bestowal of charitable gifts." Condemning hypocrisy, Jesus then models an efficacious prayer (the "Lord's Prayer," Matt 6:9–14), which exhorts us to forgive others for their moral failings (*paraptomata*, "lapses, false steps"), so that the Father will forgive us for ours.

Lear's tacit reaction to such piety signals his movement toward repentance for having neglected his social responsibilities to both the downtrodden and others. As the scene continues, Lear articulates his remorse in a series of fragmented, uncoordinated, even incoherent utterances that reflect on the hypocrisy of courtiers who flattered him with blandishment "like a dog" (4.5.94), even when he was wrong ("To say 'ay' and 'no' to everything that I said," 4.5.96). Newly accepting responsibility for honest governance ("Ay, every inch a king," 4.5.103), he summons his prerogative of royal pardon as a corrective to unfair judgments rendered by his judiciary. Against authorities who harshly punished those of low rank for transgressions that they quickly pardoned when committed by others of high rank, he reverses their verdicts ("Die for adultery? No" (4.5.107)). The scriptural subtext here is John 8:1–12, where Jesus defends the woman taken in adultery by challenging the Pharisees who are without sexual sin in deed or intent to cast the first stone. In Matt 7:1 Jesus counsels others not to judge, lest they may be judged. Drawing further consequences with regard to corrupt justice and rigid legalism, Lear asks "change places, and handy-dandy, which is the justice, which is the thief?" (4.3.145–46). To his clear-eyed conclusion, "None does offend, none," Edgar replies "Matter and impertinence mixed, / Reason in madness" (4.3.160–66), puncturing the assumption that Lear is simply mad. True madness is allowing elite members of the community to shelter themselves from the suffering of others.

The final scene of act 4 reunites Lear with Cordelia in an inversion of the parable of the Prodigal Son. Instead of depicting the act of "turning around" by an errant son who "came to himself" (Luke 15:17) and returned to his father, the scene presents an errant father who comes to himself and accepts the forgiveness of his daughter. Forgiveness and, by implication, an effectual act of repentance take place as Lear confesses his guilt: "Thou art a soul in bliss; but I am bound / Upon a wheel of fire" (4.6.43–44). Stage directions implied in the dialogue (Cordelia: "You must not kneel," 4.6.56; Lear: "Do not laugh at me," 4.6.65) countermand the sacramental postures of sinner and priest in the rite of penance, while Lear's submission to punishment ("If you have poison for me, I will drink it," 4.6.70) gestures toward sacrificial atonement.

In Mark 14:36 at Gethsemane, the site of Jesus' agony and affliction on the night before his crucifixion, Jesus accepts the cup of suffering and death as he submits to the Father's will. In the words of the Geneva Bible, whose translation echoes the Lord's Prayer, Jesus petitions: "Father, all things are possible unto thee: take away this cup from me; nevertheless not that I will, but that thou wilt be done." In Shakespeare's play, Lear is an afflicted human father who submits to his daughter's will, but she declines to punish him or force amends from him: "No cause, no cause" (4.6.74). Lear honors her request: "You must bear with me. Pray you now, forget / And forgive. I am old and foolish" (4.6.81–82). The final lines of Shakespeare's Quarto, eliminated from the Folio, point toward a less optimistic conclusion. Here Kent witnesses the arrival of Goneril and Regan's army against Cordelia's troops with an apprehension that "report is changeable," and a Gentleman forewarns him that "the arbitrement is like to be bloody" (Halio, 274, 307).

From a tragic perspective rooted in the pagan setting of pre-Christian Britain, Lear's plight can be understood as the search for a follow-up to his recognition of social asymmetry and societal dysfunction. Non-scriptural options point to Stoicism and Epicurism as possible remediations for a suffering that is divinely foreordained (as with Stoicism) or merely random (as with Epicurism). Each in its own way appears hollow for neglecting the individual's responsibility toward others in a broad communal framework. The protagonists' consideration of social inequality, the miscarriage of justice, and the practice of generosity and goodwill toward others is hardly a very low bar. Ecclesiastes would share this view that humans cannot make straight what God has made crooked and that a righteous man can perish in his righteousness (Eccles 7:13, 15). As a pre-Christian monarch, Lear has a precocious insight into the Hebrew Testament *'ahaba* and the Latin Vulgate *caritas*, both inscribed in the Greek concept of *agape*, but his understanding founders against the general unavailability of these ideas at the time. It returns inexorably to the options of Stoicism and Epicurism, and both are shown to be wanting.

By act 5, scene 3, Goneril and Regan's army has defeated Cordelia's troops. Lear embraces Cordelia in their march to prison where he proposes to "kneel down / And ask of thee forgiveness" and where, anticipating absolution, "we'll live, / And pray, and sing, and tell old tales, and laugh / At gilded butterflies . . . / And take upon 's the mystery of things" (5.3.10–16). The solution that he anticipates conflates Roman Stoic detachment from the implacability of fate and Epicurean indifference to the finality of random chance. Significantly, Lear concludes with a reference to Judg 11:29–40, where the military leader Jephthah vows a burnt offering for victory over the Ammonites, and the offering by chance turns out to be his own daughter. In Lear's words, "Upon such sacrifices, my Cordelia, / The gods themselves throw incense" (5.3.20–21). The Geneva Bible cross-refers this story to Paul's Epistle to the Hebrews, in which a host of Old Testament figures such as Gideon, Barak, Samson, David, and Samuel who "though they were commended for their faith, did not receive what was promised" (Hebr 11:39). The troubled comparisons, undermining Lear's anticipation of a happy outcome, portend an aleatory outcome with its resulting sense of pessimism and doom.

In what follows, Edgar in yet another disguise challenges Edmund to a trial by combat to prove the latter "False to thy gods, thy brother, and thy father, / Conspirant 'gainst this high illustrious prince" (5.3.124–25). The folly of such a trial increases the tension between competing claims of a universe governed by divine will as the Stoics had posited, and of one beset by random chance as the Epicureans would have it. In the event, virtuous Edgar prevails over his illegitimate brother, who volunteers to forgive his mortal blow if Edgar identifies himself: "If thou'rt noble, / I do forgive thee" (5.3.155–56). With more than a hint of bitterness ("Let's exchange charity," 5.3.166), Edgar sheds his disguise and ascribes the victory to divine providence: "The gods are just" (5.3.160). In the heat of the moment, he also reveals that their father – upon learning of his return and Edmund's treachery – has just died "'Twixt two extremes of passion, joy and grief" (5.3.188). Gloucester's double recognition of one son's goodness and the other's wickedness, now effectively active and complete, has undone him. The gods seem not so much unjust as they are downright cruel to have allowed him this tragic recognition.

Yet these same gods permit Edmund himself to repent and experience a flicker of redemption. After the news of Edgar's victory, Kent's loyalty to Lear and Gloucester, and the deaths of Goneril and Regan, the reprobate son with his dying breath vows "some good I mean to do, / Despite of mine own nature" (5.3.217–18). He intends to forestall the execution of Lear and Cordelia, but – in an ultimate nod to both random chance and the cruelty of the gods – it is already too late. Lear enters with his daughter dead in his arms, himself exhausted after having attacked and killed her executioner, now lamenting that "She's gone forever" (5.3.233). Perhaps mirroring Edmund's false hope and imagined redemption, Lear holds out a feather to test whether Cordelia still breathes: "If it be so, / It is a chance which does redeem all sorrows" (5.3.239–40). In the end, what he believes he sees proves to be illusory or, more likely in a naturalistic sense, only the shaking of his own hand as he holds the feather to her lips. Worn by age and exhaustion, Lear dies of heart failure.

The tragedy is not that Cordelia and Lear die. All human beings die, a banal truism that Montaigne's Epicurean essays welcomed because it means that death is normal and natural and therefore not to be feared. The play's tragedy is that Lear and Cordelia, despite their trials, had lived in the hope of some positive resolution and with a faith that there would be one. Ultimately, they found none, with no explanation why: neither Stoic fate nor Epicurean chance, and certainly not Biblical redemption. The closest answer may have been adumbrated in the previously cited Paul's Epistle to the Hebrews, concerning those heroes who, despite their faith, "did not receive what was promised" (11:39). But even this citation presumes that the play's tragic characters await an eschatological epoch of perfection not yet available to them. Their futility shows how strands of political history, social inequality, familial rivalry, individual greed, human fallibility, and royal prerogative have twisted into a rope that binds and scourges all of them, until their pain begins to feel natural, normal, and therefore inevitable. It's a tragedy of neither supernatural fate nor natural demise, but of metaphysical emptiness, as though all the gods have withdrawn and the entire world is Gethsemane.

Further Reading

Anonymous, *The True Chronicle History of King Leir* (London, 1605).
Beckwith, Sarah, *Shakespeare and the Grammar of Forgiveness* (Ithaca, NY, 2011).

Berry, Lloyd E., ed., *The Geneva Bible: A Facsimile of the 1560 Edition* (Madison, WI, 1969).

Boitani, Pietro, *The Gospel According to Shakespeare,* trans. Vittorio Monte-maggi and Rachel Jacoff (Notre Dame, IN, 2013).

Halio, Jay L., ed., *William Shakespeare: The Tragedy of King Lear, The New Cambridge Shakespeare,* 2nd ed. (Cambridge, 2005).

Hamlin, Hannibal, *The Bible in Shakespeare* (Oxford, 2012).

Irwin, Terence, *Classical Thought* (Oxford, 1989).

Jones, John, *Shakespeare at Work* (Oxford, 1995).

Nestle, Erwin and Kurt Aland, *Novum Testamentum Graece et Latine,* 18th ed. (Stuttgart, 1958).

Passannante, Gerard, *The Lucretian Renaissance: Philology and the Afterlife of Tradition* (Chicago, 2011).

Shaheen, Naseeb, *Biblical References in Shakespeare's Plays* (Newark, NJ, 1999).

Shapiro, James, *The Year of Lear: Shakespeare in 1606* (New York, 2015).

12 The Bible and John Milton's *Paradise Lost*

GORDON TESKEY

The seventeenth-century English poet John Milton (1608–74) is known for his epic poem, *Paradise Lost* (1667; definitive edition, 1674), which is based on the Fall of humanity in the second and third chapters of Genesis. There we read of Eve and Adam's eating the forbidden fruit, of their judgment by God, and of their *loss* of the *paradise* (a Greek-based word meaning "garden"):

> Of Man's first disobedience and the fruit
> Of that forbidden tree whose mortal taste
> Brought death into the world and all our woe
> With loss of Eden . . .
> *Paradise Lost* 1.1–4[1]

One might suppose this to be an unpromising subject for an epic poem, which it is. The Fall does not occur until the ninth book of Milton's epic; and the exile from the garden does not take place until the closing lines, in which Adam and Eve go forth into the world with the weight of history before them – history as it is told in the rest of the Bible, from Genesis to the Book of Revelation. Unpromising as it seems, in Milton's hands this subject is made into one of the great poems of the world, worthy to stand with Homer and Virgil or, as he thinks, to stand above them because it is true, and also more sublime.

---

[1] The text is John Milton, *Paradise Lost*, ed. Gordon Teskey (New York, 2005). I cite from the Authorized, or King James, version of the Bible (published by Oxford University Press). I use the standard Christian terms, Old Testament and New Testament, fully aware of their polemical significance *vis-à-vis* the Hebrew Scriptures, which I refer to as such when (rarely) focusing on their language or their Jewish context. Although Milton may well have consulted the more radically puritan Geneva Bible, when checking the text in English he appears most often to have consulted the Authorized Version, a well-thumbed copy of which is one of the books surviving from his library. For the Greek text of the New Testament I cite from *Novum Testamentum Graece*, 2nd ed., ed. Alexander Souter (1947; rpt. Oxford, 1966).

One may accept from Milton the proposition that the story of Eve and Adam is true because for him the Bible is the inspired word of God, which is accommodated to the human mind as the eye is adapted to light. In the sixteenth and seventeenth centuries, after the invention of printing with moveable type, after the Protestant Reformation and the Thirty Years' War, at a time when Scripture was being translated into the modern languages and intensively studied in the original ones, not least by Milton himself, the Bible was by far the most widespread, controversial, and important book in Europe – and increasingly, in the world. Its stories mattered to everyone, especially the story of Eve and Adam, because it is about everyone. Unlike other poets of the age who chose biblical subjects, such as Abraham Cowley, in his unfinished royalist epic *Davideis,* Milton understood that the full scale of the Bible could be captured only by seizing it at the beginning, in the story of Adam and Eve.

That simple, etiological myth, or "just so story," which explains why women have pain in childbirth, why humans must labor to eat, why snakes and humans are mutually inimical, and why we die, makes Milton's subject for his epic more relevant to people's immediate lives in a way that tales of remote heroes are not. But more sublime? What makes two naked people who eat some fruit and lose the paradise they live in for doing so "more heroic than the wrath / Of stern Achilles" (9.14–15), as Milton very seriously claims? He says that in pursuing his "adventurous song" he will soar "above the Aonian mount" – that is, mount Helicon, home of the muses of classical epic – and that he will do so not on the strength of his own powers, considerable as they are, but by virtue of the sublimity of his biblical subject (1.13–15). With the help of the Spirit, of which the classical muses are only a distorted intuition, he will vindicate the righteousness of God to all humanity throughout all the ages. Such a task can be accomplished only by following the word of God, as revealed in the Bible. That is Milton's *argument* or "subject matter":[2]

> What in me is dark
> Illumine, what is low raise and support,
> That to the heighth of this great argument
> I may assert Eternal Providence
> And justify the ways of God to men.
>
> *Paradise Lost* 1.22–26

---

[2] For *argument* as "subject matter" see OED definition 6.

This design does not amount to a wholesale rejection of the pagan epic tradition by Milton, although something like that will come later, in *Paradise Regained* (1671). It is instead an elevation of the conventions of the epic tradition to something higher, something the tradition should have been about from the start but wasn't, or that it has always wanted to be about without knowing it, because it lacked the revelation of Scripture. The laws of the genre of epic – a great concern of theorists in the Renaissance – are for the biblically inclined Milton like the good instincts of the Gentiles in Paul's epistle to the Romans, "a law unto themselves" (2:14). But the real sublimity of Milton's design, superb as is his transmutation of the classical tradition, lies in his doing something that no other poet of his day was able to do and that the poets of antiquity would not have wanted to do: to represent "the human" as a totality, and to represent history as a whole. Milton did so in the only way open to him at the time, which was to turn to the Bible.

This anthropocentrism is revealed in Milton's startling phrase, "justify the ways of God to men." In the Bible, of course, it is humans who must be justified before God, and they will be if they believe in the efficacy of Jesus' resurrection from the dead: He was "raised again for our justification"; and as a result of that, if we believe in it, we are "justified by faith" (Rom 4:25 and 5:1). The model is the faith of Abraham, who was justified through "the righteousness of faith" (*dia dikaiosunês pisteôs*) (Rom 4:13 and 22).[3] The meaning of that complex word translated as "faith" – *pistis*, "trust/belief/loyalty/confidence/uprightness" – is belief without proof, obedience without persuasion, and spontaneous assent without the conviction of the intellect, in short, everything that is *not* asked of readers of *Paradise Lost*. For Milton, it is symmetrically important, so to speak, to have the ways of God justified in the minds of human beings through a poem like his, without leaving the matter to faith. Paul wrote the epistle to the Romans to show how we may be justified to God. Milton composed *Paradise Lost* to show how God's righteousness may be justified to us. Who we are as human beings is at stake.

Other epic poets of the Renaissance, in Italy, France, Spain, Portugal, and the Americas – and of course in England, to count Milton's first model, Edmund Spenser – wrote epics of national consciousness, choosing single events within history, or supposed history: the liberation of Italy from the Goths by Belisarius; the conquest of Jerusalem in the first

---

[3] In the Greek, these two words have the same root, *dikê*, "justice," and *dikaiosunê*, "justification/righteousness."

crusade by Godfredo; the siege of Paris by the Pagan King Agramante; the circumnavigation of Africa by Vasco da Gama; and Prince Arthur's quest to find the Fairy Queen, with its political allegories of conflict in Belgium and Ireland. In these poems enemies are represented as dehumanized others, whether Saracen, African, Indian, or Native American – or Spanish and Irish. The literary interest comes from brief moments when these others show human feelings and noble sentiments, a reflection of the uncertainty as to what constitutes the human when Europeans were encountering un-baptized non-Europeans and seeking to convert, enslave, or exterminate them. Milton alone, through the figures of Eve and Adam, the first parents of the human race, takes humanity as a whole as his subject and makes history the consequence of humanity's sin, or rather, of humanity's *disobedience*, a less mysterious and more political word. Instead of the strange New Testament concept of sin, or *hamartia*, as a kind of pollution in individuals without collective meaning, *obedience* suggests a rationally determinable relation of authority between at least two parties. It is in the same category as secular terms such as *sovereignty* and bears on the theory of the state.

   To add epic grandeur, Milton develops many extra- and para-biblical themes in order to represent events on a cosmic scale that he conceives to be consistent with biblical truth. They are also consistent with the discoveries of modern navigators and geographers, and above all of astronomers, especially Galileo – twice mentioned in *Paradise Lost* (1.288; 5.262) – who vastly increased our understanding of the size of the universe and allowed Milton to place Hell not in the center of the earth but outside the universe altogether, far off in chaos (Books One and Two).

   The grandest epic portion of *Paradise Lost* is the tremendous war in Heaven, which the angel Raphael relates to Adam to explain why Satan – "the Adversary" (1.629; cf. 1.81–82; Hebrew, *ha satan*) – intends to destroy their lives and, through them, the entire human race (Books Five and Six). Milton's war in Heaven is sustainedly classical in style and decorum. But its very existence is weakly supported by apocryphal traditions and strained interpretations of small details in the Hebrew Scriptures. These include the famously obscure *nephiliim*, "sons of God," or "giants," who seduce the daughters of men as Satan seduced Eve and as the pagan gods seduce humans into worshipping them: "the sons of God saw the daughters of men that they were fair; and they took them wives of all which they chose" (Gen 6:2). There are also prophecies against human princes, especially the one against the King of Babylon: "How art thou fallen from heaven, O Lucifer, son of the

morning!" (Isa 14:12), echoed by Jesus himself: "I beheld Satan as
lightening fall from heaven" (Luke 10:18); and a prophecy against the
King of Tyre as the once divinely favored "covering cherub" in heaven,
walking among its flaming stones, but later understood to be Satan
when he is cast out of "the mountain of God" (Ezek 28:1–19). Milton
knew that the Latin name *Lucifer*, "light bearer," was Saint Jerome's
translation of the Hebrew *helel*, which means radiant light, instead of
its source, *shachar*, and that Jesus' reference to Satan falling like lightning from heaven (... *ôs astrapên ek tou oranou*) is a still more emphatic
reference to secondary, radiant light in contrast to its primary source.
Satan's "sun-bright chariot" is therefore an "Idol of majesty divine"
(6.100–1). But it is not the real thing, the Son's "Chariot of Paternal
Deity" (6.750), from which the Son hurls lightning bolts into the ranks
of the damned while the very wheels spout "pernicious fire" (6.836–88;
844–52). Milton's Son is not the dawning light, but the morning itself,
and he is not the lightning but the hand by which it is thrown.

   The fullest justification for Milton's Homeric angels is the war
recounted in the Book of Revelation (although this occurs at the end
of the world, not, as Milton's does, before the world is made). There,
Michael and his angels war against the dragon and *his* angels (12:7): "and
the great dragon was cast out, that old serpent, called the Devil, and
Satan, which deceiveth the whole world: he was cast out into the earth,
and his angels were cast out with him" (12:9). In this passage, however,
Satan and his angels are cast down to earth, not into Hell, as they are in
Paradise Lost (6.860–77). The apocalyptic account must therefore be
supplemented by the following, from the Epistle of Jude: "the angels
which kept not their first estate, but left their own habitation, he hath
reserved [the Greek verb means 'guarded'] in everlasting chains under
darkness unto the judgment of the great day" (6).

   This analysis should teach us two things: first, Milton's vast and
detailed, synthetic knowledge of the Bible, in English as well as in the
original languages, is the principal source of the densely allusive texture
of his verse; second, his willingness to imagine large coherent scenes in
his poem is based on the smallest of biblical precedents.

   On the same principles we are shown the creation of the entire
universe and within it the earth, based on the first two chapters of
Genesis, but on a far larger canvas (Book Seven). We see Sin and Death,
briefly mentioned in Romans as legal abstractions: "the law of sin and
death" (8:2). In *Paradise Lost* they spring to life as terrifying monsters
building a great bridge across chaos from Hell toward the created universe – "a ridge of pendant rock / Over the vexed abyss" – and doing so

by "wond'rous art / Pontifical," as Milton slyly adds (10.312–14). Sin lays out the route for the bridge, being guided by a mysterious "connatural force" of like with like, the sin of Man with Sin herself. She is "strongly drawn / By this new felt attraction and instinct" (10.246 and 262–3). Death follows her, drawn by a more primitive and, at a distance, less reliable guide for directions, that of smell:

> I shall not lag behind nor err
> The way, thou leading, such a scent I draw
> Of carnage, prey innumerable, and taste
> The savor of death from all things there that live.
> *Paradise Lost* 10.266–69

In a shocking scene, Death turns one expanded nostril upward like a satellite dish to capture the olfactory signal of his prey: "So scented the grim feature and upturned / His nostril wide into the murky air, / Sagacious of his quarry from so far" (10.279–81). Another subtlety to observe is how Milton describes Sin using her deeper powers of sympathetic attraction to lead her otherwise indomitable and impetuous offspring, Death, who raped and tortured her as soon as he emerged from her womb (2.785–808). Milton is setting forth the priority of sin in this biblical passage: Death can't live without Sin (otherwise, he'd kill her) and he can't get into the universe to devour all living flesh, striving to satisfy his insatiable hunger, without Sin leading the way. All this starts from the biblical verse, "in the day that thou eatest thereof thou shalt surely die" (Gen 2:17). But it visualizes brilliantly the passage in Romans describing sin and death entering the world: "as by one man sin entered the world, and death by sin [*kai dia tês hamartias ho thanatos*], so death passed upon all men" (5:12).

Paul's term for "world," by which he means our earth and the daytime sky we see above it, is *kosmos*. For Milton, "cosmos" means what it means today, the entire universe, as does, for him, the word *world*, which is what Sin and Death will fasten the end of their prodigious bridge to: "From out of chaos to the outside bare / Of this round world"; they fix it in place "with pins of adamant / And chains" (10.317–19). The bridge is fastened not to the earth but to what Milton earlier calls "the firm opacous globe / Of this round world," which protects all the stars and planets inside it from the destructive force of chaos outside (3.418–21). When we look up at the night sky we now understand the blackness that we see beyond the stars to be empty space through which light can pass from any distance, given sufficient time to do so. Milton asks us to imagine it as the concave, inner side of a solid sphere, on the convex side of which Satan first lands, after his voyage across chaos. All this is carefully extrapolated from hints in the Bible. Milton is exceptionally free in the liberties that he takes with the biblical texts; but he always likes to stay in touch.

We now see that it will be by means of this bridge (10.256–61) that the devils will reach the universe and come to earth, pretending to be gods, in particular, the idols of Palestine, Egypt, and Greece, drawing human worship away from the true God in order to promote murder and sexual perversion as religious observances. We are introduced to this interesting theory of religion in the first book, in the magnificent catalogue of the leaders of the rebel angels, whom Satan marshals after they have risen from the burning lake of Hell: "The chief were those who from the pit of Hell / Roaming to seek their prey on Earth" (1.381–82). These set themselves up first as "gods adored" in the nations surrounding Israel, eventually establishing their shrines on Mount Zion itself, beside God's holy Temple (1.382–91). The catalogue begins with Moloch, "horrid king, besmeared with blood / Of human sacrifice and parents' tears" (1.392–93), within whose bronze, furnace-like idol infants were torched, their screams drowned out by his priests' tambourines and drums: "Though for the noise of drums and timbrels loud / Their children's cries unheard that passed through fire / To his grim idol" (1.394–96). He is followed by Chemos, also named Peor, "the obscéne dread of Moab's sons" (1.404), whose religious observances, which included ritual defecation as well as sexual perversion, spread from Shittim, a place of rest during the wilderness journey, to Jerusalem and the neighborhood of the Temple itself, near the shrine of Moloch (Num 25:1–3). Both gods were brought there by Solomon (1 Kgs 11:1–9). There they remained as busy shrines to hate and lust, attracting worship away from the true God on Mount Zion until, years later, King Josiah "burnt the bones of the priests upon their altars, and cleansed Judah and Jerusalem" (2 Chr 34:4–5):

Yet thence his lustful orgies he enlarged
Ev'n to that hill of scandal by the grove
Of Moloch homicide (lust hard by hate)
Till good Josiah drove them thence to Hell.
Paradise Lost 1.45–18

This is Milton's account of the continual and compulsive idolatry of Israel, from the Golden Calf of Exodus 32 to the mixing of sex and religion during the journey to the Promised Land to the monotonously reiterated crimes of idolatry in the "high places" as recounted in the Books of Kings and Chronicles. Idolatry becomes especially troublesome after the division of the kingdom, which occasions the doubling of the original Golden Calf crime. The doubling is perpetrated by Jeroboam, the new king of the rebel northern kingdom, now called Israel (1 Kgs 12:28–30). To prevent his subjects from going to the enemy southern kingdom of Judea to worship at the Temple in Jerusalem, Jeroboam sets up *two* golden calves, one to be worshipped in Bethel, near the southern border and close to Jerusalem, the other in Dan, far to the north, under Mount Hermon.[4] In doing so, Milton speculates, Jeroboam imitates the gods of "fanatic Egypt" with their "brutish forms / Rather than human":

> Nor did Israel 'scape
> Th'infection when their borrowed gold composed
> The calf in Oreb [Sinai] and the rebel king [Jeroboam]
> Doubled that sin in Bethel and in Dan,
> Likening his Maker to the grazèd ox.
>
> *Paradise Lost* 1.480–86

Milton's intense command of the Bible is evident through this long catalogue of 124 lines (with a further sixteen lines on gods from other parts of the world). Every detail calls up multiple biblical passages. The location of the religious orgies and murders is in the valley of the son of Hinnom, an obscure name (*ge ben Hinnom* [Josh 15:8, and many subsequent references]). This valley is to the west of Jerusalem and in it was an area reserved for Moloch's shrine, named *Tophet*, "oven," "burning place" (2 Kgs 23:10). King Manasseh, like other kings, had his children burned there, this being but one item in the long list of that king's idolatrous crimes, mentioned almost as an afterthought: "And he caused his children to pass through the fire in the valley of the son of Hinnom" (2 Chr 33:6). The valley is renamed by the prophet Jeremiah, probably – so Milton assumes – because its name, *Hinnom*, had pleasant associations from earlier days when the valley contained groves: "Therefore, behold, the days come, saith the Lord, that this place shall no more be called Tophet, nor The Valley of the son of Hinnom, but The valley of slaughter" (Jer 19:6; also 7:32). The New Testament Greek derivative of *ge ben Hinnom*, via Aramaic, is *gehenna*, which is the name frequently used by Jesus as a place of punishment beyond this world, i.e. Hell: "Ye serpents, ye generation of vipers, how can ye escape

---

[4] In *The Origins of Biblical Law: The Decalogues and the Book of the Covenant* (Ithaca, NY, 1992), 229, Calum Carmichael argues that the passage on the Golden Calf in Exodus 32 was inserted after Jeroboam's idolatry, as a condemnation of it.

the damnation [judgment] of hell [*tes kriseôs tês gehenês*]?" (Matt 23:33). Hence for Christians the earthly valley lying along Mount Zion's west side, where refuse was burned and the dead were eaten by dogs, where horrible murders and obscene acts were committed in the name of religion, is a *type* or historical symbol – that is, a symbol established by God himself in real events and places in the Old Testament – of the truth to be revealed in the New Testament. For the true place of horrors awaits us beyond this world, after the Last Judgment.

All these biblical passages with their philological refinements and theological elaborations are activated in Milton's mind and powerfully compressed when he speaks of Solomon's making his grove for Moloch and Chemos in the valley of Hinnom: "The pleasant valley of Hinnom, Tophet thence / And black Gehenna called, the type of Hell" (1.404–5).

If Milton's command of the Bible is evident in the earlier books of *Paradise Lost* by amazing compression, in the final two books of the poem it is demonstrated by judicious selection during a masterly and inevitably tendentious summary of the Bible from Genesis 4 to the Apocalypse, "the race of time / Till time stand fixed" (12.554–55). The angel Michael has arrived to expel Eve and Adam from the garden, as God has commanded him to do, but not without hope for the future, lest they utterly despair. God instructs Michael:

If patiently thy bidding they obey,
Dismiss them not disconsolate. Reveal
To Adam what shall come in future days
As I shall thee enlighten. Intermix
My covenant in the woman's seed renewed.
                    Paradise Lost 11.111–14

After delivering the bad news, Michael puts Eve to sleep – "Let Eve (for I have drenched her eyes) / Here sleep below" (11.367–68) – and leads Adam up a high mountain, from which the first man has a clear view of the entire hemisphere of the earth from the point where he stands, another astonishing display – there have been several before – of geographic erudition. Adam may even see over that horizon, "in spirit perhaps" (11.406), gaining sight of Mexico, Peru, and Guiana:

It was a hill
Of Paradise the highest from whose top
The hemisphere of Earth in clearest ken
Stretched out to th'amplest reach of prospect lay.
                    Paradise Lost 11.377–80

Milton is filling in the inadequate and vague geographical information provided in the original Genesis story. The Bible may have been inspired by God, but it was written down by human agents, with all their imperfections, especially of information in the first millennium BCE. Milton supplies improvements before the biblical narrative gets under way.

When it does, he opens with the scene of a field partly used for growing grain – "part arable and tilth" – and partly for "sheep-walks and folds" (11.430–31). We have begun with the story of Cain and Abel, seen here as in a film, for the scenes follow one another in this manner, with Michael explaining what they mean. This setup recalls the angel in the Book of Revelation who explains the visions John sees – and several such figures in the apocrypha, for example, second Esdras. The narrative will close with Michael's prophecy of the Apocalypse:

> The woman's Seed, obscurely then foretold
> Now amplier known thy Savior and thy Lord,
> Last in the clouds of Heaven to be revealed
> In glory of the Father to dissolve
> Satan with his perverted world, then raise
> From the conflagrant mass, purged and refined,
> New Heavens, new Earth, ages of endless date
> Founded in righteousness and peace and love
> To bring forth fruits, joy, and eternal bliss.
>
> *Paradise Lost* 12.543–51

Of course, there is no suggestion whatever in the Book of Revelation that this present world will be purified and refined by fire, as in an alchemical retort, from out of the residue of which a new heaven and a new earth will rise. In Revelation we hear only from John that he "saw a new heaven and a new earth, for the first heaven and the first earth were passed away." This new heaven is "the holy city, new Jerusalem, coming down from God out of heaven, prepared as a bride adorned for her husband" (Rev 21:1–2). It is characteristic of the materialist and scientific Milton that he should seek a way out of the implication in the visions of the apocalypse that something can go out of existence altogether, with no conservation of matter, and that something else should come into being from nowhere, *ex nihilo*, so to speak, or that, absurdly, heaven should descend out of heaven. It is also characteristic of the rationalistic, Christian humanist Milton that he will have nothing to do with this mystical picture of the marriage of the celestial Jerusalem, arrayed as a bride "adorned for her husband," being "the Lamb's wife" (21:9). Instead, he imagines a utopia that would not be

out of place in Marxian eschatology, complete with a final struggle out
of which a new society will emerge from the conflagrant mass of the old
one, opening on "ages of endless date / Founded in righteousness and
peace and love." This is the righteousness (*dikaiosunê*) of the just
society, not the bliss of Heaven.

There is a lengthy and interesting passage – especially interesting
when we recall Milton's own blindness – in which the angel cleanses
Adam's visual nerves and instills his eyes with healing drops from the
"Well of Life" (11.411–17). That phrase is based on John's gospel, where
Jesus speaks to the Samaritan woman of "a well of water springing up
into everlasting life" (4:13–14). The symbol of such a spring is envi-
sioned in Revelation: "And he shewed me a pure river of water of life,
clear as crystal, proceeding out of the throne of God and of the Lamb"
(22:1). The author of John's gospel is perhaps recalling the river in
Genesis that waters the garden and then the whole world: "And a river
went out of Eden to water the garden; and from thence it was parted, and
became into four heads" (2:10). Both passages were undoubtedly
recalled, combined, and transfigured by the author of Revelation, who
sees the water flowing from the throne of God, like poetic inspiration.
One can imagine Milton imagining himself likewise receiving
Michael's miraculous ministrations, "that I may see and tell / Of things
invisible to mortal sight" (3.54–55).

The effect of Adam's treatment, however, wears off by the end of
Book Twelve, after the Flood, from which point Michael alone sees the
visions and recounts them verbally, with ample explanations.

This relating of the story of the Bible as a whole – with many
interestingly Miltonic omissions and emphases – is composed of 1,123
lines of verse stretching across two books and divided almost at the
middle by the Flood (at the 572nd line), with which Book Eleven ends.
We have reached only the eighth chapter of Genesis. Adam sees events
up to the Flood in visions of a largely imaginary, primitive world, a vast
stretch of time, as was thought, of which the history has been almost
totally lost. (Byron would say that some things in the first two books of
Paradise Lost are the greatest poetry in the world, at least since the
Flood, since we cannot know what great poets existed before that.[5])

---

5 "The first two books of [*Paradise Lost*] are the very finest poetry that has ever been
produced in the world – at least since the flood ... but we know no more of their
poetry than the *brutum vulgus* – I beg pardon, the swinish multitude – do of
Wordsworth and Pye." Letter to James Hogg, 24 March 1814. *Selected Letters*, ed.
Leslie A. Marchand (1973; rpt. Cambridge, MA, 1982), 100.

We noted that because of Adam's already failing, fallen human nature, Michael relates to him verbally the second part of the digest of the Bible, which is in fact most of the Bible, extending from Abraham to the end of the world. It must be said that this change, well accounted for as it is – "objects divine / Must needs impair and weary human sense" (12.9–10) – is convenient for the poet's cerebral and Pauline emphasis, which requires much longer discursive explanations, for example, this, a digest of Heb 9:13–14, although numerous other Pauline passages harmonize with it:

> And therefore was Law given them to evince
> Their natural'pravity by stirring up
> Sin against Law to fight that when they see
> Law can discover sin but not remove
> Save by those shadowy expiations weak,
> The blood of bulls and goats, they may conclude
> Some blood more previous must be paid for Man.
> *Paradise Lost* 12.287–93

Similarly, this: "But to the cross he nails thy enemies: / The Law that is against thee and the sins / Of all mankind with him there crucified" (12.415–17), a clarification, though surely incomplete, of the following: "And you being dead in your sins and the uncircumcision of your flesh, hath he quickened together with him, having forgiven you all trespasses; Blotting out the handwriting of ordinances that was against us, which was contrary to us, and took it out of the way, nailing it to his cross" (Col 2:14).

It is hard to imagine Milton creating a visual scene such as he must have seen often in the art of Italy, of Jesus suffering on the cross. We hear only of this mystical passage of nailing the Law and the sins of mankind to the cross, to be crucified there with the Lord. Milton is not attracted imaginatively to the central images of Christianity, which are of helplessness: the infant in its mother's arms and the man on the cross. But he does grasp the nettle in the lines preceding the ones just quoted, after a challenging passage of Pauline theory on imputation, faith, merit, and Legal works:

> For this he shall live hated, be blasphemed,
> Seized on by force, judged and to death condemned,
> A shameful and accurst, nailed to the cross
> By his own nation, slain for bringing life.
> *Paradise Lost* 12.411–14

The ancient rancid theme of the blood-guilt of the Jews is mentioned here, too, although I am reasonably confident that by *nation* Milton meant not a race but a political entity, one that existed at the time, but not now. It was under Oliver Cromwell, after all, that Jews were admitted back into England, having been banned for centuries.

After his prophetic vision of history, Adam descends the mountain and joins Eve for their expulsion from the garden. As Michael's troop of flaming angels draws near, their gliding movement awakens a foreboding simile of chilling evening mist and human labor to come, an allusion to tilling the earth from which we have been taken (Gen 3:23): "as evening mist / Ris'n from a river o'er the marish glides / And gathers ground fast at the laborer's heel / Homeward returning" (12.629–32). A great sword goes before the troop of angels, blazing like a comet and waving over the garden, turning it to desert. This is Milton's explanation of the cherubs and the flaming sword guarding the way of paradise: "So he drove out the man; and he placed at the east of the garden of Eden Cherubims, and a flaming sword which turned every way, to keep the way of the tree of life" (Gen 3: 24). For their protection (as much as to fulfill his mission, which is to expel them), Michael leads Adam and Eve swiftly down the cliff surrounding paradise to the plain below, and then disappears:

> They looking back all th'eastern side beheld
> Of Paradise, so late their happy seat,
> Waved over by that flaming brand. The gate
> With dreadful faces thronged and fiery arms.
> *Paradise Lost* 12.641–44

From the baldly factual account in the Bible ("Therefore the Lord God sent him forth from the garden of Eden, to till the ground from whence he was taken" [Gen 3:23]), Milton creates in his epic's final lines a poignant and yet tremendous scene. We seem to join our first parents and look through their eyes at the gathering dark as night is coming on:

> Some natural tears they dropped but wiped them soon.
> The world was all before them, where to choose
> Their place of rest, and Providence their guide.
> They hand in hand, with wand'ring steps and slow
> Through Eden took their solitary way.
> *Paradise Lost* 12

Incidentally, they take their way *through* Eden because the paradise from which they have been expelled is only one place, on top of a high mountain, within the larger country called Eden.

Despite these brilliant means of enlarging the scale of *Paradise Lost* and giving it density and weight through intensive biblical allusion, we are never really far from its central concern, which is announced in the title of the poem and is the means by which Milton's epic bears on us in our present time, whatever our present time happens to be. The loss of that ancient biblical paradise is for Milton the origin and cause of history as a continuous falling away from the ideal state of humanity. This ideal state can never again be attained in its original form, as a paradise, an environment. But by working through history it can be attained in a still higher form, which is what Michael calls "A paradise within thee, happier far" (12.587). For Milton, however, this inner paradise is not an abstracted spiritual state anticipating the next world; nor is it exclusively individual, though it lives in individuals: It is the political ideal of restored human nature, of that unperturbed wisdom that will make collective life possible on earth. The first paradise is a happy environment that is understood as external to its inhabitants. However much it penetrates them as bliss, they are above it as well, because their liberty is independent of what surrounds them. But the paradise within that is promised for the future is a political utopia on earth, a utopia that joins individuals together through the liberty that each has inside.

On the face of it, this political and humanist reading would appear to be hard to justify from the text of *Paradise Lost*, at least from its opening, which looks conventionally Pauline. I quote again the lines with which the epic opens, but allow them now to continue on a little further, to the figure of Jesus Christ, who is explicitly contrasted with Adam through the adjectival comparative, *greater man*. He is to *restore us*, presumably at the Last Judgment, after the end of the world:

> Of Man's first disobedience and the fruit
> Of that forbidden tree whose mortal taste
> Brought death into the world and all our woe
> With loss of Eden till one greater Man
> Restore us and regain the blissful seat
> Sing, Heav'nly Muse.

Paradise Lost 1.1–6

If this says what it should say, from a traditional, Pauline perspective, then it means that original sin enters into human nature, bringing misery on each of us individually in life and making each of us mortal, until the Son of God, as Jesus Christ, comes to earth again to save us from our condition, but not in this world and not within history. The idea of original sin and redemption from original sin is stated in the classic texts by Paul I have quoted in part, in connection with Milton's *daimons*, Sin and Death. Now, we must attend to the word *man*, referring first to Adam, the originator, so to speak, of original sin, and then to Jesus, our redeemer from original sin: "Wherefore, as by one man sin entered into the world, and death by sin; and so death passed upon all men, for that all have sinned" (Rom 5:12); "For by one man's disobedience many were made sinners, so by the obedience of one shall many be made righteous" (Rom 5:19). These texts inform to the point of saturation the opening lines of *Paradise Lost*, reiterating the phrase *one man* and repeating the word *disobedience*. On the face of it, Milton's epic could hardly be more Pauline in its thinking.

Yet there are subtle differences in this opening passage that will widen as the poem goes on. In Paul, Adam's disobedience brings into this world death and *sin*, which infects each person individually and will be reckoned up at the Last Judgment. But in these lines from *Paradise Lost* Adam's disobedience brings in death and *all our woe*, the latter being a collective description of the human condition in this world. The door has been opened – a door Paul did his best to keep closed – to collective political and historical evils for which no one person is responsible, evils requiring social analysis and political treatment. There are resonances with modern political philosophy, from Milton's contemporary Thomas Hobbes to Hegel and Marx, and the modern fields of sociology and political theory. From Milton's humanist, ethical point of view there must be no giving up on this world as a mere period of time, a *saeculum* to be endured while expecting the next world. Another divergence from Pauline theology follows closely on this one: perfectibility on earth. In Paul, Jesus Christ *redeems* us from sin by paying our debt only so we can go to heaven after the Last Judgment and after this world has passed away, not before. But Milton's lines promise to *restore* us to our original condition in life and in so doing to *regain* for us the *blissful seat* of paradise. The word *seat* implies a royal court, a throne, since Adam, like Jesus, is a legitimate king (for Milton, there are many illegitimate ones), and we are, or we should be, Adam's royal descendants.

The "blissful seat" to which the poet refers in these lines cannot be the garden in Eden, which we will see spectacularly destroyed at the Flood (*PL* 12.829–35). It must instead be the state of mind – entirely rational and free – that will exist in the members of a redeemed society on earth. It is of this that Michael's words of comfort to Adam, which we have already had occasion to see, are a prophecy: "Then wilt thou not be loath / To leave this Paradise but shalt possess / A paradise within thee, happier far" (*PL* 12.585–87). Even so, it remains an open question whether *Paradise Lost* on its own has enough force to achieve escape velocity from the strong gravitational field of Pauline Christianity, with its renunciation of this world in favor of the next. As its title indicates, *Paradise Lost* is inextricably about loss, not about what might be gained that is better than what has been lost.

That is why *Paradise Lost* must be followed by *Paradise Regained* (1671), to explain exactly what is meant by the prophecy of a *paradise within* that is *happier far*. *Paradise Regained* is the keystone in the arch of Milton's poetic thinking about human life in the world. The last words spoken to Jesus Christ in *Paradise Regained* are addressed to us as well: "begin to save mankind" (*PR* 4.635). This phrase, *begin to save mankind*, means "save humanity here, in this world, by following the example of Christ." It is a collective, political call.

Paradise Regained is a shorter and less celebrated poem, as sequels always are. But we have seen that Milton chooses his titles with care. For him, *Paradise Regained* is not a sequel to *Paradise Lost* any more than for Christians the New Testament is a sequel to the Old, being much shorter and, from a literary point of view, more modest. Moreover, this sequel deliberately eschews the verbal extravagances and astounding cosmic scenes of its predecessor for something more ascetic, severe, and hard-surfaced, like those stones the devil proposes Jesus soften into bread. This poem gives us intellectual debate and spiritual battle in the blinding light of the desert landscape, harsh conditions for a struggle in which everything is at stake.

The central, and in truth the only, deep interpretative question that is posed by this poem is, what is the meaning of its title? The title of *Paradise Lost* is perfectly clear, because there we have a literal, biblical paradise that is literally lost, and guarded from return by that flaming sword, which is intended "to keep the way of the tree of life" (Gen 3:24). With his usual sublime freedom, Milton turns that sword into something that does not protect the garden but destroys it. It is almost as if Milton wishes deliberately to efface the too literal, too substantial, too beautifully imagined garden of *Paradise Lost* even before the mountain it stands on is torn loose in the flood and washed down the Euphrates to become a barren rock stranded in the Persian Gulf (11.829–35). The total destruction of the past paradise bars all return, thus compelling us to cling for hope of safety to the future one.

But what is this *paradise* in *Paradise Regained* that is said to be *raised* in the desert, and how or where is it to be *regained*? Is it the *paradise within*? Here, everything seems to be figural, to have a meaning that lies beyond anything we can quite see or even hear in the words or through them. The poem opens by joining itself to the project of *Paradise Lost*, as its completion:

> I who erewhile the happy garden sung,
> By one man's disobedience lost, now sing
> Recovered Paradise to all mankind,
> By one man's first obedience fully tried
> Through all temptation, and the tempter foiled
> In all his wiles, defeated and repulsed,
> And Eden raised in the waste wilderness.
>
> *Paradise Regained* 1.1–7

Eden is, of course, never in any literal sense raised in the wilderness or seen in this poem, since it doesn't exist anymore. The only reason Jesus needs to undo that crime by his exemplary obedience – instead of saving us directly, like a classical hero, a Heracles – is because the crime itself, which later theology would call original sin, is the crime of humanity as a whole. Milton's total conception of the Bible sees history as the unfolding of the crime of Adam in all possible ways, enveloping us, like a constricting snake, and extinguishing the good in our nature. Only Jesus, by his heroic confrontation in the desert with the principle of evil in this world, can extricate us from the entanglement and at last kill the snake, crushing its head (10.180–81; Gen 3:15). It is in this intertwining of the classically political and the mythically foundational – or, in two words, of the utopian and the biblical – that the majesty of this poet's vision consists.

Further Reading

Alter, Robert, *The Art of Biblical Narrative*, 2nd ed. (New York, 2011).
Armstrong, Karen, *The Bible: A Biography* (New York, 2007).
Bloom, Harold, *The Shadow of a Great Rock: A Literary Appreciation of the King James Bible* (New Haven, CT, 2011).
Carmichael, Calum M., *The Story of Creation: Its Origin and Its Interpretation in Philo and the Fourth Gospel* (Ithaca, NY, 1996).
Ehrman, Bart D., *How Jesus Became God* (New York, 2014).
Frye, Northrop, *The Great Code: The Bible and Literature* (Toronto, 2007).
King, Karen, *The Secret Revelation of John* (Cambridge, MA, 2006).

Levenson, Jon D., *Inheriting Abraham: The Legacy of the Patriarch in Judaism, Christianity, and Islam* (Princeton, NJ, 2012).

Lewis, C. S., *Reflections on the Psalms* (London, 1961).

Nasrallah, Laura S., *An Ecstasy of Folly: Prophecy and Authority in Early Christianity* (Cambridge, MA, 2003).

Pagels, Elaine, *Adam, Eve, and the Serpent* (New York, 1998).

Römer, Thomas, *The Invention of God*, trans. Raymond Geuss (Cambridge, MA, 2015).

Schweitzer, Albert, *The Quest of the Historical Jesus: A Critical Study of Its Progress from Reimarus to Wrede* (Baltimore, 1998).

Stark, Rodney, *The Rise of Christianity* (San Francisco, 1997).

The English Bible, King James Version, Volume 1: *The Old Testament*, ed. Herbert Marks (New York, 2012).

The English Bible, King James Version, Volume 2: *The New Testament and the Apocrypha*, ed. Gerald Hammond and Austin Busch (New York, 2012).

13 The Bible, Shelley, and English Romanticism

JONATHAN FORTIER

While an undergraduate at Oxford, Shelley published a pamphlet – which he distributed to various clergymen at the University – titled "The Necessity of Atheism" (1811). Even though Shelley's essay was mostly an exercise of young philosophical skepticism in the tradition of Hume, it ultimately resulted in his expulsion from Oxford and set him on an itinerant and short career as a wandering outcast poet – a favorite Romantic trope that suited Shelley's philosophical interests and anti-Establishment politics. In his early work, *Queen Mab* (1813), Shelley refers to religion as a "prolific fiend,/Who peoplest the earth with demons."[1] His later poem, "Mask of Anarchy" (1819), inspired by the Peterloo Massacre, portrays the British Home Secretary (allegorically represented as "Hipocracy") "Clothed with the Bible." Many other aspects of Shelley's writing, such as his criticism of the Church in its various forms, or his problematic portrayals of love and sexual union, inclined others to see him as explicitly anti-Christian. Indeed, Shelley's sympathetic portrayal of Satan, or Satanlike rebels such as Prometheus, earned him much disdain (Shelley's wife, Mary, was the author of *Frankenstein*, which was subtitled "The Modern Prometheus"). Robert Southey, another poet of the era, referred to Shelley and Byron as members of a "Satanic School" of poetry for their liberal morals and unorthodox creative work.

But despite this apparently hostile position against the Church – and the Establishment more generally – Shelley was knowledgeable about Judeo-Christian scripture and deeply interested in it, which makes him an intriguing figure to consider in light of the Bible's influence on certain aspects of Romantic writing. According to Thomas Medwin, who was the poet's cousin and biographer, Shelley believed that a very decent library could be assembled with just a dozen or so books, including

---

[1] *Queen Mab* (hereafter *QM*), VI.69–70. All references to Shelley's poetry are taken from the easily acquired *Shelley's Poetry and Prose*, ed. Donald H. Reiman and Neil Fraistat (London and New York, 1977; repr. 2002).

Milton's *Paradise Lost* and "last, yet first, the Bible."[2] Last, because of its associations with a corrupt Church and first because it contained poetry of uncommon power and was the work on which so many others depended. In the tradition of many writers before him such as Milton, Shelley clearly distinguishes between the character of Christ ("he is the enemy of oppression and falsehood ... the advocate of equal justice") and what he perceived to be the various wrong-headed ways in which Christ's example is appropriated for insidious purposes.[3] Various other prose works (*A Treatise on Morals, A Philosophical View of Reform, Defence of Poetry*) also make it clear that Shelley was sympathetic to Christian values and yet approached scripture with a critic's eye; he questioned the moral basis of the Old Testament stories, marveled at its literary majesty, and was clearly influenced by the eschatological vision that involved struggle, self-mastery, and renewal. Thanks to Mary Shelley's journal, we know that Shelley read the Bible regularly, and in addition to frequent reading of the New Testament, was particularly interested in Ecclesiastes, Ezekiel, Isaiah, Jeremiah, and Song of Solomon.[4] Several critics in recent decades, like Tim Webb, Earl Wasserman, and Bryan Shelley, have provided rich analyses of Shelley's indebtedness to – and complicated relationship with – the Bible. Others, such as M. H. Abrams, Harold Bloom, Northrop Frye, Adam Potkay, and Ian Balfour, helpfully situate Shelley within a broader tradition of biblical writing during the eighteenth and early nineteenth century. This essay will revisit some important biblical themes and images in Shelley's work and puzzle through a selection of readings that highlight the significant role the Bible played in Shelley's philosophical and aesthetic formulations, and connect this to a number of salient themes in the Romantic period.

SHELLEY'S IDEA OF GOD

Early in his poetic career Shelley developed a stance that was explicitly atheist, materialist, and necessitarian, or hostile to the notion that human beings have free-will. Caught up in a clockwork universe of

---

[2] Thomas Medwin, *The Life of Percy Bysshe Shelley*, ed. H. B. Forman (1847; London, 1913). Shelley's familiarity with the Bible was also observed by Leigh Hunt: "His book was generally Plato, or Homer, or one of the Greek tragedians, or the Bible, in which last he took a great, though peculiar, and often admiring interest." See *The Journals of Mary Shelley*, ed., Paula Feldman and Diana Scott-Kilvert (Baltimore and London, 1995), 167. Hereafter *MSJ*.

[3] "Essay on Christianity" (1817), *Shelley's Prose*, ed. D. L. Clark (London, 1988), 198. Hereafter *SP*.

[4] *MSJ*, 636–37.

causes and effects, we are necessarily impelled to act in certain ways due to our fundamentally material nature, in the same way that pulleys and levers act on blocks of stone or pieces of wood. This was a common philosophical school of thought in the eighteenth century, and Shelley comes to it mostly through his reading of Lucretius, Spinoza, Holbach, and Mary Shelley's father, William Godwin, whose *Political Justice* (1793) was greatly influential in this period. As Sharon Ruston and others have observed, Shelley was also knowledgeable about, and inspired by, the discoveries made by scientists such as Joseph Priestley and medical doctors such as John Abernethy and William Lawrence. In important ways, the language of science (electricity, magnetism, light) finds its way into Shelley's poetry and underpins theories of the soul, of life, and the relationship of the individual to the material world.

Despite the commitments to science and materialism, Shelley's poetry is often intuitive, spiritual, and ethereal, and the later works (such as *A Defence of Poetry*) promote theories of inspiration, creativity, and change that are as amenable to idealist readings as they are grounded in the science of eighteenth-century empiricist rationalism. Shelley also repeatedly invokes biblical allusions while simultaneously castigating traditional forms of Christianity. And so in his early long poem *Queen Mab* (1813) Shelley employs Voltaire's famous attack on the Church, "L'Ecrasez l'infame!" ("Crush the infamous thing"), but then offers a work that implicitly asserts human immortality, endorses a Christian ethic, and describes the soul's flight through the cosmos where the secrets of past and present are laid bare.

The structure and tone of *Queen Mab* recalls aspects of Ezekiel (one of Shelley's favorite Old Testament Books). Shelley shifts the explicit critique and prophecies centered on Jerusalem to an analysis of human vice and the possibilities for positive change in a general and expansive sense. In Shelley's poem the opening meditation on Ianthe, the sleeping woman, is abruptly interrupted by the arrival of Queen Mab: "Hark! whence that rushing sound?" (QM, I.45), echoing Ezekiel: "Then the spirit took me up, and I heard behind me a voice of great rushing" (Ezek 3:12).[5] Queen Mab's chariot is pulled by horses described as "Celestial coursers" with "filmy pennons" (or ethereal wings) that transport the soul of Ianthe to the outer cosmos:

From the celestial hoofs
The atmosphere in flaming sparkles flew,

[5] All biblical references are to the Authorized King James Edition (1611).

> And where the burning wheels
> Eddied above the mountain's loftiest peak,
> Was traced a line of lightning.
> (*QM* I.213–17)

Again, the lines echo Ezekiel where the Prophet "heard also the noise of the wings of the living creatures that touched one another, and the noise of the wheels over against them, and a noise of great rushing" (Ezek 3:12). The multiple references to cosmic wheels in Ezekiel find expression throughout much of Shelley's work, used variously for scenes of violence, aspiration, and cosmic flight. We find "the clash of clanging wheels" as artillery unleashes on the innocent in *The Mask of Anarchy* (1819, l.309), and in *Prometheus Unbound* the mysterious character "Demogorgon" deposes the tyrant Jupiter with language reminiscent of Ezekiel:

> Hear ye the thunder of the fiery wheels
> Griding the winds? – from Demogorgon's throne. –
> Victory! Victory! Feel'st thou not, O World,
> The Earthquake of his chariot thundering up
> Olympus?
> (*PU*, III.i.47–51)

While Shelley echoes Ezekiel as well as Isaiah and Revelation, the images are combined with accounts of exploitation and misery, as in the building of Solomon's temple in Jerusalem:

> Behold yon sterile spot;
> Where now the wandering Arab's tent
> Flaps in the desert-blast.
> There once old Salem's haughty fane
> Reared high to heaven its thousand golden domes,
> And in the blushing face of day
> Exposed its shameful glory.
> (*QM*, II.134–40)

The glory is "shameful" because the work required the forced labor of men "worn out with toil and slavery" (*QM*, II.143). Shelley despises all abuses of power and repeatedly castigates kings, priests, and magistrates that bend others to their will. In these passages, however, Shelley uncharacteristically levels an attack on the Jewish nation itself ("an inhuman and uncultured race") and juxtaposes the Old Testament Hebrews with "Athens, Rome, and Sparta," which are idealized as high cultures where "the ghost of Freedom stalks" (*QM*, II. 149, 162, 169). Shelley's Hellenism has been well documented by Timothy Webb and others, but what is remarkable is the extent to which the language and imagery of the Bible permeates Shelley's poetry while he struggles to distance himself from the culture that produced the very language and narratives he clearly admires.

Shelley repeatedly reworks the idea of God, especially as understood in the Old Testament, and attempts a variety of equivalents, such as "Mind," "Power," or some version of "Necessity" itself. In the sixth canto of *Queen Mab* the Fairy explains that man's "frenzied brain" gathered all the "elements of all that thou didst know" and "called it God" (*QM*, VI.89, 95, 102). God, claims Shelley, may have power, but it is really only the "power" of human consciousness that appropriates the idea of a willful transcendent entity and wields it over others for tyrannical purposes. God is the "prototype of human misrule," he is like an "earthly king," and "Hell, gapes for ever for the unhappy slaves/Of fate, whom he created, in his sport/To triumph in their torments when they fell!" In the remaining lines of this short canto, Shelley proposes an alternative to the idea of a tyrannical god, which he calls the "Soul of the Universe! eternal spring/Of life and Death" (*QM*, VI.105, 107–10, 190–91), but he also associates this "force" or "presence" with "Power" and "Necessity":

> Spirit of Nature! all-sufficing Power,
> Necessity! thou mother of the world!
> Unlike the God of human error, thou
> Requirest no prayers or praises;
> [...]
>   all that the wide world contains
> Are but thy passive instruments, and thou
> Regardst them all with an impartial eye,
> Whose joy or pain thy nature cannot feel,
> Because thou hast not human sense,
> Because thou art not human mind.
>   (*QM*, VI.197–203, 214–19)

In these lines there is a repeated attempt to disqualify the possibility of a transcendent deity, especially a god that possesses volition and power as seen in the Old Testament. But the passage contains subtle ambiguities and ironies that seem to undermine or qualify summary statements. For example, Shelley's address to the trio of forces – "Spirit of Nature! all-sufficing Power,/Necessity" – claims that no "prayers or praises" are needed. But this long address to the "Soul of the Universe" is a prayer in itself, and the praises that are subsequently offered are the very ones that this "Soul" does not need (*QM*, VI.190). In fact, the lines that follow have the quality of supplication before the very omnipotence that is held up for assault: The Fairy anticipates when the "storm of time" will blow over the "broken altars" of the vengeful God who "usurps" the proper "honours" of this "Spirit" (See *QM*, VI.220–38). This canto goes on with incantatory repetitions that deny the existence of a deity – "There is no God!" – (*QM*, VII.13) and invokes Ahasueras – the "Wandering Jew" associated with the non-Jewish King Ahasuerus of the Book of Esther – as witness for the defense, or the prosecution, depending on your perspective. Shelley qualifies his statement about the Deity in a note: "This negation must be understood solely to affect a creative Deity. The hypothesis of a pervading Spirit coeternal with the universe, remains unshaken."[6] Shelley's allowance for a "Spirit" in the universe was a typical proviso, allowing for an escape from a reductive materialism and the possibility of transcendence or self-realization if one could only align oneself with this life-force.

The long passage from the sixth canto of *Queen Mab* is delivered to a singular Being or Force in the language of religious worship ("thy," "thou"), and yet there are, ostensibly, four or five forces at work here: the Soul of the Universe, the Spirit of Nature, Necessity, Power, and the "mother of the world." This may be an example of Shelley's characteristic accumulation of similes in a description of a single image, each successive simile drawing attention to the inadequacy of the one it replaces. But even if this is so, it emphasizes the obscurity of the idea he is attempting to represent. Furthermore, it seems that each name carries with it slightly different inflections. The "forces" to whom the poet addresses his "prayer" seem to echo certain aspects of the Christian trinity, so that Power, Necessity, and the Spirit of Nature could stand in for the Father, the Son, and the Holy Ghost, or variations on that theme.

Three years after writing *Queen Mab* Shelley composes "Hymn to Intellectual Beauty" and "Mont Blanc," where he explores similar ideas about God, with a particular interest in the mind's relationship to power and inspiration. Much as with *Queen Mab*, Shelley seeks to distinguish his conception of God from biblical representations, but the lines are blurred, and Shelley's imagery borrows heavily from both the Old and

---

[6] *QM*, n. 13, ll. 1–3 (*Poems of Shelley*, i.381).

New Testaments. Both poems adapt a stance of reverent prayer before the mysterious and incomprehensible. Shelley opens the "Hymn" with a blank assertion: "The awful shadow of some unseen Power/Floats though unseen amongst us" (ll.1–2). The devotional state of awe recalls the structure, tone, and language of the Psalms: "He that dwelleth in the secret place of the most High shall abide under the shadow of the Almighty" (Ps 91:1). "Mont Blanc," like the "Hymn," enacts a personal encounter with the transcendent, and for this reason the Psalms and the Book of Job serve as better models for these poems than other biblical books such as Genesis, which also address questions of origins. In "Mont Blanc" the mountain is uneasily identified with Power, and the river Arve "for ever/Rolls its loud waters to the ocean waves" (ll.124–25). In Psalm 46 we see this imagery cast in a similar devotional voice:

> God is our refuge and our strength, a very present help in trouble. Therefore will not we fear, though the earth be removed, and though the mountains be carried into the midst of the sea; Though the waters thereof roar and be troubled, though the mountains shake with the swelling thereof. Selah. There is a river, the streams whereof shall make glad the city of God, the holy place of the tabernacles of the most High. God is in the midst of her; she shall not be moved. (Ps 46:1–5)

Typical of the Psalms, the poet searches for reassurance and consolation in the powerful presence of God, and we sense that the act of writing, speaking, or singing the devotional accomplishes its purpose. By contrast, in both the "Hymn" and "Mont Blanc" Shelley repeatedly comes up against silence and limitation. "Why dost thou [Spirit of Beauty] pass away and leave our state/This dim vast vale of tears, vacant and desolate?" And why is it that men have such capacity "For love and hate, despondency and hope?" Shelley concludes his series of questions with a flat finality: "No voice from some sublimer world hath ever/To sage or poet these responses given" ("Hymn," ll.16–17, 24, 25–26). It is the imperfect words such as "God and ghosts and Heaven" that serve as a testimony to our "vain endeavor" to understand the transcendent ("Hymn," ll.27–28).

In the early chapters of Job we have a sustained and inconclusive attempt to understand the nature of unjust suffering and the motivations of the divine. Zophar rebukes Job for his desire to know the nature of God: "Canst thou by searching find out God? Canst thou find out the Almighty unto perfection? It is as high as heaven; what canst

thou do? deeper than hell; what canst thou know?" (Job 11:7–8). Others
speak on God's behalf but Job repeatedly returns to a search for answers:
"Oh that one would hear me! Behold, my desire is, that the Almighty
would answer me." (Job 31:35). Following the excoriations of Elihu, God
emerges out of the whirlwind and poses a series of questions about the
origins and mystery of existence: "Where wast thou when I laid the
foundations of the earth? Declare, if thou hast understanding" (Job 38:4).
The divine questioning makes reference to springs and the sea, to the
clouds, snow, ice, and overflowing waters, all images that figure importantly in "Mont Blanc." The questions are, of course, unanswerable, and
reveal to Job his ignorance of the transcendent and first causes. All of
this is poor consolation indeed for the apparently inexplicable and
unjustified suffering he has had to endure, and doesn't help us answer
the problematic ethical issues at stake in God's punishment of Job.

In his sustained interrogation of the mountain, Shelley poses similar
questions: "Is this the scene/Where the old Earthquake-daemon taught
her young/Ruin? Were these their toys? or did a sea/Of fire, envelope
once this silent snow? ("Mont Blanc," ll.71–74). Shelley's poem inverts
the dynamic of God and Job, where poet now questions the transcendent
and inscrutable, but his questions go unanswered: "None can reply – all
seems eternal now" (l.75). Despite the inability to "know" the mountain's mysteries – it represents a sort of epistemological impasse –
Shelley continues to speculate with heavily qualified assertions:

> Thou has a voice, great Mountain, to repeal
> Large codes of fraud and woe; not understood
> By all, but which the wise, and great, and good
> Interpret, or make felt, or deeply feel.
> ("Mont Blanc," ll.80–83)

Again, Shelley's successive qualifications circle around meaning – possibly drawing closer to some clearer understanding – but are never able
to deliver ultimate knowledge about the issues at stake.

Mountains are associated with the divine in many places in the
Bible and Moses' encounter with God as the burning bush at Mount
Horeb is paradigmatic. Mountains are associated with wisdom or law –
for the Ten Commandments issue from Sinai – and yet they represent a
sphere that is guarded as sacred and inaccessible to common
understanding, for God has "Set bounds about the mount" (Exod
19:23). In Shelley's "Mont Blanc" there is a similar paradoxical confla-
tion of transcendent wisdom, insight, and silence. The Ravine of Arve
that descends from Mont Blanc is a "many-coloured, many-voiced vale"

(ll.14) but the Mountain – or some dimension of "Power" associated with the Mountain – remains "Remote, serene and inaccessible" (l. 97). The language of the mountain is, in part, the language of nature, so that in Exodus "all the people saw the thunderings, and the lightnings, and the noise of the trumpet, and the mountain smoking" (Exod 20:18).

Shelley seems to have incorporated much of the tone and language from the Bible, but he may also have written "Mont Blanc" as a response to Coleridge's "Hymn before Sunrise, in the Vale of Chamouni" (1802) in which the majesty of the mountain's existence and its surroundings is explained by orthodox reference to a creative God (ll.55–63). Coleridge concludes with a direct invocation: "Great Hierarch! Tell thou the silent sky/And tell the stars, and tell yon rising sun/Earth, with her thousand voices, praises God" (ll.83–85). But in Shelley's poem, as we have seen, each assertion is followed by a countervailing qualification, and most claims about knowledge are incomplete and provisional. In lieu of Coleridge's "thousand voices," Shelley gives us "The strange sleep/Which when the voices of the desert fail/Wraps all in its own deep eternity" (ll.27–29). This odd phrase, which follows a long series of speculative lines about the nature of the Ravine of Arve, prompts more questions than it answers. What is the sleep that "Wraps all in its own deep eternity"? And what are the "voices of the desert"? Are they yet another reference to the sounds of the natural world, a wind that sweeps across vast stretches of wilderness (and therefore cleansed of the human), or are the voices of the desert the wisdom of the Hebrew poets?

THE WIND OF INSPIRATION

A common Romantic theme is the desired sublimation of the self into the natural world, where the poet seeks to dissolve individual identity and become attuned with transcendent forces. We see this in a wide variety of different Romantic poets. Coleridge explores early pantheist-animist ideas when he speculates that we may all be like Aeolian harps or "wind lyres" that act as instruments for spiritual energy:

> And what if all of animated nature
> Be but organic Harps diversly fram'd,
> That tremble into thought, as o'er them sweeps
> Plastic and vast, one intellectual Breeze,
> At once the Soul of each, and God of all?
> (Coleridge, *Eolian Harp*, ll.44–48)

Similarly, Wordsworth begins his long autobiographical poem *The Prelude* (1805) with a reference to the wind of inspiration – "Oh there is a blessing in this gentle breeze, /That blows from the green fields and from the clouds" (*The Prelude*, I.1–2) – that signals the Poet's intimacy with the natural world, and his new found freedom. He is a "captive . . . coming from a house/Of bondage, from yon city's walls set free/A prison where he hath been long immured" (*Prelude*, I.6–8). The explicit allusion to Israel's liberation from the "house of bondage" (Exod 13:3) signals that Wordsworth conceives of his work within a biblical – and specifically Miltonic – tradition that privileges the themes of independence and sovereignty. Wordsworth's search is characteristically Romantic, celebrating a type of natural spontaneity: "I look about, and should the guide I chuse/Be nothing better than a wandering cloud/I cannot miss my way" (*The Prelude*, I.17–19). The city that the poet escapes can be literally understood as London, but metaphorically the liberation is psychological, and prefigures the development of the poet's own mind as he overcomes creative and spiritual limitations. Later in *The Prelude*, Wordsworth equates "Nature's self" with the "breath of God" and he himself seeks to "make/Breathings for incommunicable powers" – a perplexing phrase that may refer to his attempt to "voice the ineffable" or "express a desire to be inspired in a way that is inexpressible" (*The Prelude*, V.222; III.187–88). In the Bible, God "breathed into his [Man's] nostrils the breath of life; and man became a living soul" (Gen 2:7) but the restorative life-giving wind is also prophetic: "Prophesy unto the wind, prophesy, son of man, and say to the wind, Thus saith the Lord God; Come from the four winds, O breath, and breathe upon these slain, that they may live" (Ezek 37:9).

The image of the wind and its relationship to poetic inspiration is closely connected to pantheist beliefs that sought to identify God with nature. In *Tintern Abbey*, Wordsworth perceives a "sense sublime/Of something far more deeply interfused" that animates the natural world, dwells in the mind of man, and is described as "A motion and a spirit, that impels/All thinking things, all objects of all thought/And rolls through all things" ("Tintern Abbey," ll.95–102). Fittingly, Wordsworth writes these lines while perched on a hill above the ruins of Tintern Abbey in Wales. The abandoned church has no roof, allowing for a clear view of the heavens; the natural world is quite literally growing through the windows and doors, and sheep graze where the congregation once prayed.

The ruined church is a favorite Romantic image that accommodates aspects of Christian belief – a foundation of biblical teaching and ecclesiastical practice – to an increasingly secular, skeptical, and scientific worldview. In this way, vestiges of the Church are preserved, but animated only by those aspects of Christian teaching that harmonize with various vital forces or sublimated versions of the traditional deity. For the young Coleridge, pantheist speculations came naturally given his Unitarian inclinations, which questioned the existence of the Trinity and the divinity of Christ.

The symbiosis of the spiritual and the natural have many antecedents, but Paul's words to the Athenians would have resonated with Wordsworth, Shelley, and other Romantics: "God that made the world and all things therein, seeing that he is Lord of heaven and earth, dwelleth not in temples made with hands" (Acts 17:24). God is not remote, but interfused with all of nature and intimately bound up with our identity, for it is in God "we live, and move, and have our being" (Acts 17:28), lines that Wordsworth adapts to describe his own relationship to nature, where he finds "the anchor of my purest thoughts, the nurse, /The guide, the guardian of my heart, and soul/Of all my moral being" ("Tintern Abbey," ll.109–11). The desire to be taken over or somehow animated by the energy of the natural world also bears resemblance to Paul's many references to the spirit or word of Christ dwelling in his followers (Col 3:16; Rom 12:5; Eph 1:10).

As we saw with Coleridge, Shelley explicitly refers to the wind lyre to describe the way we are "animated" and inspired by ineffable forces: "There is a Power by which we are surrounded, like the atmosphere in which some motionless lyre is suspended, which visits with its breath our silent chords at will ... This Power is God" (*SP*, 202). To be "inspired" is to be "with the spirit," of course, and Shelley makes explicit use of this metaphor in one of his most famous poems, "*Ode to the West Wind*" (1819), where he offers a meditation on cyclical change as figured in the changing seasons. Here the Poet asks to be animated by natural forces – an analogue to God, or a Deity, or Power as we saw earlier – to bring about social and political transformation. Typical of Shelley, the poetry combines allusions to different mythical and literary traditions – Greek, Latin, and Hindu – but biblical imagery also informs many of the lines and the general structure of the prayer recalls many passages in the Bible. The poem opens with an invocation to the West Wind that drives the "dead leaves" of autumn "like ghosts from an enchanter fleeing/Yellow, and black, and pale, and hectic red/ Pestilence-stricken multitudes" (ll.2–4). The colors are literally those of autumn leaves, but as many critics have observed, they also represent the different colors of the human race (and possibly the different elements or humors within the human body). The stronger resonances, however, derive from Isaiah and Zechariah, as the poem reworks the themes of death and rebirth, with the poet-prophet as a central player in that dynamic.[7] The passage recalls the four (red, black, white, and bay) horses of Zechariah, which "are the four spirits of the heavens, which go forth from standing before the Lord of all the earth" (Zech 6:2–5). The Ode imagines the west wind as both a destructive and a generative power as it exerts its influence on the land, the sky, and the sea. In the fourth stanza, the poet compares his own limited power to the wind's: "Oh! Lift me as a wave, a leaf, a cloud!/I fall upon the thorns of life! I bleed!" (ll.53–54). The lines are overwrought and sentimental for contemporary taste, but not out of place in the context of eighteenth-century sensibility, and typical of Shelley's attempts to capture poetic rapture. Characteristically, Shelley abruptly moves from a secular pan-theist mode to a biblical reference, and chooses the image of the bleeding Christ with the crown of thorns (Matt 27–29) to contrast human limitation with the immortal and expansive powers of nature. Christ's proximity to the divine reflects Shelley's own felt proximity to the west wind, only Shelley cannot achieve – like Christ – the sublimation into natural or divine forces as completely as he wishes. Recognizing that full identification with the wind is denied to him, the poet – as did Coleridge – turns to the trope of the Aeolian harp in the final stanza: "Make me thy lyre, even as the forest is:/What if my leaves are falling like its own!" (ll.57–58). Shelley hopes that the wind will "breathe" through him, literally and metaphorically "inspiring" the poet, so that the pages – or leaves – of his creative works will enact the themes of birth and renewal hinted at in the first stanza:

> Drive my dead thought over the universe
> Like withered leaves to quicken a new birth!
> And, by the incantation of this verse,
>
> Scatter, as from an unextinguished hearth
> Ashes and sparks, my words among mankind!
> Be through my lips to unawakened Earth
>
> The trumpet of a prophecy! O Wind,
> If Winter comes, can Spring be far behind?
>
> (*Ode to the West Wind*, ll.63–70)

---

[7] Mary Shelley's journal records that Shelley was reading the Bible with great frequency between 1819 and 1820, particularly Isaiah, Ezekiel, and Ecclesiastes. *MSJ*, 636–37.

We have seen how the wind of inspiration is naturally connected to the "breath of life" and identified with God, nature, and prophecy. Shelley's model for communicating his prophetic message also recalls biblical passages in which a "rushing mighty wind" allows the assembly to "speak with other tongues" (Acts 2:1–4).

There may be additional echoes to Zechariah in these closing lines. We read that the priests and the people refused to follow God's law as heard through the prophets, and so the Lord "scattered them with a whirlwind among all the nations whom they knew not" (Zech 7:14). The themes of destruction and renewal (figured in the restoration of Jerusalem and the foreknowledge of Christ's birth and death) offer parallels to Shelley's own thematic concerns. In Isaiah the prophet is told to "lift up thy voice like a trumpet, and shew my people their transgression" (Isa 58:1) but Shelley reworks the lines so that the poet tells of a future transformation with the "leaves" of his writing spreading the ideas as seeds for political change. Shelley's vision of a regenerated earth (a sort of millenarian ecstasy that would have psychological, political, and spiritual dimensions) is quickly qualified, with the final question, which implicitly acknowledges the imminence of Winter – in all its symbolic power – and the uncertainty about Spring's expected return. Shelley's question is partly rhetorical, for we know Spring follows Winter, but it suggests a desire to be assured that the symbolic equivalents of Spring (social and political reform, spiritual regeneration) will indeed follow the current "Winter" of oppressive regimes and stunted vision.

REVOLUTIONS OF MIND AND STATE

Shelley's Ode is a personal invocation to the West Wind, but the change the Poet hopes to precipitate is universal, and has both political and spiritual dimensions that are informed by much of the writing about revolutionary change from the earlier generation of Romantic figures. Shelley, in a letter to Byron, referred to the French Revolution as the "master theme of the epoch in which we live,"[8] and his various poems can be seen as a reworking of revolutionary promise in which he presents a vision of the regenerated post-millennial world. In the preface to *Laon and Cythna* (1817, later republished as *The Revolt of Islam*) Shelley explicitly situates his poem within the context of the failure

---

[8] *The Letters of Percy Bysshe Shelley*, ed. F. L. Jones (Oxford, 1964), 1:504.

of the French Revolution, and observes that the violent excesses that followed the initial hopes of freedom arose from the ignorance of a people incapable of self-government. The new Eden is only possible if the individual is first enlightened.

A significant number of writers during the 1790s – such as Blake, Wordsworth, and Coleridge – believed that the French Revolution heralded a radically new age of political liberty and social progress and perhaps signaled wider millenarian change – the belief that great upheaval would be followed by a long period of peace and spiritual renewal as described in various biblical books. Much writing of this period repeatedly links human events with natural correlatives such as storms, earthquakes, and floods, recalling the language of Revelation, where the human and the natural are combined to great effect. The initial optimism for the Revolution was crushed when France descended into bloodshed and anarchy. One of the central objectives of Robespierre and others leading the Terror was to supplant Christianity with the "Cult of the Supreme Being." Churches were renamed "Temples of Reason" and statues of a mythical French woman ("Marianne") appeared, allegorically standing for liberty and the new republic (the Statue of Liberty – a late nineteenth-century gift from France to the United States – is a version of this figure). The scenes of licentiousness and idolatry were observed to have close parallels with the story of the Golden Calf, where a whole people turn away from the true God, or the justice and law he represents:

> They have turned aside quickly out of the way which I commanded them: they have made them a molten calf, and have worshipped it, and have sacrificed thereunto, and said, These be thy gods, O Israel, which have brought thee up out of the land of Egypt. (Exod 32:8)

It soon became clear to those observing the violent changes in France that "apocalypse" did not describe the relatively peaceful initial stage of the Revolution, but the violent events after September 1792. Wordsworth, one of the few English poets who had lived and travelled in France during this period, writes about his meditations from a "high and lonely room" in Paris in 1792: "I thought of those September massacres/Divided from me by a little month/And felt and touched them, a substantial dread" (*The Prelude*, X. 64–66). Wordsworth's meditations are set aside in an address to himself, a blend of apocalyptic vision and cautionary remonstrance:

> 'The horse is taught his manage, and the wind
> Of heaven wheels round and treads in his own steps;

Year follows year, the tide returns again,
Day follows day, all things have second birth;
The earthquake is not satisfied at once' –
And in such way I wrought upon myself,
Until I seemed to hear a voice that cried
To the whole city, 'Sleep no more!'

(The Prelude, X. 70–77)

The obvious reference to Shakespeare's *Macbeth* ("Sleep no more;/ Macbeth doth murder sleep" [II.ii.35–36]) is combined with a series of images that emphasize a destructive circularity (playing on the literal meaning of "revolution"). The horse is trained by man (unnaturally, we assume), and the wind, like the horse, treads back "in his own steps." The natural recurrence of year, tide, and day culminate in a reference to Christian rebirth, but it is a false or negative resurrection quickly consumed in an earthquake. Wordsworth seems to have gathered images from a variety of sources, but biblical echoes of Isaiah seem prominent throughout this passage, a fitting inspiration, as Isaiah opens with a scene that must have resonated given the circumstances in France: "Ah sinful nation, a people laden with iniquity, a seed of evil-doers, children that are corrupters: they have forsaken the Lord, they have provoked the Holy One of Israel unto anger, they are gone away backward" (Isa 1:4). The "backward" direction of the people parallels France's backward return to despotism, and is captured in Wordsworth's horse wheeling by force of man back in its own steps. Isaiah expresses amazement at the turn experienced by Zion: "How is the faithful city become an harlot! it was full of judgment; righteousness lodged in it; but now murderers" (Isa 1:21). In a later passage, God summons the "nations from afar" and "their horses' hoofs shall be counted like flint, and their wheels like a whirlwind" (Isa 5:26–28).

As we saw earlier, the "burning wheels" of Shelley's *Queen Mab* recall the language of Ezekiel, and here too Wordsworth combines horses and "wheels" (refashioned as a verb) to suggest apocalyptic change connected to widespread natural forces such as tides and earthquakes. In Ezekiel, "By reason of the abundance of his horses their dust shall cover thee: thy walls shall shake at the noise of the horsemen, and of the wheels, and of the chariots" (Ezek 26:10). The horsemen of Revelation are galloping everywhere in the background here, of course, and Shelley makes use of the "pale horse" in *The Mask of Anarchy* (1819). There, a catalogue of allegorical figures such as Murder, Fraud, and Hypocrisy correspond to figures of British establishment authority:

Last came Anarchy; he rode
On a white horse, splashed with blood;
He was pale even to the lips,
Like Death in the Apocalypse.
                    (*Mask of Anarchy*, ll.30–33)

Wordsworth concludes his passage with a recollection that his "high and lonely room" in Paris was "a place of fear/Unfit for the repose of night/Defenceless as a wood where tigers roam" (*Prelude* X.80–82). There are no tigers in the Bible, but this chapter of Isaiah combines similarly haunting lines: "Their roaring shall be like a lion, they shall roar like young lions ... And in that day they shall roar against them like the roaring of the sea" (Isa 5: 29–30). Here, as in the passage from *The Prelude*, the animal, the inanimate forces of nature, and the political vicissitudes of a nation are bound together in something akin to a cycle of destruction and rebirth. In the two chapters that follow, Isaiah points to the promise of a son born to a virgin, who "shall know to refuse the evil, and choose the good" (Isa 7:15). For Wordsworth and other Romantic writers, rebirth is figured differently, usually in a manner that exploits the individual imagination as a faculty for change. Here in these lines about the French Revolution, however, the birth is engulfed not in a promise of regeneration or liberty but in violence.

As we saw with regards to Shelley's "*Ode to the West Wind*," imaginative reworking of revolutionary promise is a central Romantic theme. The initial hopes connected with the storming of the Bastille were celebrated in the belief that positive social and political change would signal a new period of liberty – liberty conceived as a kind of panacea that would engender personal transformation leading to earthly prosperity and spiritual enlightenment. In the writings of most Romantic authors, this formulation comes to be inverted almost completely: It is not political change that brings liberty to the individual, but individual transformation that must precede change in the polity.

For the Romantics, "individual transformation" was variously understood as a cultivation of the inner moral life that was associated with self-mastery, temperance, or virtuous action. All of these values were, in turn, a pre-condition of individual freedom, one of the master themes of political revolution and of Romanticism more generally. In Shelley's work, the struggle toward self-mastery and ultimate freedom is best displayed in *Prometheus Unbound* (1819), where we see the Titan overcome the "conflicting throngs within" and this leads – somehow – to his eventual liberation. Curiously, the question of how, or why, Prometheus is "liberated from chains" is the subject of endless conjecture. An anonymous writer in the *Gentleman's Magazine* (1848) observed that the "actual unbinding of Prometheus, the business of the drama, is so drawn out and so commented on that one hardly knows where it is."[9] It isn't terribly difficult to locate the "actual unbinding" of Prometheus, which is performed by Hercules in the third act (Act III. scene iii), but it does risk being overlooked for its bathos and serves only to fulfill the standard account of the Greek myth. In a sense, Prometheus' physical liberation signals the end of the dramatic action, and seems almost inconsequential relative to the steps that precede his release. What matters most for our purposes here is to trace a few biblical allusions that might help answer the question of why Prometheus achieves freedom from his "eagle baffling mountain."

In the Preface to his drama, Shelley explicitly acknowledges that Prometheus shares many qualities with Milton's Satan, but Prometheus is a "more poetical character than Satan because, in addition to courage and majesty and firm and patient opposition to omnipotent force, he is ... exempt from the taints of ambition, envy, revenge ... Prometheus is, as it were, the type of the highest perfection of moral and intellectual nature, impelled by the purest and the truest motives to the best and noblest ends" (*SPP*, 207). But while Prometheus' rebellion against God – Jupiter – recalls Milton's Satan, his act of stealing fire for the benefit of humans, and his subsequent punishment on their behalf, align him most directly with the figure of Christ. In the opening of the drama, Prometheus is "Nailed to [a] wall" and "The crawling glaciers pierce" him, recalling Jesus' crucifixion (Matt 27:35; John 19:34). Jesus cries out "My God, why hast thou forsaken me?" (Matt 27:46) and Prometheus poses a similar set of suffering-induced questions: "I ask the Earth, have not the mountains felt?/I ask yon Heaven – the all-beholding Sun/Has it not seen?" (I. 25–27). Later, Prometheus is presented with the most acute of all punishments – witnessing the suffering of the dying Christ, to whom he sends words of encouragement: "let that thorn-worn brow/ Stream not with blood – it mingles with thy tears!/Fix, fix those tortured orbs in peace and death/So thy sick throes shake not that crucifix" (I.598–60). At the moment of greatest pain and temptation (I.631) the Furies – who torture Prometheus with a vision of human depravity and

---

[9] *Gentleman's Magazine*, February 29, 1848, 151. See also *Shelley's "Prometheus Unbound": A Variorium Edition*, ed. Lawrence Zillman (Seattle, 1959) for this (521) and other reviews.

suffering – appropriate Jesus' own words to describe the ignorance of mankind: "they know not what they do" (Luke 23:34).

In aligning Prometheus so clearly with Christ, Shelley combines classical and biblical narrative in a manner consistent with his syncretic myth-making. Whereas Christ dies – to be reborn – to save mankind, Prometheus first "saves" humanity through his sacrifice, is punished, and ultimately released from his chains – a symbolic rebirth that precipitates the regeneration of the Earth and the Cosmos.

There are many theories that aim to explain how it is that Prometheus achieves freedom, but most of them seem to acknowledge that an important first step is the capacity for self-mastery. For Prometheus, this is figured as a refusal to "obey" authority and successfully preserving autonomy in the face of torture executed by the "Furies" as agents of Jupiter. The Furies promise to "dwell beside" Prometheus' soul and crawl "like agony" through his "labyrinthine veins" (I.485, 490). But even so, Prometheus asserts: "I am king over myself, and rule/The torturing and conflicting throng within" (I.492–93). Prometheus is "King over himself" not as Jupiter – or any political or religious ruler – governs others, but in the way that Jesus is "King of the Jews" (Matt 27:29) – a spiritual leader guiding discordant elements through example. The denunciation of an absolute ruler and the assertion of righteous sovereignty also recalls aspects of Ezekiel, where the poet – instructed by God – sets himself up in opposition to the Pharaoh: "Behold, I am against thee Pharaoh king of Egypt, the great dragon that lieth in the midst of his rivers, which hath said, My river is my own, and I have made it for myself" (Ezek 29:3).

Prometheus' struggle to control his inner self has many antecedents both in classical and biblical literature. But the particular complex of ideas we have discussed bear striking resemblance to the Pauline books of the New Testament, particularly Romans and Galatians. There the self is frequently portrayed as internally divided, a contest between spirit and flesh, or virtue and sin (Rom 6:12–14). When we are bound to sin, we are slaves. At times, spiritual righteousness is set in opposition to carnal sin and bondage (Rom 7:14). There is a law of the Spirit, but there is another "law" at work in the body: "But I see another law in my members, warring against the law of my mind, and bringing me into captivity to the law of sin which is in my members" (Rom 7:23). The self is portrayed as a collection of disparate fractious elements vying for control. Our body is like a "creature" but through righteous alliance with the Spirit, it will "be delivered from the bondage of corruption into the glorious liberty of the Children of God" (Rom 8:21). In Galatians we are instructed to "Stand fast ... in the liberty wherewith Christ hath made us free, and be not entangled again with the yoke of bondage" (Gal 5:1). Paradoxically, when we achieve the freedom of righteousness and self-mastery – when we are "free from sin" – we "become servants to God" (Rom 6:22). More emphatically still, Paul repeatedly identifies as the "Prisoner of Jesus Christ" (Eph 3:1; 4:1; Phil 1:1, 1:9).

Shelley's short fragment, "On the Doctrines of Christ" (1817), composed approximately a year before *Prometheus Unbound*, bears remarkable similarity – both in theme and in tone – to this Pauline opposition:

> Let us beware, if we love liberty and truth, if we loathe tyranny and imposture, if, imperfect ourselves, we still aspire to the freedom of internal purity, and cherish the elevated hope that Mankind may not be everlastingly condemned to the bondage of their own passions and the passions of their fellow beings, let us beware.[10]

This practice of equating righteousness and truth with liberty is common to many of the Romantic poets. Coleridge, for example, recanting his earlier enthusiasm for the French Revolution, writes that the "Sensual and the Dark rebel in vain/Slaves by their own compulsion! In mad game/They burst their manacles and wear the name/Of Freedom, graven on a heavier chain!" (*France: An Ode*, ll. 85–88). Biblical literature would have served as a model for much of this writing, but so too would earlier English poets, especially Milton, who describes "true Christian freedom" as the right to follow the Spirit of God as revealed within one's inner self.[11]

While self-mastery is clearly an important element in achieving freedom, it should also be noted that Hercules is the figure who literally unbinds the Titan, and Jupiter – representing tyranny – is mysteriously deposed by Demogorgon. Demogorgon is described as "Filling the seat of power" and he has "neither limb/Nor form, nor outline; yet we feel it is/A living spirit" (*PU*, II.iv.3–7). "Demogorgon" may derive from the "Demiurge" or "Creator" of Plato's *Timaeus*. He has been variously interpreted to represent molten magma under the earth, as Power, Necessity, Potentiality, and as the collection of democratic forces

---

[10] "On the Doctrines of Christ," ll. 34–39 (*Prose Works*, ed. E. B. Murray (Oxford, 1993), i. 273).

[11] This is a phrase Milton employs frequently in his prose writing, see, for example, *A Treatise of Civil Power in Ecclesiastical Causes* (vi: 22ff), where Milton quotes extensively from the New Testament (especially Corinthians and Galatians) to substantiate his claims.

capable of supplanting oppressive regimes.[12] But Demogorgon also clearly recalls the presentation of God as the burning bush beside Mount Horeb (Exod 3:2) and his mysterious tautologies – typical of the oracular figure he represents – also recall God's subsequent self-definition to Moses "I AM WHO I AM" (Ex. 3:14).

With these different aspects of the drama in mind, we can see that the path to freedom follows self-mastery and righteousness but also importantly depends on powers outside the self, or aspects of the self symbolically represented by these other characters. Shelley's imaginative reworking of revolutionary change – like the other Romantic poets of the period – draws heavily on biblical narrative and imagery to repeatedly assert that political transformation will never be possible until there is a transformation of mind and spirit.

Further Reading

Abrams, M. H., *Natural Supernaturalism: Tradition and Revolution in Romantic Literature* (New York and London, 1971; repr. 1973).

Abrams, M. H., "The Correspondent Breeze: A Romantic Metaphor," in *English Romantic Poets: Modern Essays in Criticism* (Oxford, 1960; repr. 1970), 37–54.

Balfour, Ian, "Shelley and the Bible," in *The Oxford Handbook of Shelley*, ed. Michael O'Neill and Anthony Howe (Oxford, 2013).

Paley, Morton, *Apocalypse and Millennium in English Romantic Poetry* (Oxford, 1999).

Shelley, Bryan, *Shelley and Scripture* (Oxford, 1994).

Shelley, Mary, *The Journals of Mary Shelley*, ed. Paula Feldman and Diana Scott-Kilvert (Baltimore and London, 1995).

Shelley, Percy Bysshe, *Shelley's Poetry and Prose*, ed. D. H. Reiman and Neil Fraistat (New York, 1977).

Wasserman, Earl, *Shelley: A Critical Reading* (Baltimore, 1971).

Webb, Timothy, *A Voice Not Understood* (Manchester, 1977).

---

[12] Geoffrey Matthews, "A Volcano's Voice in Shelley," *ELH*, 24 (1957), 205–8, 222; Wasserman, *A Critical Reading*, 321. Stuart Sperry, *Shelley's Major Verse* (Cambridge, MA, 1988), 99; Cameron, *The Golden Years*, 512–15; Foot, *Red Shelley*, 195ff.

14 Herman Melville and the Bible

RUTH BLAIR

The context of a volume on the Bible and literature affords an opportunity to explore the conjunction of these terms in relation to a writer, Herman Melville, whose great work *Moby-Dick* (1851) – the story of the hunting down of a white whale by an obsessed sea captain – came to have, after Melville's lifetime, mythic status for his nation and for the Western world. Melville's life (1819–91) spanned the nineteenth century and he was one of its outstanding thinkers. His work throughout is profoundly influenced by the Bible.

Of the many writings on Melville's attention to biblical texts, two works are of particular importance for this essay. Gail Coffler's indexing in *Melville's Allusions to Religion* (2004) is an invaluable guide to the extent of his use of biblical texts. Nathalia Wright's *Melville's Use of the Bible* (1949) – still the best introduction to the topic – focuses on a range of ways in which biblical texts function in his writings. At the heart of her study is the assumption that the Bible is the bedrock of Melville's career as a writer. She argues convincingly that his early and deep acquaintance with the Authorized (King James) Version (1611), the standard one for his time and place, influenced his choice of the literary arts as the vehicle for his thought. He found, says Wright, "this first of all his sources phenomenally the most wealthy, yielding history, literature, humor, speculation, spiritual exercises, a multiplicity of styles."[1] The Bible Melville had to hand was the Authorized Version with Apocrypha, published in Philadelphia in 1846.[2] Because of its stylistic significance, citations in this essay will be from the Authorized Version (AV).

There are many overviews of Melville's religious thought, which included an interest in a range of religions and mythologies. This essay addresses an aspect of that thought. Through attention to particular passages, it highlights the influence of the Wisdom books of the Old

---

[1] Nathalie Wright, *Melville's Use of the Bible* (Durham, NC, 1949), 7.
[2] M. R. Sealts, *Melville's Reading* (Columbia, SC, 1988), 155.

Testament (particularly the Books of Job, Proverbs, and Ecclesiastes) in order to show both their capacity to help Melville think through the problems of his age and their influence on his understanding of the power of story and the capacities of language. "No other group of scriptural books," Wright observes, "is so extensively represented in his pages, or so profusely marked in his Bible."[3]

The essay first addresses the role of Melville's South Seas experiences in his formation as a writer, as it was there, as a young man, that he began seriously to question the Dutch Reformed Protestant faith of his upbringing and to consider his experiences in relation to a broader social and philosophical context. A reading of a passage in *Moby-Dick* follows, illustrating the depth of Melville's interest in and understanding of the Wisdom books. The long poem of Melville's mature years, *Clarel*, based on his travels in the Holy Land, prompts a reflection upon his grappling, in later years, with the nature of wisdom and the possibility of faith.

Though this essay focuses on ways in which Melville's writing is enriched by biblical stories, themes, and styles, it is also important to note that the relationship is not a one-way phenomenon. Biblical texts, Yvonne Sherwood observes in her book on Jonah, are "sustained by interpretation" – by their "afterlives."[4] Through their powers of storytelling their ancient matters persist. Literary works like Melville's, revisiting those matters, re-telling those stories, casting them in different lights, are part of that process.

"THE ISLES OF THE SEA"[5]

Herman Melville was born into a turbulent and confident post-revolutionary American society, with heroes of the War of Independence on both sides of his family. His mother was descended from Dutch colonists who settled in Albany, New York. His father, from a Scottish family of Boston traders, was a well-traveled and cultured man who set up his trading business in New York City. Bad decisions led to bankruptcy and an early death when Herman was eleven years old. This tragedy cut short the life of relative privilege the family had led, as well

---

[3] Wright, *Melville*, 94.

[4] Yvonne Sherwood, *A Biblical Text and Its Afterlives* (Cambridge, 2000), 2.

[5] Isa 24:15 in Herman Melville, *Typee* (Evanston, IL, and Chicago, 1968), 26:195. For ease of reference to Melville's texts, chapter numbers are given in addition to page numbers where relevant.

as Melville's education. In 1839 he took ship on a merchant vessel bound for Liverpool, for one voyage. In 1841, at twenty-one years of age, he signed aboard a whaling vessel, the *Acushnet*, bound on a three-year voyage in the Pacific. He lasted eighteen months on the *Acushnet* before jumping ship with a mate, Toby, on the island of Nukuhiva in the Marquesas. (Absconding from whaling vessels was not uncommon.) From there, he found his way to Tahiti, then Hawaii, returning home on a United States man-of-war in 1844. Encouraged to write about his South Seas experiences, he published his first book, *Typee*, in 1846. The book met with great success and was closely followed by two other South Seas tales, *Omoo* (1847) and *Mardi* (1849). At this point also he embarked on the wide range of reading that would inform his future work.

Melville's religious thought, his relationship with biblical texts, and his artistry cannot be understood without some sense of the radical nature of his South Seas experiences. The Marquesas, far-flung islands of Polynesia, had proved, unlike Tahiti or the Sandwich Islands, inhospitable to settlement by Europeans and a difficult missionary outpost. Melville was able there to experience Polynesian life relatively untouched by commerce (in the narrow and broad senses of the word) with Europeans.

Although Melville's account is grounded in fact, it was his instinct not to call his narrator by his own name but to give him an appellation, Tommo. (He follows this practice in all his narratives of seafaring life.) He also gave his story two frames in counterpoint that invite the making of meaning out of the material of his adventure. The first framing story, the Genesis myth of the Garden of Eden, provided a common reference point for Europeans encountering the islands for the first time. The seeming innocence and good life of the Polynesians were, however, a problem for prospective colonizers. Tommo observes: "The penalty of the Fall presses very lightly [...] for, with the one solitary exception of striking a light, I scarcely saw any piece of work performed there which caused the sweat to stand upon a single brow" (195).[6] To put the argument that the Typee are indeed fallen, Melville creates a captivity plot that explores the dangers of being tempted by the allures of the unchristian life.

The Garden of Eden is invoked when Tommo and Toby come upon an enchanting scene in a glade: two young Marquesans, a boy and a girl,

[6] *Typee*, 26:195.

"slender and graceful, and completely naked, with the exception of a slight girdle of bark, from which depended at opposite points two of the russet leaves of the bread-fruit tree."[7] However Eden-like the scene, the absconders have ended up in the valley of a reputedly ferocious group, the Typee. Though they are treated well, both feel themselves to be captives. Toby escapes. Tommo, hampered by a swollen leg, settles in for a largely happy captivity. Cannibalism and tattooing (the favored markers by colonizers and missionaries of the fallen state of Pacific islanders) finally enter the story as potential threats, and Tommo makes his escape. An intervening series of ethnographic chapters, largely borrowed from other sources, makes it clear that Melville, like his narrator Tommo, has developed, during his captivity, a genuine interest in and respect for this culture so different from his own. Inseparable from these insights is a change in his perception of the Christianity in which he was raised. Thus begins his long exploration of where, in his own time, faith and an understanding of the realities of life and death might reside.

In a Preface and an Appendix to *Typee*, Melville attacks the behavior of the vanguard of "civilization" in the area, particularly missionaries. Christianity's "glorious cause," he states in the Preface, "has not always been served by the proceedings of some of its advocates." In the Appendix he describes the handling of the occupation of the Sandwich Islands by the United States under the auspices of "a junto of ignorant and designing Methodist elders." Tommo remarks: "Heaven help the 'Isles of the Sea'!"[8] In citing Isaiah here (24:15), Melville draws the South Seas islands into the resonances of the biblical text. This gesture will recur in *Clarel*, where the islands have a significant figurative presence.

The Christianizing effort in the South Seas continued to preoccupy Melville in *Omoo* and *Mardi*. In *Omoo*, where he elaborates on the collusion between commerce and religion, he seems caught between the desire to acknowledge the value of introducing the island peoples to Christianity and a more strongly felt abhorrence of the intransigence with which native culture and social structures were dismantled. "Doubtless," he writes, "in thus denationalizing the Tahitians, as it were, the missionaries were prompted by a sincere desire for good; but the effect has been lamentable."[9] Priests, proclaims the philosopher Babbalanja in *Mardi*, are "pious heralds" of this process, and "[t]he

[7] Ibid., 10:68.
[8] Ibid., xiv; 255; 26:195.
[9] Herman Melville, *Omoo* (Evanston, IL, and Chicago, 1968), 47:183.

march of conquest through wild provinces may be the march of Mind; but not the march of Love."[10]

To read any of these early texts is to see that the Bible is the lifeblood of Melville's writing. His experiences in the South Seas also remain with him, informing his profound humanity and feeding uncertainty about the questions and doubts that will mark the nineteenth century in America as well as elsewhere in the Western world. It is not surprising that the Wisdom books have a significant role in the development of Melville's thought. Their context is Israelite society after the Babylonian captivity. They too reflect upon a particular world, within a framework of belief.

WISDOM

For the young United States, the nineteenth century was a time of both exhilarating growth and demoralizing crisis, culminating in the Civil War of the 1860s and its aftermath. Only rarely (in some of his short stories and poems) does Melville tell personal or domestic (in the narrower sense of the word) stories. From *Typee* on, his writing is engaged with the politics and the soul of his country.[11] Two more novels of seafaring life followed the South Seas tales: *Redburn* (1849), based on his voyage to Liverpool, and *White-Jacket* (1850), an account of life on a man-of-war. As he began, next, a whaling story, Melville's writing moved into a new register, reflecting the range of his reading.

In the manner of many books of the Bible, or of any great mythic or scriptural texts, *Moby-Dick* sets on the back of its central story a multiplicity of social and metaphysical meanings. Teeming with biblical references, it is also crisscrossed with allusions to many other mythic formulations. Chapter 96, "The Try-Works," marks a reflective moment on the narrator Ishmael's part before the turn of the narrative toward a tragic ending. It is a place to observe Melville at work, weaving together the everyday and the metaphysical, and to see how and where the Wisdom books – here Ecclesiastes and Proverbs – become major directive texts in his work.

The story that impels the narrative tells of Ahab, the captain of a whaling ship, the *Pequod*, who, out of vengeance for the loss of a leg, is

---

[10] Herman Melville, *Mardi* (Evanston, IL, and Chicago, 1970), 168:552.
[11] On the socio-political dimension of Melville's work see Michael Rogin, *Subversive Genealogy* (Berkeley, CA, 1983).

"chasing with curses a Job's whale round the world."[12] (Ahab is also a Promethean figure, and the eponymous white whale resonates with a range of mythic meanings.) Ishmael, who guides the reader through the story, figures only rarely in the action. He too has been a man obsessed, but his friendship early in the narrative with the South Sea islander harpooner Queequeg calms his soul. "I felt a melting in me," he says as the bond between them grows. "No more my splintered heart and maddened hand were turned against the wolfish world. This soothing savage had redeemed it."[13]

Though Ishmael often speaks, comments, and reflects on the action throughout the narrative, in Chapter 96 he gives an extended meditation on a dramatic experience of his own. The chapter begins with the kind of detail, resonant with meaning, to which the reader is by now habituated. The try-works are large cauldrons for rendering whale blubber, "planted between the foremast and mainmast, the most roomy part of the deck. The timbers beneath are of a peculiar strength, fitted to sustain the weight of an almost solid mass of brick and mortar, some ten feet by eight square and five in height." When they are fired up, "[i]t smells like the left wing of the day of judgment; it is an argument for the pit." (The reference here is to Matt 25:33 and 41.) The pagan harpooners as stokers are "Tartarean shapes" (a Hellenistic reference). "The continual sight of the fiend shapes before me," says Ishmael, at the helm of the ship one night, "begat kindred visions in my soul."[14] Losing concentration, he almost turns the ship around. The chapter ends with his meditation on the near-catastrophe. The passage is quoted in full:

> Look not too long in the face of the fire, O man! Never dream with thy hand on the helm! Turn not thy back to the compass; accept the first hint of the hitching tiller; believe not the artificial fire, when its redness makes all things look ghastly. Tomorrow, in the natural sun, the skies will be bright; those who glared like devils in the forking flames, the morn will show in far other, at least gentler, relief; the glorious, golden, glad sun, the only true lamp – all others but liars!
>
> Nevertheless the sun hides not Virginia's Dismal Swamp, nor Rome's accursed Campagna, nor wide Sahara, nor all the millions of miles of deserts and of griefs beneath the moon. The sun hides not the ocean, which is the dark side of this earth, and which is two

---

[12] Hermann Melville, *Moby-Dick* (Evanston, IL, and Chicago, 1988), 41:186.
[13] Ibid., 10:51.
[14] Ibid., 96:421–23.

thirds of this earth. So, therefore, that mortal man who hath more of joy than sorrow in him, that mortal man cannot be true – not true, or undeveloped. With books the same. The truest of all men was the Man of Sorrows, and the truest of all books is Solomon's, and Ecclesiastes is the fine hammered steel of woe. "All is vanity." ALL. This wilful world hath not got hold of unchristian Solomon's wisdom yet. But he who dodges hospitals and jails, and walks fast crossing grave-yards, and would rather talk of operas than hell; calls Cowper, Young, Pascal, Rousseau, poor devils all of sick men; and throughout a care-free lifetime swears by Rabelais as passing wise, and therefore jolly; – not that man is fitted to sit down on tomb-stones, and break the green damp mould with unfathomably wondrous Solomon.

But even Solomon, he says, "the man that wandereth out of the way of understanding shall remain" (*i.e.* even while living) "in the congregation of the dead." Give not thyself up, then, to fire, lest it invert thee, deaden thee; as for the time it did me. There is a wisdom that is woe; but there is a woe that is madness. And there is a Catskill eagle in some souls that can alike dive down into the blackest gorges, and soar out of them again and become invisible in the sunny spaces. And even if he for ever flies within the gorge, that gorge is in the mountains; so that even in his lowest swoop the mountain eagle is still higher than other birds upon the plain, even though they soar.[15]

The tripartite passage is a poised moment of vision, which Melville had essayed in *Mardi* (Chapters 75 and 119) and has perfected here. It marks the growing significance for him of the Wisdom books, and though Job is not referenced in it, of the role of argument in Job. Ishmael's meditation has a Hellenistic dialectical structure of thesis, antithesis, and synthesis. The tone, however, from the opening admonition, is biblical. The biblical cast of the passage is reinforced by Melville's use of the rhetorical strategy of parallelism that is a feature of many Old Testament writings. He would have known of Robert Lowth's discussion of parallelism in Hebrew poetry from John Kitto's *Cyclopaedia of Biblical Literature*, which he had at hand while writing *Moby-Dick*.[16] The first paragraph begins with five parallel admonitions

---

[15] Ibid., 96:424–25.
[16] Robert Lowth, *Lectures on Sacred Hebrew Poetry* (New York, 1971), II: 24–59; Kitto, John, ed., *Cyclopaedia of Biblical Literature* (Philadelphia, 1866), 571–72; M. K. Bercaw, *Melville's Sources* (Evanston, IL, 1987), 95.

about the seductive danger of fire-gazing, followed by three reminders that human beings are earth-bound, and of the consolations of that condition in the diurnal round. The paragraph ends with an ecstatic alliterative homage to the "glorious, golden, glad sun" and a final small parallelism: "the one true lamp – all others but liars." Though this is Ishmael speaking about his own experience, the paragraph resonates with the Promethean dimensions of Ahab's quest for vengeance. It recalls, in warning, Ahab's alliance with his boat crew of fire-worshiping Parsees led by the diabolical Fedallah, the gathering metaphysical dimensions of his quest ("I'd strike the sun if it insulted me." "Who's over me?"), and the impossibility of consolation: "This lovely light, it lights not me."[17]

The ecstatic conclusion to the first paragraph is followed by its antithesis in five parallel negations. There is a dark side to the earth – "deserts and griefs" that the sun cannot hide, and the ocean, which will remain Melville's figure for the vastness of the unknowable. An alternative conclusion emerges: that truth can reside only in the acknowledgement of sorrow. After quoting Eccl 1:2 ("All is vanity"), Ishmael continues: "The truest of all men was the Man of Sorrows." The reference is to Isa 53:3: "He is despised and rejected of men; a man of sorrows, and acquainted with grief." The capitalization points to the reading in the Gospel of Matthew of this pronouncement as an allusion to the future Christ: "That it might be fulfilled which was spoken by Esaias the prophet [...]" (Matt 8:17). Then follows a strange conjoining that looks at first glance like what Lowth calls "synthetic" or "constructive" parallelism, in which sentences or phrases "answer to each other," not by sameness or opposition, "but merely by form of construction."[18] "And," says Ishmael, "the truest of all books is Solomon's, and Ecclesiastes is the fine hammered steel of woe." The linking of Christ with "unchristian Solomon" through this construction gives pause. It forces a consideration of the darkness as well as the light that surrounds the figure of Christ. Melville then enrolls in his dark scriptural pantheon some literary figures, "poor devils all of sick men," lacking in a carefree spirit, who are fitted to "break the green damp mould with unfathomably wondrous Solomon," referencing Eccl 2:2: "I said of laughter, It is mad: and of mirth, What doeth it?"

Synthesis follows, as Ishmael quotes Prov 21:16: "But even Solomon, he says, 'the man that wandereth out of the way of understanding

---

[17] *Moby-Dick*, 36:164; 37:167.
[18] Lowth, Lectures, II, 49.

shall remain' (i.e. even while living) 'in the congregation of the dead'." Do not be absorbed by the artificial fire, Ishmael admonishes, bringing the reader/listener back to the story with which the chapter began, "lest it invert thee, deaden thee; as for the time, it did me." An antithetical parallelism follows: "There is a wisdom that is woe; but there is a woe that is madness." Eccl 1:17–18 is the reference here: "And I gave my heart to know wisdom, and to know madness and folly: I perceived that this also is vexation of spirit. / For in much wisdom is much grief: and he that increaseth knowledge increaseth sorrow."[19] In his own riddling sentence Melville is testing his own prophetic arm.

"And there is a Catskill eagle ..." – not any eagle but a particular eagle common in the Catskill mountains. This compelling figure, expressing a balance between the tragic and the radiant, echoes Isaiah's "they shall mount up with wings of eagles" (40:31). The "And" bursts into the argument as the prose soars with the bird, descending with a riddling coda: "so that even in his lowest swoop, the mountain eagle is still higher than other birds upon the plain, even though they soar." In the final phrase of this sentence, two trochees, with their rising notes in the metrical foot, are followed by the magnificent, almost onomato-poeic quality of the long, open vowel of "soar." George Saintsbury notes the power and beauty of the long diphthong vowel in English in the AV's rendition of the first verse of Isa 60: "Arise, shine; for thy light is come, and the glory of the Lord is risen upon thee." "The clarion sound," Saintsbury calls it, "of the glorious vowel *i*," and the "euphonious contrast" with the long *o*'s of "the glory of the Lord."[20] In Ishmael's meditation, as elsewhere throughout Melville's writing, the music and the poetry come predominantly from the tones and cadences of the AV, which mesh with those of Shakespeare, his other great inspiration.

In the tiny chapter that follows, "The Lamp," Melville takes the reader down from the sublime heights of the long meditation into the democratic coziness of the forecastle, lit by purest whale oil. Previously, describing the crew, Ishmael has signaled that his epic story will not be about kings but about "meanest mariners, renegades and castaways," and "if even the most mournful, perchance the most abased, among them all, shall at times lift himself to the exalted mounts; if I shall

[19] Gail Coffler attributes Solomonic references in the meditation to the Wisdom of Solomon as well as to Ecclesiastes (*op. cit.* 49, 14). I follow Harold Beaver who sees all the wisdom references here as from Ecclesiastes or Proverbs (*Moby-Dick*, ed. Beaver [Harmondsworth, 1972], 879–80). Melville knew of the questionable attribution of these books to Solomon. He would have found this information in Kitto.

[20] George Saintsbury, *A History of English Prose Rhythm* (London, 1912), 145.

touch that workman's arm with some ethereal light [...] then against all mortal critics bear me out in it, [...] thou great democratic God!"²¹ In "The Lamp" he echoes this conviction, drawing the reader to consider that in this domestic light, flickerings of great eagle-like souls may be found:

> Had you descended from the Pequod's try-works to the Pequod's forecastle, where the off duty watch were sleeping, for one single moment you would have almost thought you were standing in some illuminated shrine of canonized kings and counsellors. There they lay in their triangular oaken vaults, each mariner a chiselled muteness; a score of lamps flashing upon his hooded eyes.²²

"[K]ings and counsellors" comes from Job 3:14 and shows how Melville braids biblical references into his writing in complex ways, to give that kind of "afterlife" to scriptural texts that Sherwood discusses. We need to read around the particular verse to gather the range of implications in the use of the words of Job here. In this chapter, Job curses the day of his birth and asks, in a triple parallelism: "Why did I not die in the womb? ... / For now should I have lain still and been quiet, I should have slept; then had I been at rest" (Job 3:11, 13). "With kings and counsellers of the earth," he adds, for death is an equalizer. "The small and the great are there; and the servant is free from his master" (Job 3:14–15, 19). In their "chiselled muteness," the "meanest mariners" resemble the effigies on the coffins of kings and princes in old Christian churches. In the images and intertextual references of the tiny chapter, the lives and fates of the sailors are distilled. There is an intra-textual echo, also, of "bleak tablets" announcing that "there is death in this business of whaling," in the seamen's chapel where, before Ishmael and Queequeg set out to sea, they hear the preacher, Father Mapple, deliver a sermon on Jonah.²³ That the sailors' bunks resemble coffins foreshadows the men's tragic destinies. And the book will end with the paradox of Ishmael being saved, buoyed up by a coffin Queequeg has had made for himself. The allusion to Job, then – and this is invariably the case throughout Melville's writing – is more than a handy reference. It opens a door to understanding the high seriousness of the lives of these men, through the connection of Melville's story with one of the greatest expressions of the human condition in the face of immensity and woe.

---

²¹ *Moby-Dick*, 26:117.
²² Ibid., 97:426.
²³ Ibid., 7:36, 37.

Moby-Dick, full of encyclopedic knowledge of the sea and of human stories, is also about America. *The Pequod* is the ship of state. Ahab is Emersonian self-reliance run amok. C. L. R. James announces a broader political theme in his subtitle: *The Story of Herman Melville and the World We Live In.* "The voyage of the *Pequod*," he says, "is the voyage of modern civilization seeking its destiny." It prefigures "how the society of free individualism would give birth to totalitarianism and be unable to defend itself against it."[24] The Wisdom books, in their particular historical setting, shed a significant light on these deeper meanings.

THE HOLY LAND

Melville was thirty-two when *Moby-Dick* was published. The complex and oddly structured book, at times challengingly metaphysical, received a poor critical and popular reception and did not find an avid readership until the early twentieth century. Two novels, *Pierre* (1852) and *The Confidence-Man* (1857), and a number of short stories followed *Moby-Dick* in the 1850s. In 1856, Melville fulfilled a long-held desire to travel to the Holy Land. Around this time he turned his hand to writing poetry. He published a collection of poems on the Civil War, *Battle Pieces*, in 1866. In the same year, he began work as an Inspector of Customs in New York. Between 1870 and 1875 Melville wrote *Clarel: a Poem and Pilgrimage in the Holy Land*, published quietly and scarcely noticed in 1876. It is an extremely long poem, still little read or known, and along with *Billy Budd* (found among his papers after his death), the great work of Melville's later years. It resumes, in a different guise from the prose fiction, his ongoing reflections on the nature of good and evil and the meaning of life. There are many pathways through the poem. I follow that of the Wisdom books.

Accounts of travels in the Holy Land were popular in the mid-nineteenth century. Against the grain, Melville chose to write a long dramatic poem that would enable him to reflect on the nature of the modern – Western/Christian – experience of that ancient landscape and on questions it provoked. His young protagonist, Clarel, embarks, much as Melville did, on a pilgrimage, from Jerusalem to the Dead Sea, returning via Mar Saba and Bethlehem. His companions represent a range of Western men whose debates on theological and philosophical topics Clarel follows with interest in an attempt to anchor his own troubled soul. Before setting off on the pilgrimage, Clarel falls in love

---

[24] C. L. R. James, *Mariners, Renegades and Castaways* (London, 1985 [c. 1953]), 25; 60.

with a young Jewish woman, Ruth, the daughter of an American Zionist
father. This tragic love story begins and ends the poem.

As in all his writing, Melville made copious use of source material
to flesh out his experience and to shape patterns of thought. His facility
for ranging across biblical texts in the poem is impressive. Following
Coffler's indices, I count easily two hundred direct references – to
twenty-eight books of the Old Testament and to nine of the New. *Clarel*
is daunting – at first. It is long and in a verse form (rhyming iambic
tetrameters) demanding of both writer and reader. The form is in a way a
spiritual exercise for both. Melville hammers words and wrenches
syntax to fit the form. Walter Bezanson, in his substantial commentary
on the poem, sees the "constricting" form as reflecting "the tragedy of
modern man."[25] Yet the verse form is often fluid and flexible. From
both these aspects, the poem engages the reader in a difficult journey,
rather like the pilgrimage itself, on horseback – a mode of travel in
which one cannot afford to lose concentration, and whose rhythm the
tetrameter line echoes.

The drama of *Clarel* lies not in the framing story of its young
protagonist but in the arguments among the pilgrims. These are what
draw the reader on, as in the Book of Job. *Clarel* too is a Wisdom book.
How will the great questions of what we are and where we are going be
resolved? It is also a lively poem with engaging descriptions of landscape
and people, and patterns of imagery – often in Homeric extended
similes – that weave a redemptive beauty around an increasingly dark
vision of the world. Much of the imagery, drawn from Melville's experience, is of the sea. Rolfe, one of the company, wakes from sleep to "a
refluence of disquiet," imaged as when

> The roller upon Borneo's strand
> Halts not, but in recoiling throe
> Drags back the shells involved with sand,
> Shuffled and muffled in the flow
> And hollow of the wallowing undertow.
>
> $(3.15.7; 3.15.1-5)$[26]

Rolfe is a sailor who, like Melville, has sailed the oceans and experienced the southern islands. He recalls a sojourn in the South Seas that
echoes Tommo's adventures. Reflecting on a palm tree at the monas-
tery of Mar Saba, he muses: "Remindings swell; / Sweet troubles of

---

[25] Walter Bezanson, in Herman Melville, *Clarel* (Evanston, IL, and Chicago, 1991), 569.
[26] References to *Clarel* will be given in the text to Part.Canto.Line/s.

emotions mount – / Sylvan reveries [. . .] / Whom weave ye in, / Ye vines, ye palms?" (3.29.37–42) Later, his thoughts reaching "from Bethlehem [. . .] to Tahiti's beach," he essays: "Tahiti should have been the place /For Christ in advent."(4.18.35–36, 43–44) A similar comment appears in Melville's 1856–57 journal: "J. C. should have appeared in Taheiti [*sic*]."[27]

Melville does not, however, allow Polynesia to become simply a romantic touchstone for disillusion. The questioning of those Euro-American procedures in the South Seas that had provoked early the unsettling of religious certainties remains. Echoing the narrators Tommo and Omoo, and *Mardi's* Babbalanja, Rolfe speaks in anger of the collusion between missionaries and colonialists: "These pirates of the sphere! [. . .] / Mammonite freebooters, / Who in the name of Christ and Trade [. . .] / Deflower the world's last sylvan glade." (4.9.121–25) Political issues become indivisible from an examination of contemporary Christianity and its relationship to the "gentle Jesus," as he is called in *Typee*, of the Gospels.[28]

Melville voices the many arguments of *Clarel* through a number of "counter natures." (3.20.39) The sailor Rolfe and Derwent (an Anglican priest) are at different times in dialogue with the more extreme characters Mortmain (a Swedish revolutionary) and Ungar (a part-Cherokee disillusioned former officer of the Southern Confederacy). Vine (an enigmatic American intellectual) is largely, like Clarel, a listener. The main lines of argument gather around debates among Derwent, Rolfe, and Ungar. A challenger whose "forest eyes" yet bear "No cynic fire sarcastic" (4.5.3, 17), Ungar becomes, for the young Clarel, an increasingly convincing comrade.

Ungar bears most of the weight of argument in the final Part (4) of the poem. Through the voice of this self-exiled mercenary, Melville continues his consideration of the American project, its present and its future. For Ungar, as for Melville, this issue is connected to wider issues of European civilization. In three key cantos of sustained and dramatic debate (4.20–22), Ungar voices a suspicion of Protestant "reform" of both church and society. Reflecting on the Reformation, he says:

> From Luther's great initial down,
> Through all the series following on,

---

27 Herman Melville, *Journals* (Evanston, IL, and Chicago, 1989), 154.
28 *Typee*, 27:203.

The impetus augments – the blind
Precipitation: blind, for tell
Whitherward does the surge impel?
(4.20.21–25)

Derwent replies that the "object clear" is "belief revised, / Men liberated – equalized / In happiness." (4.20.28–30) Ungar darkly responds: "Now the world cannot save the world; / And Christ renounces it." (4.20.34–35) This is bold material, rejecting the Anglican Derwent's moderate and optimistic view of modern life. The counterpoint of views echoes the meditation in *Moby-Dick* discussed earlier; the seeds of it were sewn in the South Seas where Melville glimpsed dangers in the partnership between the Enlightenment and Protestant reform. In *Clarel* this alliance becomes the most unsettling and challenging topic in the poem. Science is the pointy end of the target, embodied most abjectly in the character Margoth, a geologist who figures Melville's distrust of the emptying-out of spirit in the historical/geographical line of biblical criticism. Margoth declares: "the plain – the vale – Lot's sea / It needs we scientists to remand / Back from old theologic myth / To geologic hammers." (2.20.46–50) In Canto 21, Ungar darkly sums up a sense of the threadbareness of modern life ("our denuding day" [4.20.11]):

Know
Whatever happen in the end,
Be sure 'twill yield to one and all
New confirmation of the fall
Of Adam. Sequel may ensue,
[...]
Man disennobled – brutalized
By popular science – Atheized
Into a smatterer.
(4.21.121–33)

There is no counter to this argument as the poem draws to its close. In Canto 21, Ungar reflects upon "the impieties of 'Progress'," (4.21.28) quoting loosely from Job 21. Job describes those who "spend their days in wealth, and in a moment go down to the grave" and therefore "say unto God, Depart from us; for we desire not the knowledge of thy ways. / What is the Almighty that we should serve him? and what profit should we have, if we pray unto him?" (Job 21:13–15). Ungar: "What say *these*, in effect to God? / 'How profits it? And who art Thou / That we should serve Thee?'" (4.21.29–31. Emphasis in text.) He continues, voicing the impious who say:

> [...] Of Thy ways
> No knowledge we desire; *new* ways
> We have found out, and better. Go –
> Depart from us; we do erase
> Thy sinecure.
>   (4.21.31–35. Emphasis in the text.)

Given Melville's abiding interest in the book of Job, I doubt that it is by accident that the invocation of Job 21 occurs in the important Canto 21 of Part 4. Job appears at odd moments throughout the poem in points of reference that add meaning and color. Vine, glimpsed in a moldy library, is likened to "the bankrupt man of Uz." (3.27.71; Job 1.1) The pilgrims wait at the foot of Mar Saba "[l]ike Job's pale group, without a sound." (3.3.62. Job 2:13) Arabs "show a lingering trace / Of some quite unrecorded race / Such as the Book of Job implies." (2.27.74–76) (Melville here refers to speculations in his time on the sources and nationalities of the Book of Job.)[29] Eliphaz the Temanite's dream vision lends one of Clarel's dreams consequence. (1.22.110–12. Job 4: 12–16). But more significantly, Job is enrolled in the service of argumentation, supporting a line of thought that leads to the poem's conclusion. Derwent's character is pegged when he is introduced as one who "Abreast kept with the age, the year / And each bright optimistic mind. / Nor lagged with Solomon in rear, / And Job, the furthermost behind." (2.1.36–39) There is an echo here of the "Try Works" meditation: In putting Solomon and Job behind him, Derwent is "not true, or undeveloped." Derwent tries to persuade Clarel that pessimism is "obsolete." (3.21.284–85) The clouds, he says, of Byron, Shelley, and Goethe's Werther are gone, even "Hamlet's sigh" now "perverse." (3.21.293–96) To which Clarel, by now having heard the counter-arguments of Rolfe and Ungar: "Forbear! / Ah, wherefore not at once name Job, / In whom these Hamlets all conglobe [...] / Doubt bleeds, nor Faith is free from pain!" (3.21.300–4)

   To simplify a complex history, theological approaches to the Book of Job turn around a dichotomy: Job as a patient man or as defiant. In an essay on Melville and Job, Janis Stout writes that in *Moby-Dick* it was

---

[29] Bezanson in *Clarel*, 781.

"the questioning Job rather than the patient Job that caught Melville's imagination."[30] But Melville rarely lets the scales fall on one side of a dichotomy. You know you are warm only when the tip of your nose is cold, as Ishmael muses in *Moby-Dick*; "nor Faith is free from pain."(3.21.304)[31] Job and his "pale group" of questioners haunt the sometimes theodical arguments of the pilgrims. But glimpses in Job of the sublime power of God, celebrated in the climax of *Moby-Dick* as Melville's divinely beautiful leviathan brings down ship and men, are echoed in the final stages of Melville's poem. Here the sublime is in the stars. It is the end of the journey and Ungar reflects: "Arcturus and his shining sons; And lo, Job's chambers of the South: / How might his hand not go to mouth / Adoring ye, bright zones?" (4.7.95–98; Job 9:9) Ungar is the one character in the poem who, like the Catskill eagle, can hold the bright and the dark in balance, even if only momentarily.

After the debates of Part 4 touched on earlier, Clarel's story resumes. Returning to Jerusalem, Clarel comes across the funeral procession of his beloved Ruth. His sojourn in the Holy Land thus ends in personal tragedy. But he is not Ishmael, who survives the destruction wreaked by Moby Dick to become the prophetic storyteller. Clarel's is, at least for now, a narrow and shadowy path:

> Dusked Olivet he leaves behind,
> And, taking now the slender wynd,
> Vanishes in the obscurer town.
>
> (4.34.54–56)

The Epilogue is delivered by the narrator, who speaks, here, in the more traditional and settling rhythm of the iambic pentameter. Rejecting the solace of the "common uninquiring life" (which Clarel ponders momentarily [4.28.76]) the narrator asks, taking up again the debated connection between Protestantism and the Enlightenment and science: "If Luther's day expand to Darwin's year, / Shall that exclude the hope – foreclose the fear?" (4.35.1–2) Yet faith

> With blood warm oozing from her wounded trust,
> Inscribes even on her shards of broken urns
> The sign o' the cross – *the spirit above the dust.*
>
> (4.35.9–11. Emphasis in the text.)

---

[30] J. Stout, "Melville's Use of the Book of Job," *Nineteenth Century Fiction*, 25.1 (1970), 69–83 (70).
[31] *Moby-Dick*, 11:53–54.

The figure of Christ and the significance of Christianity in Melville's time are important threads in the poem. Christ's presence increases in Part 4, accompanied by the emblems of cross and star. However, in the Epilogue, despite the earlier invocation, the Wisdom books set the tone. The narrator continues:

> Degrees we know, unknown in days before:
> The light is greater, hence the shadow more;
> [...]
> But through such strange illusions have they passed
> Who in life's pilgrimage have baffled striven –
> Even death may prove unreal at last,
> And stoics be astounded into heaven.
>
> (4.35.18–19, 23–26)

The last line of this quotation echoes the old Crusader cry *"Denique Coelum"* (Heaven at Last) – a motto that goes back through Melville's *White-Jacket* to the Melville family crest.[32]

> The final stanza of the Epilogue offers Clarel, and the reader, a
>   degree of hope:
> That like the crocus budding through the snow –
> That like a swimmer rising from the deep –
> [...]
> Emerge thou mayst from the last whelming sea,
> And prove that death but routs life into victory.
>
> (4.35.29–34)

Victory at the end has nothing to do with sin and redemption. As in the valley of Typee, "[t]he penalty of the Fall presses very lightly'" on this poem. Melville offers, not Derwent's loose and superficial reconciliations, but something like what he calls in the Supplement to *Battle Pieces* "sacred uncertainty."[33]

From *Typee* on, ambiguity was a significant feature of Melville's writing, but, like Sir Thomas Browne whom he admired, he was a speculative, never a cynical, writer. Melville's reputation began to be re-made in the early twentieth century. Perhaps the modernist sensibilities of the early decades of the century responded to Melville because he was neither optimist nor cynic, and to the very quality of uncertainty in his writing. But at the same time, Melville, as becomes clear in

---

[32] Bezanson in *Clarel*, 839.
[33] Herman Melville, *Published Poems* (Evanston, IL, and Chicago, 2009), 185.

Clarel, was quarrelling with modernity and its loss of a sense, not of transcendence, but of the sacred, which, as he saw it, was simply the unknowable. The persistence of this sense of the sacred is why Margoth the geologist, bent on scientific "explanation" of biblical texts, is a despised figure in *Clarel*. And it is why the questioning book of Job, with its final burst into sublimity, is braided through Melville's work.

Further Reading

Bercaw, Mary K., *Melville's Sources* (Evanston, IL, 1987).

Blair, Ruth, "Introduction." Herman Melville, *Typee* (Oxford, 1996).

Braswell, William, *Melville's Religious Thought* (New York, 1959).

Coffler, Gail H., *Melville's Allusions to Religion: A Comprehensive Index and Glossary* (Westport, CT, and London, 2004).

Cook, Jonathan A. and Brian Yothers, *Visionary of the Word: Melville and Religion* (Evanston, IL, 2017).

Herbert, Walter, *Moby-Dick and Calvinism: A World Dismantled* (New Brunswick, NJ, 1977).

Melville, Herman, *Clarel: A Poem and Pilgrimage in the Holy Land* (Evanston, IL, and Chicago, 1991).

Melville, Herman, *Journals* (Evanston, IL, and Chicago, 1989).

Melville, Herman, *Mardi: And a Voyage Thither* (Evanston, IL, and Chicago, 1970).

Melville, Herman, *Moby-Dick* (Evanston, IL, and Chicago, 1988).

Melville, Herman, *Omoo: A Narrative of Adventures in the South Seas* (Evanston, IL, and Chicago, 1968).

Melville, Herman, *Published Poems* (Evanston, IL, and Chicago, 2009).

Melville, Herman, *Typee: A Peep at Polynesian Life* (Evanston, IL, and Chicago, 1968).

Pardes, Ilana, *Melville's Bibles* (Berkeley, CA, 2008).

Parker, Hershel, *Herman Melville: A Biography*, 2 Vols. (Baltimore and London, 1996, 2002).

Rogin, Michael, *Subversive Genealogy* (Berkeley, CA, 1983).

Sealts, Merton R., *Melville's Reading* (Revised and enlarged edition) ([Columbia, SC], 1988).

Wright, Nathalia, *Melville's Use of the Bible* (Durham, NC, 1949).

15 The Song of Songs and Two
    Biblical Retellings

EMILY O. GRAVETT

The Song of Songs is a biblical book like no other. Its lyrics offer a picture of earthly, egalitarian love, unencumbered by place and time, spoken by both female and male lovers from a place of burning but (predominately) unfulfilled desire. The book appears in the third and final section of the Hebrew Bible called the "Writings" (*ketuvim*), but it is an odd inclusion in the canon. The rabbis debated whether it even should have been included, whether it "defiled" the hands, whether it was truly taboo and thus sacred scripture (e.g. *Mishnah Yadayim* 3:5). The second verse of the book, spoken by a woman about her beloved, shows it to be a text drunk on love: "Let him kiss me with the kisses of his mouth! For your love is better than wine." Erotic epithets and euphemisms abound, as illustrated in the line: "my beloved thrust his hand into the opening, and my inmost being yearned for him" (5:4). In phrases such as "your breasts are like two fawns" (4:5), the book draws on recurrent imagery from the natural world to create lavish metaphors that accentuate the sensuality, infatuation, and eroticism of the book.

Moreover, as Michael Fishbane notes, "readers of this love and bounty will find no references to God and Israel, the Exodus and Sinai, or any other event of the sacred history recorded in Scripture. Nor will they find references to covenant obligations and religious observance – even the love of God – in these lyrics."[1] The book's specific setting and time period are similarly opaque: It refers to Jerusalem and Lebanon, mountains and valleys, streets and squares. Dating the Song is difficult too, with no easily identifiable or verifiable historical referents. Characters are unnamed, and though the woman, as we read earlier, seems to be the main speaker, it is not always clear who is saying what. No wonder that the canonization of the Song was questioned from the start.

[1] Michael Fishbane, *The JPS Bible Commentary: Song of Songs* (Philadelphia, 2015), xix.

In an attempt to justify its designation as scripture, early Jews and Christians generally interpreted the Song as an allegory, as representative of the covenantal love between Israel and God or Christians and the Church, respectively. But, on the surface, it reads as a eulogy to earthy, not divine, love – in the same vein as medieval Arabic erotic poetry and Boccaccio's fourteenth-century *The Decameron*. Biblical scholars have wondered whether the Song was used in ancient wedding or fertility rituals. Through its use of dialogue (an unusual tactic even for ancient love poetry) and the first-personal plural ("we"), the Song celebrates admiration and intimacy, longing and love. It has a dreamy, universal air. In J. Cheryl Exum's words, "their love is timeless."[2]

As one of the Bible's most infamously ardent lovers, Solomon is often credited with this book, the result of a first verse that reads "the Song of Songs, which is Solomon's." He was also said to have written 1005 songs (1 Kgs 4:32). Indeed, many may know this biblical book by another name, "The Song of Solomon," though most scholars now think that the Song was composed by various authors over many centuries and that the reference to Solomon was a later attribution intended to authorize a controversial text. Still, the link to the legend has persisted. Solomon was a larger-than-life king, like his father David, known in the biblical text for being wealthy and wise. The Jewish Talmud and the Muslim Qur'an consider him a prophet. He built the First Temple in Jerusalem. And he was a lover, with over 1000 wives to his name, princesses and concubines alike. It was said that he "clung" to these women (1 Kgs 11:2).

The Song's love is not without its complications. The lovers speak primarily from a place of separation. The woman speaker says, "I sought him, but found him not" (Song 3:1) and, later, "if you find my beloved, tell him this: I am faint with love" (5:8). There is a sense of urgency or sickness about her feelings. She even recounts that "making their rounds in the city the sentinels found me; they beat me, they wounded me" (5:7). Although often understood to be part of a dream (earlier she says, "I slept, but my heart was awake," 5:2), this verse introduces anxiety, danger, even violence into the lyrics.

In just eight chapters, the Song includes myriad ambiguities and provokes many questions. As we will see, these ambiguities have allowed later authors to offer their own versions of the book, in the form of biblical retellings.

---

[2] J. Cheryl Exum, *Song of Songs: A Commentary* (2005), 8.

BIBLICAL RETELLINGS

Retelling stories from the Bible is not an especially new phenomenon. Before they were even considered part of a closed canon, many biblical stories were being repeated, reused, and revised. First and Second Chronicles, themselves biblical books, explore material also found in Samuel and Kings. Ancient Jewish documents, like *The Life of Adam and Eve* and the *Testament of Job*, extend and also diverge from stories found in the canonical books of Genesis and Job, respectively. Later, rabbinic commentary (like *Midrash Rabbah*) often contains retellings. More recent novelists like William Faulkner and Mark Twain have spun their own tales using those from the Bible. The Song of Songs itself has captured artists' attention, from Marc Chagall's "Song of Songs" paintings (1958) to Kate Bush's "Song of Solomon" recording (1993) to Neil Gaiman's novel *American Gods* (2001) to Richard Ramsey's 2014 film *The Song*.

The ubiquity of retellings has captured the interest of scholars with a similar fervor. Their body of work, collectively, is referred to as "biblical reception history." As defined by Brennan Breed, "reception history explores all the different ways that people have received, appropriated, and used biblical texts throughout history."[3] This history has spawned a great many books, series, journals, encyclopedias, handbooks, and commentaries, especially over the last decade, such as Wiley Blackwell's Bible Commentary series, Walter de Gruyter's *Encyclopedia of the Bible and Its Reception*, and *The Oxford Handbook of the Reception History of the Bible*. While some scholars have theorized about the phenomenon of reception history itself, such as *Nomadic Text* by Brennan Breed and *Sustaining Fictions* by Lesleigh Cushing Stahlberg, others have homed in on a specific figure, story, or retelling over time or in one place, as in Janet Howe Gaines's *Music in the Old Bones: Jezebel through the Ages*, Yvonne Sherwood's *A Biblical Text and its Afterlives: The Survival of Jonah in Western Culture*, or Melanie Wright's *Moses in America: The Cultural Uses of Biblical Narrative*. While I have chosen to use the term "biblical retelling" throughout this chapter, be aware that you may find information about this phenomenon – in which texts creatively rework their biblical precursor while retaining enough of the original that people will notice – under other

---

[3] Brennan Breed, "What Is Reception History?" *Bible Odyssey*: www.bibleodyssey.org/en/tools/bible-basics/what-is-reception-history (accessed November 13, 2017).

terms, including "afterlife," "allusion," "intertextuality," "midrash," "transfiguration," or even "Rewritten Bible."

I will explore two biblical retellings of the Song of Songs: the novel *Song of Solomon* (1977) by Toni Morrison and the short story "Song of Songs" (2004) by Darcey Steinke. As we will see, Morrison's novel moves away from nominal connections with the biblical book to respond instead to the fear that the black community is losing its stories and its connection to the past. Steinke's story is a much more obvious retelling. It is situated in an anthology that responds to a current conundrum: People are drawn to but also repelled by religion. Steinke offers an updated "Song of Songs," one that implies God can continue to be found in and through sexuality. By the end, we will be poised to consider the field of biblical retellings and to offer a specific definition of the term – a term that so far scholars have approached not unlike US Supreme Court Justice Potter Stewart approached the definition of "obscenity" in 1964: "I know it when I see it." The chapter will conclude with a consideration of why authors choose to retell at all.

Toni Morrison's *Song of Solomon*

The American milieu in which Toni Morrison – author also of *The Bluest Eye* (1970), *Beloved* (1987), *Jazz* (1992), and *Paradise* (1997) – found herself while writing *Song of Solomon* was complex and contributed to the novel's main themes: identity, community, naming, and the past. Morrison thought that the novel as a genre was "needed by African-Americans now in a way that it was not needed before ... We don't live in places where we can hear those stories anymore; parents don't sit around and tell their children those classical, mythological, archetypal stories that we heard years ago."[4] "Children," the next generation, were losing touch with an important part of their heritage. Her novel, *Song of Solomon*, is a response to this anxiety about "loss"; in it, Morrison records important stories that used to be heard.

Song of Solomon also counters a tendency that Morrison saw in other literature of her time: that authors tended to represent characters in isolation. Community was important to her – and to the African American experience. She says, "It is easily the most obvious thing about us – which is the connectedness, the history of family and personal relations, people's attitudes toward one another based on

---

[4] Quoted in Michael Awkward, "'Unruly and Let Loose': Myth, Ideology, and Gender in *Song of Solomon*," in *Modern Critical Interpretations: Toni Morrison's Song of Solomon*, ed. Harold Bloom (Philadelphia, 1999), 96.

anecdotes and legends about them that you may not have even known. And how all of that pulls into and mixes and becomes a community."[5] This communal past is central in *Song of Solomon*, as it is in the rest of Morrison's works. Folklore, oral culture, magic, nature, ancestors, ghosts, and other elements of her African and African American ancestry were present in Morrison's life from an early age, passed down from her parents.

Song of Solomon reflects Morrison's commitment to these sources, although it has often been understood in terms of its white American or European predecessors. Critics have compared *Song of Solomon* to the English romance, the epic quest, and the *bildungsroman*, the hero's journey, and rites of passage. The novel does incorporate elements of these traditions; main character Milkman, for instance, becomes initiated into the black community after a period of seeming liminality. Yet Morrison does not include, wholesale, other myths in her fiction; instead, she prefers to add and to alter them to suit her own purposes.

The title of the novel is the first clue of Morrison's presumed engagement with the Bible, though biblically named characters appear throughout. Readers might assume that the title relates to the biblical figure Solomon, and the biblical book attributed to him, but it is not so. The name actually refers to the flying African Solomon, an ancestor of Milkman's whom he eventually discovers. The story of the flying African is one Morrison grew up hearing:

> Everybody told me, my grandmother, all of them. They never said to me, 'Did you know Black people could fly?' They'd say, 'You know, during the days when Black people could fly ... ' It was a given. But they always talked about it. When I grew up I didn't think about it that much. Then I began to read slave narratives. They always talk about it. They all either knew somebody who flew, or they saw somebody who flew, or they know somebody who said they knew somebody who flew. It's all over the stories, everywhere.[6]

In the novel, Solomon is not important because he is the famous king mentioned in the biblical book; rather, he is important because he embodies a well-known, but at risk of being forgotten, African legend.

---

[5] A. J. Verdelle, "Loose Magic: A.J. Verdelle Interviews Toni Morrison," *Doubletake* (Summer 1998); reprinted in *Toni Morrison: Conversations*, ed. Carolyn C. Denard (Jackson, MI, 2008), 166.

[6] Quoted in Pepsi Charles, "An Interview with Toni Morrison," *Nimrod International Journal of Prose and Poetry*, 21. 1 (1977); reprinted in *Toni Morrison: Conversations*, 21.

The story of flying Africans is so crucial for Morrison that she begins and ends her novel with that image. It is a story that she wishes to record for her community.

Morrison's emphasis becomes even more apparent when we closely compare *Song of Solomon* to the biblical book, the Song of Songs. The relationship between Milkman and his cousin Hagar (the name of a figure from the biblical book of Genesis) best approximates the erotic relationship depicted in the Song. Morrison indicates that Milkman falls in love with Hagar when he is just a teenager: "the girl stretched her back and turned around ... But Milkman had no need to see her face; he had already fallen in love with her behind."[7] Just as the characters in the biblical text covertly love one another, particularly physically, Milkman and Hagar love one another mostly in secret (primarily because they are cousins).

Although the couple forms a key romantic pair in the novel, Milkman is not exclusively committed to Hagar and they never become officially attached, much like their biblical counterparts. In fact, Milkman considers Hagar "not a real or legitimate girl friend – not someone he might marry" (91). Morrison does not dwell long on their actual relationship or the mutual love it may have once entailed. Her focus is different than the Bible's. Indeed, the next time Milkman and Hagar appear in the novel, their love has run its course, at least for Milkman: "After more than a dozen years, he was getting tired of her" (91). Milkman comes to find Hagar boring, smothering, and ultimately unappealing. She was like "the third beer ... the one you drink because it's there, because it can't hurt, and because what difference does it make?" (91). This fading luster is absent from the biblical Song.

In fact, Milkman is reluctant to participate in relationships of any kind. He is the type, Morrison writes, who "avoided commitments and strong feelings" (180). He cares little for his two sisters. At one point, Magdalene called Lena says to him, "you have never asked one of us if we were tired, or sad, or wanted a cup of coffee" (215). Worse, when Milkman learns about the death of fourteen-year-old African American Emmett Till – who was lynched in Mississippi in 1955, reportedly for flirting with a white woman – his response is dismissive and self-centered: "Yeah, well, fuck Till. I'm the one in trouble" (88). No sense

---

[7] Toni Morrison, *Song of Solomon* (New York, 1977), 43. All future references to Morrison's *Song of Solomon* in this chapter will be cited parenthetically by page number.

of shared racial identity or community bond seems to move Milkman; he has yet to develop such race consciousness.

Milkman decides to break off his relationship with Hagar, a finality not present in the biblical text. For Christmas, he gives her cash and a thank-you note, expressing his gratitude. This gesture is not received well. Hagar has a breakdown and finds herself taking to the streets: "every month Hagar looked for a weapon and then slipped out of her house and went to find the man for whom she believed she had been born into the world" (127). She sets out to kill Milkman, not out of revenge, but as a way of possessing his life. While the biblical persona similarly pursues her lover – "I will rise now and go about the city, in the streets and in the squares; I will seek him whom my soul loves" (Song of Songs 3:2) – she does not wish to kill him. Hagar's "weapon" adds a violent note to the relationship that is not present in the Bible. Her attempts to kill Milkman are unsuccessful, however, and he goes off on a journey, where he winds up discovering the truth about his family history. Morrison focuses the rest of her novel on this journey. The most obvious similarity with the titular Song of Solomon/Songs – Milkman and Hagar's romantic but tumultuous relationship – does not extend for the entire duration of Morrison's novel, nor does it seem to be the main point.

There are other important differences too. Morrison's story is filled with particular places (e.g. Michigan, Not Doctor Street) and colorful but non-biblical names (e.g. Guitar, who is Milkman's best friend). The novel reads less like an ephemeral or archetypal account of love than an account of Milkman's very specific life. Moreover, there are so many characters, relationships, and sub-plots in *Song of Solomon* that cannot be linked to the Song, like Milkman's sisters First Corinthians (the name of a New Testament book) and Magdalene called Lena (the name of a New Testament figure). Morrison creates biblically named characters that resemble, rather, African figures: Milkman's great-aunt Pilate is portrayed as a living ancestor and priestess. It is difficult to firmly establish retellings in these instances. The character of Solomon ultimately provides the best clue – not for any biblical stories retold, but for what is most important to Morrison.

Although Solomon never appears in person in the novel, he illuminates Morrison's concern about community and about the preservation of communal stories for the future. Solomon is Milkman's great-grandfather and he disappeared long ago by flying (literally) back to Africa. Morrison uses him to show the importance of the ancestors within African and African American communities. She incorporates some of her own ancestry into the story too. (It is no coincidence that

Morrison's grandfather's name was John Solomon.) The Solomon of the novel, however, does not correspond well with the man of the biblical text. That Solomon is best known for being the son of King David, marrying numerous women, possessing great wisdom, and building the Temple. He is responsible for securing quite a legend for himself. The notion of legend is important in *Song of Solomon*, but not in the way that one might expect.

Morrison is invested in the legend of the flying African. It "comes to Milkman, and the reader, as fragments – a blues song, a children's ring game, words and names that suggest but do not clearly name Milkman's ancestors."[8] But, once Milkman journeys down to Virginia, to his ancestor's place, he learns the connection between this song and his own heritage. About Solomon, Milkman says:

> Oh, man! He didn't need no airplane. He just took up; got fed up. *All the way up!* No more cotton! No more bales! No more orders! No more shit! He flew, baby. Lifted his beautiful black ass up in the sky and flew on home. Can you dig it? Jesus God, that must have been something to see ... My grandfather. Wow! Woooee! Guitar! You hear that? Guitar, my great-granddaddy could flyyyyyy. (328)

The freedom entailed in flying, specifically from the abuses that Africans and African Americans knew well ("cotton," etc.), is what most impresses Milkman. Precipitated by a sense that such traditions were being lost, Morrison uses Solomon to preserve a legend popular in her own life.

Milkman even comes to embody his ancestor Solomon by the end of the novel. After a confrontation with Guitar, Milkman decides to leap off a cliff: "Without wiping away the tears, taking a deep breath, or even bending his knees – he leaped. As fleet and bright as a lodestar he wheeled toward Guitar and it did not matter which one of them would give us his ghost in the killing arms of his brother. For now he knew what Shalimar knew: If you surrendered to the air, you could *ride* it" (337). "Now" he has learned what Shalimar (a city whose name relates to Solomon) already "knew." He has gained communal knowledge, which, like flying, can carry him. Although Morrison's ending is not clear, she does, at the least, convey Milkman's recognition of and integration into his ancestral community.

In the *Song of Solomon*, Morrison chooses to meditate on the importance of ancestors and community and to bolster that community

---

[8] Philip Page, "Putting It All Together: Attempted Unification in *Song of Solomon*," in *Bloom's Modern Critical Views: Toni Morrison*, 113.

through the recording (and the retelling) of stories important to Africans and African Americans, using whatever source material might fit. Although the Milkman–Hagar pairing provides the most persistent connection to the biblical Song, there are so many crucial differences that it is not an obvious or central retelling.

Darcey Steinke's "Song of Songs"

Darcey Steinke's "Song of Songs" takes a different tack. It was published in *Killing the Buddha: A Heretic's Bible* (2004), an anthology edited by Peter Manseau and Jeff Sharlet. Their title comes from a shocking old Buddhist *koan* or riddle: "if you meet the Buddha on the road, kill him," meaning you should get rid of all attachments, even your concept of the Buddha, on your path toward enlightenment. Manseau and Sharlet's own process of "killing of the Buddha" began in 2000 when they created their website of the same name. Their (online) manifesto reads: "*Killing the Buddha* is a religion magazine for people made anxious by churches, people embarrassed to be caught in the 'spirituality' section of a bookstore, people both hostile and drawn to talk of God. It is for people who somehow want to be religious, who want to know what it means to know the divine, but for good reasons are not and do not."[9] Manseau and Sharlet are interested in bringing together people with mixed responses to religion. These people seek religion out – they "want" such fulfillment in their lives – yet they feel conflicted about it. Manseau and Sharlet identify a contemporary crisis: People may be ambivalent about religion, but they cannot get away from it.

Manseau and Sharlet gesture toward the specifics of this crisis when they talk about the Bible, which is the source material for *Killing the Buddha*:

> In America, the first nation founded on secularism, the Bible is always there, the book waiting for a sweaty-palmed rendezvous in every motel room. There's no refuge from the Bible's reach. It's there in the movies you like and the books you don't. It's on our money and in our courts and in our classrooms, everywhere at once, whether you want it or not. Consider its stories – Adam meets Eve, Jonah meets the whale, Jesus meets a bad end – you've heard them all before. The Bible is in your bones before you crack its binding.[10]

---

[9] "Manifesto": http://killingthebuddha.com/manifesto/ (accessed November 13, 2017).
[10] Peter Manseau and Jeff Sharlet, "Mortal, Eat This Scroll!," in *Killing the Buddha* (New York, 2004), 4.

Indeed, *Killing the Buddha* itself exemplifies "the Bible's reach." The title indicates that it was made for and by "heretics." Yet it is also called a heretic's "Bible." In fact, Manseau and Sharlet said they "made this book not to replace the Bible but to light it and its successors on fire."[11] In that sense, they are not really "killing the Buddha" (destroying all longing for religion, God, etc.), as clever as the name may be. They are not trying to escape the Bible or religion's reach, not trying to "replace" it, not trying to eject everyone from the spiritual aisles of bookstores.

Steinke was one of thirteen authors that Manseau and Sharlet invited to take on "a solo, a single book of the Bible to be remade, revealed, replaced, inverted, perverted, or born again, however the spirit so lead them."[12] Previously, she had included religious themes in her work: She co-edited a volume with Rick Moody entitled *Joyful Noise: The New Testament Revisited* in 1997 and her 1999 novel was called *Jesus Saves*. She was tasked with the Song of Songs.

Steinke's story exemplifies what Daniel Asa Rose said in his review of *Killing the Buddha*, that the project is "not so much a rewriting of the Bible as giving it a super-charged hip-hop makeover."[13] The Bible is not being dismissed; it is being given a new look to stay appealing, to keep up with the times. The reference to "hip-hop" gives a glimpse into the culture to which the authors are responding – one of new musical genres, new technologies and media, new modes of communication, new forms of relationships. These are some of the urgent impetuses driving an update of the biblical text, as well as some of the reasons why people may be interested in, yet also repelled by, religion. The Bible must be rethought and refashioned to fully speak to and about contemporary times. Her piece lights the ancient scripture on fire by making it (or, perhaps, revealing how it already is) relevant to readers today.

Like Morrison's novel, at first, there are a number of signs that seem to immediately link Steinke's piece to the biblical Song. To start, it bears the same name of a biblical book ("Song of Songs") and it begins with an epigraph of a direct quotation from the biblical Song, "Let him kiss me with the kisses of his mouth!" (1:2).[14] It is filled with epithets

---

[11] Ibid.

[12] Ibid.

[13] Daniel Asa Rose, "Travels with the Holy Ghost: An Orgy of Skeptical Ecstasy," *The New York Observer* (January 5, 2004): http://observer.com/2004/01/travels-with-the-holy-ghost-an-orgy-of-skeptical-ecstasy/ (accessed November 13, 2017).

[14] Darcey Steinke, "Song of Songs," in *Killing the Buddha*, ed. Peter Manseau and Jeff Sharlet (New York, 2004), 139. All future references to Steinke's "Song of Songs" in this chapter will be cited parenthetically by page number.

that sound like they are pulled directly from the biblical Song, like "my love, my own" (142). And it is situated in an anthology explicitly devoted to retelling biblical stories. These initial cues prime readers to anticipate extensive interplay between Steinke's piece and the biblical Song. Steinke does not disappoint.

From the beginning, there are (at least) two characters in Steinke's story, "me" and "you," mimicking the biblical material. Steinke's story starts, for example, with "Bougainvillea petals blew around on the stone floor with a sound dry and melodic as you came into me" (139). We realize quickly that the addressee in Steinke's piece is male and remains male, while her persona is steadfastly female. In the Bible, the poem is a conversation, moving between both male and female speaking parts, with the speaker's identity often unclear. As in the Bible, too, Steinke's readers feel like eavesdroppers of an intimate dialogue, which reflects and participates in increased and more explicit sexual freedom.

While the speaker of Steinke's story does not change and initially the beloved seems to be one man, on closer examination, the addressee is not necessarily the same throughout. This imprecision lends an air of dynamism and universality to the piece, as in the Song of Songs, while also offering a snapshot of the sexual freedoms available today. The female persona first recalls her beloved's "gray eyes," then his "brown eyes with black lashes," and later, his "green eyes [that] looked like tiny planet earths" (140–41). Alcohol may play a role here and certainly time is not straightforward. The persona may be experiencing multiple presents. It could also be that the persona has numerous partners. Regardless, the effect is that the reality of the piece becomes blurry and the characteristics of the beloved open up. He is not limited to one eye color, physique, or personality; rather, he is an everyman, unlike Milkman of Morrison's *Song of Solomon*. This uncertainty corresponds with the biblical text, which is often noted for its hazy, dreamlike qualities (achieved, in Steinke, by her use of stream-of-consciousness and the presence of intoxicants) and its portrayal of universal love, but Steinke also builds off of it, offering an even more fluid understanding of romantic and/or sexual relationships.

Indeed, Steinke's persona sees her beloved everywhere, just as the biblical lovers do. She says, for example, "I desired ... the you in the glittering asphalt, the you in the gas oven's blue flame, the you in the pattern of bubble in the glass of Coke" (139). Her lover is omnipresent. She need not look for him in grand gestures or edifices, but simply on the ground level, in the nitty gritty, in the mundane. She views the world differently, with her lover as a reference point. Steinke highlights how, in the Bible, the lovers also see one another everywhere – in the fields, in the animals, in the streets – but she is also commenting on the ways in which the divine (that other "you") can be sought in today's world.

It is, after all, a complex world Steinke's persona finds herself in. While she makes frequent references to cityscapes like "Norfolk" and "Brooklyn" (140), where she eats Chinese food, drives a Volkswagen, and watches *E.T.*, Steinke's persona also draws heavily on the natural world and the human body for her descriptions. It is a technique right from the Bible. We read of a "heart like a peony" and a "pelvis like a bowl of clean water" (140). Cantaloupes, rain, blossoms, and cedar appear to – as well as cleavage, skin, fingers, lashes – mimic the original, though often less euphemistically. Steinke's character takes to exaggeration to express herself, just as extravagant language is used in the biblical Song, where, for instance, the male lover says, "Your channel is an orchard of pomegranates with all choicest fruits, henna with nard, nard and saffron, calamus and cinnamon, with all trees of frankincense, myrrh and aloes, with all chief spices" (Song of Songs 4:13–14). Steinke's persona speaks of being drunk "on a thousand gin and tonics" (139) and how she and her lover "came two hundred times" (140). The details are mostly impossible, but Steinke's point is not to convey an empirical reality. It is, rather, to suggest the experiences of the persona – how drunk she felt, how many times she had sex – and to use those experiences to reflect on the contemporary condition.

Steinke focuses on the persona's passionate relationship(s) for the duration of her story, delving into the pleasures as well as the frustrations of young love. When the persona says, for example, "I desired not your body, which I already knew I could never make mine" (139), she indicates her inability to fully possess her lover, which corresponds with the biblical version. After all, the female persona in the Song reveals: "I sought him, but found him not; I called him, but he gave no answer" (3:1). Steinke's character too recognizes the transience, the delicacy, and the difficulty of love. And she suffers because of it, dealing with, for instance, the presence of other women in her beloved's life. She says, "When I saw you pull the girl onto your lap, my heart broke" (141–42). While all is not perfect in the biblical world either – the biblical female says she is beaten by sentinels when they find her out at night (5:7) and she admits that other women love him (e.g. 1:3) – there is no indication of any suspicion, asymmetry, or unrequitedness. Steinke updates the biblical Song by describing (and thus showing that she is responding to) the difficulties she believes face people today.

What is most striking is the analogy Steinke draws between the persona's experiences, lived out in a distinctly contemporary setting, and the divine. The persona tells her beloved that "at first when I loved you without knowing you it was like loving God" (140) and that there is a "holy space engendered after mutually fulfilling sex" (141). Steinke is implying that sex is one of the ways, in contemporary society, to find some semblance of the holy, some glimpse of the divine. This kind of implication may explain, in part, the continuing but complicated attraction toward religion that Manseau and Sharlet articulate – certain experiences hint that something more is out there. Most revealing is what the female persona says at the end of the piece. The male beloved breaks her heart and she takes the subway to flee back to the natural world, "to the shore of the lake" (142), where she says: "My love, my own, I have looked for you everywhere, particularly in the pelvic region of the male species" (142). "My love" no longer signifies just a man. The "male species," and her sexual encounters with them, is the vehicle for something bigger, something more profound. While the association between sex and the transcendent is not a new one – in fact, the biblical Song may imply such an association – Steinke addresses the tensions between attraction and repulsion by offering a complex, poignant, but familiar portrait of American life, in which the divine is still present, but just not always in the places or ways one might initially expect.

THE FIELD OF "BIBLICAL RETELLINGS"

Because of the preceding analyses, we now have a better idea of how to characterize biblical retellings, specifically of the literary narrative variety. There are many different attributes that can intersect to create a retelling; no single element always appears or is required. There is no hierarchy, such that without a particular similarity, a contemporary work could not be considered a biblical retelling. While it is true that some elements more easily indicate a biblical retelling than others (e.g. the title of the work versus its tone), all are equally valid.

A literary narrative could therefore be considered a "biblical retelling" for several reasons. It will most likely be a retelling if it advertises its retold nature in its title, subtitle, foreword, chapter headings, or epigraphs. When names, overall personalities, or even specific attributes of the characters correspond with their biblical counterparts, it is also a retelling. Geographic locations and significant objects can be markers of the existence of the biblical world in the narrative. Without explicit identifiers, the presence of formal similarities in plot, character, and/or action between the contemporary narrative and the biblical one may also indicate a retelling. These similarities, however, must be enough that the correspondence does not seem coincidental or incidental (e.g. a character in love does not automatically indicate a retelling of the Song). There are other, less decisive (but still salient) ways to classify narratives as retellings. These include the presence of quotations, key themes, images, or even important words borrowed from the Bible. Narrative perspective, style, and tone can also be considered.

Similarities between the biblical text and a later narrative retelling must be more than two and they must be present, to borrow a phrase from Theodore Ziolkowski, to "a *noticeable* extent."[15] Try performing a simple thought experiment: Imagine removing any one of the similarities (e.g. the name of a main character) between the biblical text and the new work. If the newer work still seems like a biblical retelling, then it is a retelling to a "noticeable extent."

The metaphor of a "field" suggests itself at this point. It allows a definition of retelling to be precise without being unduly limiting. Retellings can have fuzzy boundaries. Indeed, it is not always possible, or desirable, to draw a clear line and to definitively say what a retelling is and what a retelling is not. Some works seem more prototypical than others, more central on the field. By central, I do not mean better; rather, I mean those closer to the original biblical text, that is, those that are more obviously biblical retellings. Given the confluence of significant similarities – in title, epigraph, voice, imagery, style, theme, language – and given the fact that a story similar to the biblical Song (a lustful but complicated relationship) is the focus of Steinke's piece, it is appropriate to consider her story an unmistakable biblical retelling, one close to the center of the field, in contrast to Morrison's novel, which is much more on the periphery.

To help guide and situate future discoveries on this field, I offer the following, working definition of "biblical retelling": (1) a post-biblical narrative that (2) purposefully uses a specific biblical story as a predominant source in order to (3) create a new and different story, while also (4) explicitly emphasizing enough connections with the biblical text, through (5) a matrix of sufficient and suitable correspondences (6) to ensure that readers who know of the corresponding biblical story will be able to recognize the connection and understand the narrative not just as a work in its own right, but as a work in dialogue with the Bible.

---

[15] Theodore Ziolkowski, *Fictional Transfigurations of Jesus* (Princeton, NJ, 1972), 6; my italics.

WHY RETELL?

As is so often the case in the study of religion and the Bible, origin stories are important. We have seen, in this chapter, how retellings emerge out of, are tied to, and directly respond to specific and usually current crises. Anthony C. Swindell claims that his own study of "reworkings" focuses on "texts generated at moments of great cultural change or upheaval."[16] Yet it is my contention that this is not just a coincidental similarity Swindell found in the texts on which he happened to focus, but rather a general trend. The biblical text resonates with later authors because of their own crises – personal, cultural, or both – and thus becomes a means by which they can grapple with these crises. Readers of retellings may encounter different crises in different retellings, but each seems to explain why the retellings exist at all, whether the authors (or the audience) are religious or not, whether the biblical literature, in their view, is something to uphold and revere or something to subvert and ridicule.

Yet it is not simply external crises that precipitate a seizing of the biblical past. It is that the biblical text is still available and amenable to being seized. Despite dire predictions and warnings of secularization, religion is not going away. As Peter Berger recognizes, "the world today ... is as furiously religious as it ever was, and in some places more so than ever."[17] And the Bible is not just a religious text, for religious people; it holds great cultural influence, as well, particularly in North America and Europe. It is still turned to, drawn on, and thought about, even if in more subversive or heretical ways than were available to our predecessors. An adult toy superstore is named Adam and Eve. Darren Aronofsky made a blockbuster movie about the flood. Sheba showed up in a *New Yorker* poem. Although religious literacy may be on the decline, the Bible is still the best-selling book in the world.

The Bible contains many rich, imaginative stories, not just blood-less platitudes. In those stories, readers have continued to find and mine biblical "crises": gaps, inconsistencies, repetitions, contradictions, silences, ellipses, problems, ambiguities, multiple perspectives from multiple figures – so often left undecided or unreconciled. The Bible is multivocal, polyphonous. Its delightful messiness, not found in all

---

[16] Anthony C. Swindell, *Reworking the Bible: The Literary Reception-History of Fourteen Biblical Stories* (Sheffield, 2010), 2.

[17] Peter Berger, "The Desecularization of the World: A Global Overview," in *The Desecularization of the World: Resurgent Religion and World Politics* (Washington, DC, Ethics and Public Policy Center, 1999), 2.

ancient Near Eastern texts, provides numerous entry points for authors to use in working through their issues, each in their own way. It is a two-way street: The Bible has the power to shape us, but it is shaped by us too. Once we read these biblical retellings, it is hard to look at the biblical text the same way again.

Further Reading

Breed, Brennan W., *Nomadic Text: A Theory of Biblical Reception History* (Bloomington, IN, 2014).

Manseau, Peter and Jeff Sharlet, *Killing the Buddha: A Heretic's Bible* (New York, 2004).

Pope, Marvin, *Song of Songs: A New Translation with Introduction and Commentary* (Garden City, NY, 1977).

Sherwood, Yvonne, *A Biblical Text and Its Afterlives: The Survival of Jonah in Western Culture* (Cambridge, 2000).

Stahlberg, Lesleigh C., *Sustaining Fictions: Intertextuality, Midrash, Translation, and the Literary Afterlife of the Bible* (New York, 2008).

Swindell, Anthony C., *Reworking the Bible: The Literary Reception-History of Fourteen Biblical Stories* (Sheffield, 2010).

Wright, Melanie, *Moses in America: The Cultural Uses of Biblical Narrative* (New York, 2003).

Index